HOMEMADE IN HALF THE TIME

HOMEMADE IN HALF THE TIME

Smart Ways to Cook
Delicious Meals Every Time

Edited by
SHEA WAGGONER

RODALE

Photographs by Mitch Mandel

Cover and Interior Food Stylist: Diane Vezza

Book design by Christina Gaugler

Cover recipe: Chicken Pot Pie with Biscuits (page 216)

Library of Congress Cataloging-in-Publication Data

Homemade in half the time : smart ways to cook delicious meals every time / edited by Shea Waggoner.

      p.   cm.

Includes index.

ISBN-13 978-1-59486-365-3   hardcover

ISBN-10 1-59486-365-2   hardcover

1. Quick and easy cookery.   I. Waggoner, Shea.

TX833.5.H645   2006

641.5'55—dc22   2006004958

2 4 6 8 10 9 7 5 3 1 hardcover

RODALE
LIVE YOUR WHOLE LIFE

We inspire and enable people to improve their lives and the world around them

For more of our products visit rodalestore.com or call 800-848-4735

CONTENTS

INTRODUCTION

Nothing tastes as good as a home-cooked meal, a bittersweet fact given that most of us have only a few minutes in the evening to pull together dinner. But it is possible to have that "all-day-in-the-kitchen" flavor in 10 minutes or less—if you know how to make it homemade in half the time.

Packed with more than 200 delicious, kitchen-tested recipes and dozens of speedy tips, this book will show you how to prepare great-tasting meals without spending a lot of time doing it. You'll learn about the best new convenience foods that deliver fresh flavor without the fuss. Plus, there's a special A to Z guide to all the secret pantry staples to have on hand. Simply knowing how to choose the right ingredients is a big part of having memorable home-cooked meals on the table in record time.

Many of the recipes here are traditional favorites streamlined for the modern kitchen. See how to shave 3 hours off the prep and cooking time for Chicken Pot Pie with Biscuits (page 216) or nearly 2 hours off traditional Green and White Lasagna (page 208) with widely available ingredients and simple techniques.

Look for the chapter called "Double-Duty Dinners" to see how to make two meals for the work of one. All of the recipes in this chapter come in pairs. Make the first recipe one night, save half of the finished dish, and use it to create a completely different meal later in the week. For instance, on Monday night, you can enjoy The Easiest Meatloaf (page 260) then transform it into Rigatoni with Chunky Meat Sauce for Thursday's dinner.

Are make-ahead meals more your style? You'll find 20 tasty dishes that are ready to finish whenever you are. Just preheat your oven and you're practically done. If slow cookers are more your speed, you'll be delighted to find that almost every recipe in that chapter requires less than 10 minutes of hands-on time.

With these quick-cooking recipes, you can even make homemade bread in a fraction of the time. Just buy some prepared frozen bread dough, add your favorite seasonings, and bake. Simple.

For dessert, transform a box of brownie mix and some orange marmalade into Chocolate-Almond Torte with Orange Sauce (page 326) with only 10 minutes of hands-on time.

And don't worry, these recipes don't use a lot of ingredients. One of the biggest complaints about cooking is all the ingredients you need. Well, toss those labor-intensive recipes aside. More than 50 of the recipes here are made with only five ingredients—or less! You need only four ingredients to make fabulous Baked Brie with Peach-Zinfandel Chutney (page 126), an impressive appetizer worthy of any dinner party. You need only five ingredients (plus salt and pepper) to pull together delicious Bistro Steaks with Mushrooms and Onions (page 192) for a satisfying weeknight meal. And just four ingredients can be turned into Clementine Tart with White Chocolate-Macadamia Cookie Crust (page 320) in only 8 minutes of hands-on time.

All of the five-ingredient recipes are tagged as "Five Ingredients or Less!" so you can find them easily. Other handy recipe tags on the dinner recipes include "Vegetarian Dish" and "Pressure Cooker Dish" so you can quickly find the food you are looking for. Plus, every recipe comes with "Hands-On Time" and "Total Time" so you can see exactly how long the recipe will take from start to finish.

To make this new way of home cooking ultraeasy, turn to the weekly menus at the back of the book. Complete with shopping lists and total cooking times for the week, these menus show how little time you need to spend to serve great-tasting meals in your kitchen.

A whole new world of high-quality convenience foods is right there in your supermarket. All you need to do is bring them home and combine them into fabulous meals that the whole family will love.

CHAPTER 1

GETTING STARTED

Some cooks look so efficient in the kitchen. They glide from the refrigerator to the countertop, quickly chopping onions, sautéing them breezily in a pan, and building a fabulous meal in no time. Using quick-cooking ingredients, techniques, and equipment is essential for speed. But there are other behind-the-scenes strategies for achieving this sort of easy grace. Organizing your work space, shopping smart, and making a plan before you start are the big three. Here's how the pros do it.

Set Up an Efficient Kitchen

Long before you start cooking, your kitchen layout determines how quickly you can get dinner on the table. Professional kitchens are designed for speed. That doesn't mean you have to remodel your kitchen to match a professional one, although it might help! Most folks simply need to maximize the space they have at hand.

Consider the four major areas. Your goal is to arrange your kitchen so it revolves smoothly around four major areas: the storage area, the preparation area, the cooking area, and the cleaning area. If possible, keep these areas relatively separate but linked by countertops. In smaller kitchens, it's likely that these areas will have some overlap, which is okay. For instance, your microwave oven is technically a piece of cooking equipment, but it may be on your countertop (a prep area) or nestled among your cabinets (a storage area). Work with your kitchen space to determine the best spot for each area, and move small appliances accordingly.

Draw a diagram. If you're working with an existing layout, start by drawing a picture of your kitchen, showing only the walls, doors, windows, cabinets, and countertops—things you can't easily move. Next, pencil in the major appliances in the places where they fit best. Ideally, the refrigerator, sink, and stove will form a triangle to minimize walking as you go from one to the other. When picturing this work triangle, take into account the kitchen's walking paths. Try to keep the work triangle away from walking paths, so that foot traffic doesn't cross through key work areas, especially the area between the stove and the sink.

Create linked countertops or workstations. Most kitchens link the refrigerator, sink, and stove (or at least two of the three) with countertops. At the very least, your kitchen should have two key surfaces: a prep surface and a resting surface, each near the stove or the sink. Depending on your kitchen layout, you may find it more efficient to create workstations. For instance, if your stovetop has no available countertop surrounding it, you can create a prep area near the stove with a center island or butcher-block rolling cart. Or, if you bake often and have a wall oven, you can streamline prep time by keeping a similar work surface and all of your baking supplies near the oven.

Organize Equipment for Easy Access

After you organize the major and small appliances in your kitchen, it's time to think about storage. Should the pots be kept in a deep drawer or hung on the wall or from the ceiling? Should the spices be near the stove or in a cabinet? Where is the best place to store cooking oils? The answer is to put things where they will be needed most.

Separate the pots from the knives. Think back to the four major areas of your kitchen: the storage area, the preparation area, the cooking area, and the cleaning area. Pots will be used for cooking, so they should be stored as close to the cooking area as possible, either in a drawer, on a shelf, on the wall, or hanging from the ceiling. Knives will be used for preparation, so they should be kept near the prep area. If they are in a drawer, keep each knife in a sheath to protect the blades from becoming dull. Mixing spoons, whisks, and other preparation utensils also go near the prep area, preferably on a magnetic wall strip or upright in a crock for quick access. Slotted spoons, spatulas, tongs, and other cooking utensils go near the cooking area, again in a crock or on a magnetic strip if possible.

FIND HIDDEN SPACES

"I need more counter space!" This is the most common complaint among home cooks. If you've ever worked in a tiny kitchen, you know how unnerving it can be when there aren't enough places to chop, mix, assemble, and set down hot pots, pans, or baking sheets. To solve the problem, take a look around the kitchen and maximize the available space.

Declutter countertops and drawers. It's easy to be a kitchen pack rat, especially if you love cooking. But most gadgets and small appliances are hardly ever used. Keep work surfaces clear by putting only essential small appliances on the countertops. If you don't use the food processor and stand mixer often, put them in a cabinet or on a closet shelf. Clean out the gadget drawer, too. Do you use that nifty waffle cutter or cheese slicer only once a year? Keep a separate drawer or box of rarely used gadgets, and store it away from the main prep area. The less clutter in your central kitchen, the faster you'll be able to find what you need.

Think small. If you have very limited counter space, buy only compact appliances: a mini food processor instead of a full-size processor, a good-quality hand mixer instead of a bulky stand mixer, an immersion blender instead of a tall drink blender, and a wooden or plastic citrus reamer instead of an electric juicer. Buying handheld items may help to free up precious counter space in your kitchen.

Use the walls. Put shelves on the walls to create more surface area. Instead of storing knives in a knife block on the counter, put them on a magnetic strip on the wall. Get extra magnetic strips to hold metal gadgets such as cheese graters. Wall-mounted magazine racks can hold your favorite cooking magazines or books. Hanging baskets can be used to store onions, bananas, and other food that might take up cabinet or counter space. Or follow the late Julia Child's lead and use a Peg-Board on the wall to hang your equipment. Julia's ingenious Peg-Board setup is now immortalized along with the rest of her kitchen at the Smithsonian National Museum of American History in Washington, D.C.

Use all horizontal surfaces. Need a place to hold platters of cooked food or to warm plates? Use the stove or microwave oven. Looking for a place to set down a hot pot or a sheet of cookies? Use a trivet on an unused table or on top of the refrigerator. Set up a portable table or ironing board if necessary. Or pull out the junk drawer and rest a serving tray or sturdy baking sheet on it. Inspect your kitchen for other ways to create horizontal surfaces when you need them during mealtimes.

Store seasonings between the prep and cooking areas. Spices and seasonings will be used during preparation and cooking, so they will ideally go between the prep and cooking areas. The best place for these items is often in a cabinet or drawer to protect them from heat and light, thereby extending their shelf life. The same goes for oils, salt, pepper, soy sauce, and other seasonings. Since salt is shelf-stable and used for both prep and cooking, keep some salt within reach in both areas. Low-sided bowls or plastic containers offer the easiest access to salt. In the prep or baking area, fill the bowl with table salt and keep a $\frac{1}{2}$ teaspoon measuring spoon in the bowl to speed measuring. In the cooking area, fill the bowl with coarse or Kosher salt so you can quickly pinch up some salt when needed to salt pasta water or season a sauce.

Prep Like a Pro

Most actual cooking doesn't take that long. It's the preparation and cleaning that really eat up your time. In professional kitchens, prep cooks and dishwashers do this kind of dirty work. But how do home cooks beat the clock? Simple. Just remember two key principles followed by professional chefs: one, eyeballing; and two, *mise en place,* which is French for "things in place."

Review your plan. Apprentices in French kitchens learn the basic principle of mise en place before they ever pick up a knife. The idea is that cooking will proceed more quickly and efficiently when there is order in your kitchen. If you are cooking from a recipe, step number one is to get yourself in order by reading the recipe all the way through. Think of recipes as road maps. First read the map so you know where you're going. Then make sure you have all of the ingredients and equipment needed. Next review the basic sequence of the tasks in the recipe so there are no surprises once you start cooking. Look out for additional steps that require you to precook an ingredient or make a minirecipe (such as pesto) as part of the larger recipe. If you'll be substituting ingredients or changing amounts, pencil those changes right onto the page so you won't forget them when the cooking begins.

Gather your ingredients. Step two is to gather all of your raw ingredients and equipment near the prep area. Go to the refrigerator or pantry only once and pull out everything you need. If you have a lot of ingredients to gather, use a tray to transfer them from the storage area to the prep area. This initial gathering step saves time by eliminating extra trips to the storage area and double-checking that you have everything you need to make the recipe. And it prevents "recipe frazzle," that frustration felt when you're in the middle of making a recipe and find that you don't have a key ingredient or piece of equipment.

Prepare your ingredients. Step three is to measure all of your ingredients and prepare your equipment. Wash and trim vegetables, toast nuts, melt chocolate, marinate meats, grease pans, or do anything that can be done ahead of the main cooking. This step is especially important when stir-frying, sautéing, or grilling because the cooking time for these techniques is so short and you don't want to be distracted by last-minute preparation steps. You can drastically reduce this preparation step by using precut produce, premarinated meats, and other modern convenience foods.

Combine tasks to save time. Now we come to the heart of mise en place, which is combining like tasks. Smart cooks save time by completing a single task in its entirety before moving on to the next task. For instance, if you need to chop several items, such as vegetables, nuts, and herbs, do all the chopping at once. If several items go into the pan at the same time, combine them so you can quickly add them to the pan all at once. If two recipes call for baking something at the same temperature, bake them together. Or if several items are boiled, boil them one after the other in the same pot. Combining tasks streamlines the preparation process by eliminating needless repetition.

Eyeball it. Now that you have a handle on mise en place, here's how to really kick your food preparation into high gear. Learn how to eyeball amounts rather than slowly measuring every ingredient. Practice eyeballing by measuring a teaspoon of salt and pouring it into your palm. Observe its size, shape, and weight. Try to remember these details. To test your accuracy, clean your palm and then pour what you think is a teaspoon of salt directly from the container into your palm. Measure that amount with a measuring spoon by pouring it from your palm into the spoon. Repeat this process now and then until you can eyeball accurately.

To practice eyeballing liquid ingredients, use a similar strategy. Measure a tablespoon of oil and then pour it into a sauté pan. Observe how the oil spreads in the pan and the total area that it takes up. Try to remember these details and then proceed with the cooking. The next time you sauté, pour what you think is a tablespoon of oil directly from the container into the pan, then measure the oil to test your accuracy.

Approximating measurements like this saves on prep time and cleanup time, because you don't need to dirty any measuring spoons. Don't worry if your approximations are slightly off. Many recipes will survive just fine when 3 teaspoons of oil are used instead of 2 teaspoons or if $\frac{1}{3}$ cup of chopped bell pepper ends up in the pan instead of $\frac{1}{4}$ cup.

The one exception is baking. Eyeballing is not recommended when preparing quick breads, yeast breads, cakes, cookies, and batters and doughs. The quality and structure of baked goods is less forgiving when the ratios of ingredients are not precise. For all baked goods, measure with measuring cups and spoons.

Get help. If mealtime still has you frazzled, don't hesitate to enlist the help of your kids, family members, or friends. When meals are simple, extra helpers can mix ingredients in a bowl, make a salad, or at least set the table and get drinks. You may even find this a pleasant way to sneak more family time into your life.

Clean As You Go

Another key principle of quick cooking is to keep your kitchen clean. Less clutter means less time wasted. If you've ever tried to pull together a holiday meal with piles of soiled dishes and utensils littered all over your work surface, you know how a dirty kitchen can slow you down. Here's how professional cooks save on cleanup time.

Keep bowls on the counter. Always have cleaning at the back of your mind—even the moment you begin preparing ingredients. As you chop or slice vegetables, move them off the cutting board into handy bowls or plates on the counter. Use a scrap bowl to contain vegetable peels and other waste so it's out of the way. This kind of planned cleaning avoids last-minute damage control in a cluttered kitchen.

Use the right cutting board. Quick cooks keep at least two cutting boards on hand: a small one and a large one. Match the cutting board to the size of the job. Use the small board when you simply need to mince some garlic or ginger. Use the large board for bigger jobs like peeling and chopping several potatoes or slicing a roast. When in doubt, use the large board. Nothing slows you down more than chopping at awkward angles to avoid piles of food on the cutting board. A large board also ensures that chopped food stays on the board so you don't have to scoop it together from across the countertop.

Wipe spills immediately. To avoid time-consuming cleanup, wipe down splatters before they dry out and are difficult to remove. Keep the sink filled with water for soaking dirty pots or at least fill pans with hot water while they are still easy to clean. Put dishes in the dishwasher or sink as soon as you dirty them rather than leaving them strewn over your prep area. If you watch television cooking shows, you'll notice that TV chefs clean habitually. They rarely have dirty bowls in front of them.

They always clean or clear equipment and utensils immediately after using them, a practice that allows you to jump right to the next cooking task instead of getting distracted by a work surface muddled with dirty dishes.

Plan Easy Menus

Whether you're whipping up a weeknight meal, entertaining friends, or preparing a multicourse holiday dinner for the extended family, it saves time to plan ahead. Keep your menus simple. When trying new recipes, plan only one new recipe per menu. It also helps to do as much ahead of time as possible.

Go for variety. The best meals excite all of your senses. When planning meals, try to include a variety of textures, flavors, and temperatures in the dishes. A crunchy, cold salad can be assembled ahead of time and makes a satisfying contrast to a tender, hot entrée. Simplify things by starting the meal with room-temperature cheese and crackers, crudités, or an antipasto platter of pitted olives, roasted peppers, and sliced deli meats.

Build make-aheads into the menu. Experienced cooks keep cooking to a minimum by preparing as much ahead as possible. This is especially important when entertaining, so that the cook can enjoy the party, too. Even for weeknight meals, plan at least one make-ahead for every menu. Soups and stews can be made days ahead of time and actually improve in flavor when reheated. Casseroles such as lasagna can be assembled ahead of time, refrigerated, and then baked just before serving. Cakes, cookies, quick breads, and yeast breads can be frozen for weeks, then thawed before serving. Fresh vegetables can be chopped hours in advance and refrigerated until needed. You can even precook pasta. Slightly undercook it (the pasta should be quite firm in the center), cool it under running water, toss it with oil to prevent sticking, then refrigerate it. Simply reheat the precooked pasta for 1 to 2 minutes in boiling water before serving.

Serve cold foods. Plan on serving some cold foods for variety and to lighten the workload during mealtime. Hours before the meal, you can assemble marinated salads right in their serving bowls or green salads directly on their serving plates. Pour on the dressing for green salads right before mealtime or pass it at the table. Instead of preparing a hot vegetable, make a cold one ahead of time. Make potato salad instead of baked potatoes, or serve chilled broccoli or asparagus in vinaigrette instead of hot steamed vegetables. Even roasted meats can be cooked well in advance of the meal, then served at room temperature or chilled. Cold ice creams, puddings, custards, and tarts make dessert a snap. Or go for room-temperature desserts like cookies, cakes, and quick breads.

Cook unattended foods. In your menus, try to serve at least one dish that can cook unattended. Roasts, stews, and braises can all cook on low or moderate heat for hours, freeing you up to do other things before mealtime. Let your slow cooker do the work, set your oven to low or medium-low, or slow cook on the stovetop by simmering or braising meats or vegetables.

Double up. Cook your favorite dishes in quantity. If you're making pasta for dinner, double the amount so you have enough for lunch the next day. When cooking rice, make enough for two meals and refrigerate the leftovers for another meal later in the week. Soups and stews freeze well for months. In the winter, make a double or triple batch of these hot foods so you always have a last-minute meal on hand.

Make a game plan. For multicourse or extensive holiday meals, remember the three p's: plan, prioritize, and prep. Plan by jotting down your menu and shopping list. Prioritize by determining how far ahead of time each task can be done. (For example, 2 weeks before, you can shop for shelf-stable items. A week ahead, you can make and freeze pies, cakes, and cookies. Three to 4 days ahead, you can shop for fresh items and fully prepare good-keeping dishes like dips, soups, and stews. The day or night before, plan to defrost or marinate meats, wash and store salad greens, trim vegetables, chop onions, and prepare casseroles or other dishes that can be refrigerated overnight.) And prep by preparing as much ahead of time as possible. If you follow the three p's, the big day should be a breeze. Then you simply cook off the casseroles, roast long-cooking meats, reheat soups or stews, make last-minute vegetable dishes or sauces, and dress the salads.

Stock up. Not everyone likes to plan so far in advance. If you prefer to cook spontaneously, save time by stocking your kitchen with the foods you love most, including plenty of quick-cooking staples like canned beans and broth, jarred sauces, dried pasta, quick-cooking rice and other grains, dried spices and seasoning mixes, refrigerated doughs, cheeses, premarinated meats, precut produce and bagged salad mixes, and frozen stuffed pastas. For more information on these and other modern convenience foods, see "An A–Z Guide to Ingredients" on page 24.

Shop Smart

Shopping is much easier when you use a few simple strategies like shopping during the grocery store's slow times and buying in bulk. Here's how smart shoppers get in and out of the store in no time flat.

Make a list. Speedy shoppers know exactly what they're looking for and use a shopping list. To make it easy, keep a pad of paper in the kitchen. Whenever you run out of an ingredient, jot it down on the list. When planning meals for the week ahead, jot down all the items you'll need. Some cooks tape an ongoing shopping list to the inside of a cabinet door, then take that list to the store.

Group like items together. Even if you have a list, it'll take you twice as long to follow it if you get all the way over to the frozen foods section and have to run back to the produce section for something you forgot. To avoid those delays, organize your shopping list by the sections of the typical supermarket: produce, dairy, deli, meats, seafood, bread/bakery, frozen foods, canned vegetables and fruits, boxed grains and cereals, spices and baking, paper goods, bags and wraps, cleaners, and personal care items. Make these categories headings on your list. For larger store sections like the produce section, make subheadings or group like items together, such as fruits, herbs, storage vegetables (onions, potatoes, squash, etc.), and perishable vegetables (tomatoes, peppers, broccoli, cucumbers, etc.).

Shop fresh last. Most stores put the produce section at the entrance because it's attractive. But fresh food should be shopped for last because it is the most perishable. Putting fresh vegetables and fruits into your cart last also helps to prevent them from being crushed beneath six-packs of soda or bags of flour.

Use a diagram. If possible, get a diagram of your favorite grocery store. Ask the store manager for a store layout or draw one up yourself. The diagram should include the store's major sections. Run off copies of the layout to use for your shopping lists. Then simply jot down shopping list items in the very section of the store in which they are located.

Shop the same store. Of course, the quickest way to shop is to know where everything is. Don't waste time hunting down ingredients in unfamiliar stores. Find the one supermarket closest to your home that stocks the items you buy the most. Do your high-volume shopping at that store only—with your visual diagram to help you. Over time, you won't need the diagram anymore because you'll know the store like the back of your hand.

Stick to your favorites. Put only one or two new foods into your cart on each shopping trip. You'll get through the grocery store more quickly if you know what you want and aren't standing in the aisles reading labels or making impulse purchases. Try different brands carried by your local store to find your favorite ones. After you know what you like best, getting in and out of the store quickly will be a snap.

Avoid the rush. Even if you have a list and stick to it, shopping at the wrong time can sabotage your best efforts. Smart shoppers don't shop right after work or on Saturdays, the two busiest times for supermarkets. The best shopping time is Tuesday night after 7 p.m. By that time, the store has restocked after the weekend rush, and most people are at home eating dinner or watching television. Or, if your nights are too busy and you're an early riser, shop in the morning before going to work. Or try shopping during the weekday. Save time by spending your lunch hour or break time quickly stocking your kitchen for the week ahead.

Buy in bulk. Stock up on the foods you eat most. Dried pasta and frozen stuffed pasta keep well for months, for example. When you buy pasta, buy several pounds at a time. Keep the freezer stocked with big bags of frozen vegetables and frozen boneless chicken breasts. Keep loaves of bread in the freezer. Filling the pantry means fewer trips to the store and less time spent shopping.

Get it delivered. Many retailers offer free or inexpensive local delivery. Call your local markets and ask if they offer delivery service. Home delivery can cut your shopping time in half or more. For shelf-stable and nonperishable items, consider the Internet. Many online grocery stores sell the same shelf-stable items that you find in your local store, including cold cereals, salad dressings, and canned beans. Some online retailers, such as Fresh Direct and Peapod, also deliver fresh items to your door. The extra shipping cost may be worth it, especially if you factor in the cost of the gasoline and the time it would take to shop locally for these items.

CHAPTER 2

USING THE RIGHT EQUIPMENT

Quick cooking, like all cooking, involves three main elements: ingredients, equipment, and techniques. But if you want to get a meal on the table in record time, all three elements have to be geared for speed. Of the three, it's wise to invest in kitchen equipment that functions reliably and saves time whenever possible because the time savings can be huge. For example, a good food processor will save loads of chopping, slicing, and shredding time; a convection oven will save preheating time as well as cooking time; and an immersion blender will save on prep and cleanup time.

Here's a look at what you need to know about the equipment that makes great home cooking easier and more efficient—from a simple $2 plastic citrus reamer to an elaborate $2,000 grill.

Big-Ticket Items

Let's tackle the expensive equipment first. You'll see some big price tags here. Of course, a convection oven, gas grill, and separate freezer are not absolutely essential. But they will undoubtedly shorten your cooking time if you're serious about cooking faster. Give some thought to investing in the following equipment:

Consider convection. Many modern ovens, including gas, electric, and microwave ovens, come with an option for convection cooking. In these ovens, the main heat source remains the same, but fans circulate the hot air around the food. The constantly moving hot air cooks foods about 25 percent faster than foods cooked in a conventional oven. Convection cooking also eliminates an oven's hot spots, browns food more evenly, encourages a crisper crust on breads and pizzas, and locks in the juices of roasted meats. Convection ovens don't need preheating either. If you're in the market for a new oven, it pays to get the convection option. Not only will you speed cooking, you'll also get better results.

Keep in mind that most recipes are written for cooking in conventional gas or electric ovens. To convert these recipes for cooking with convection, reduce the oven temperature by 25° to 50°F and reduce the cooking time by about 25 percent. Start checking for doneness after about three-quarters of the original cooking time has elapsed. When roasting meats with convection, use a rack that suspends the meat in the air so that hot air can freely circulate around the food and lock in juices. Or put the meat directly on your oven rack and position a drip pan on the lowest rack to catch dripping juices. With either method, heat will reach all surfaces, eliminating the need to turn the meat.

Invest in frozen assets. A freezer offers two main advantages for the quick cook: One, you can buy in bulk, and two, you can freeze double batches of your favorite meals for quick dinners anytime. Buying in bulk cuts down on shopping time, and with main dishes always at the ready, you have more time to relax.

The big question is: Do you need to buy a stand-alone freezer? It depends on the size of your household and the amount of frozen foods you buy and store. Most folks should plan on about 2 cubic feet of freezer space per family member. Assuming you have the typical refrigerator/freezer combo, check the volume label on the inside of your refrigerator to find the volume of your freezer space. If you have a family of four and less than 8 cubic feet of freezer space, consider buying some extra freezer space. Large residential freezers generally cost less than $500 and use only about $8 per month in electricity. The freezer could pay for itself in less than a year if you take full advantage of it. Freeze bulk grains such as oatmeal, flour, and rice to extend their shelf lives. Most breads freeze incredibly well—a plus for people who want to make the most of their local bakeries without traveling there every day. You can also freeze nuts to retard rancidity. And, of course, freeze fresh market vegetables and fruits when in season so you can enjoy their flavor all year long. When preparing desserts, make a double batch and freeze one so you can have brownies, cake layers, cookies, and fruit pies ready at the end of a meal. Once you stockpile these frozen assets, you'll see how a freezer earns its keep by streamlining mealtime.

Get gas. Searing food over the high heat of an open flame is one of the oldest—and fastest—cooking methods around. Plus, cleanup is a snap. Scrape and oil your grill rack and it's ready for the next round of food. For many backyard grillers, tending a wood or charcoal fire is half the fun. But charcoal grilling takes time, which is why easy-to-use gas grills now outsell charcoal grills in America. If you love grilled food but can't stand the wait, buy a gas grill.

When shopping for a gas grill, first look at basic features before ogling the bells and whistles. The grill should be constructed of heavy-gauge metal and be sturdy enough to withstand sleet, snow, and rain, because it will most likely live out in the elements. Look for a thick, solid firebox, a tight-fitting lid, and at least two burners (preferably three or four) with a minimum of 350 square inches of cooking space. That will give you just enough room to grill a simple meal for a family of four. If you plan to host big backyard barbecues, look for 500 squares inches of cooking space or more.

The BTUs aren't crucial, but shoot for at least 30,000 total BTUs, which will allow you to grill consistently at about 500°F. If you intend to grill in cold weather, get a grill with 40,000 BTUs or more. A gas gauge and built-in thermometer are also useful features, as are side tables for extra workspace.

If you like bells and whistles, the first thing to look for is a smoker box, which burns wood chips or chunks. A smoker box provides the convenience of gas as well as the flavor of smoke normally achieved over a wood or charcoal fire. As for other extras, warming racks come in handy, and a side burner is convenient for boiling marinades or making stovetop dishes without having to run back into the house. To totally deck out your grill, buy one with a motorized rotisserie for effortless spit-roasting.

Plan to spend at least $250 for a modest-sized, well-built grill. If you go for all the options, you could be looking at a sticker price of $2,000 or more.

Of course, apartment dwellers can make do with a $20 grill pan or a slightly more expensive electric contact grill such a George Foreman-type. The grill pan, essentially a heavy skillet, features parallel raised ridges on the bottom that resemble the bars of a grill rack. When preheated on the stovetop, the heated ridges quickly sear foods, simulating the grill marks of an outdoor grill. A contact grill works in a similar way but also includes a contact lid with raised ridges so that both sides of the food cook at once.

The obvious features lacking from grill pans and contact grills are the live fire and smoke flavor achieved through real burning embers. The same goes for cooking over a gas flame for that matter. But it is possible to approximate that smoke flavor indoors or on a traditional gas grill. Pick up some liquid smoke seasoning, a natural product available in the spice aisle of most supermarkets. Add a drop or two of liquid smoke to your marinade or sauce, and voila! Instant smoke flavor in your indoor-grilled or gas-grilled food.

You can also add smoke flavor by using smoky-tasting seasonings such as chipotle chiles (smoke-dried jalapeños). Ground chipotle powder injects a smoky, woodsy spiciness to dry rubs, wet marinades, and sauces. Chipotle powder is available in the spice aisle of most grocery stores. Or use canned chipotle chiles packed in adobo sauce.

If you prefer, skip the flavorings altogether and use a smoker bag for indoor grilled flavor. Savu smoker bags made in Finland are sold on the Internet and in upscale grocery store chains like Whole Foods, Trader Joe's, and Wegmans. This ingenious invention traps a layer of wood dust in a perforated lining on the inside of the bag. Put a roast or other ingredients into a baking dish, and then slide the dish into the smoker bag. Seal the bag and, during baking, the wood dust heats up and smolders, emanating flavorful smoke over your food. After the normal cooking time, simply cut the bag open and remove your smoky-tasting food. Toss the bag in the trash and there's no mess or extra time spent achieving outdoor grilled flavor from your indoor oven!

Small Appliances

Further down the price scale are all those electric appliances taking up precious space on your countertop. You know the ones we're talking about: the microwave oven, toaster oven, and stand mixer. Here's what quick cooks should keep—and what they should drop.

Max out your microwave. The first commercial microwave ovens appeared in 1947 and cost about $3,000. Today, you can buy a dorm-room model for $50 or a top-of-the-line model with a convection-cooking option for less than $1,000. Simply put, microwave cooking is the single fastest cooking method available. It's also the most energy-efficient, according to the American Council for an Energy-Efficient Economy.

In case you're curious, microwave ovens work by generating short, high-frequency radio waves that penetrate food and cause the food's water molecules to vibrate rapidly. As the food vibrates—quietly yet intensely—the resulting friction creates heat, which quickly spreads throughout the food. Microwave ovens can reheat foods such as casseroles in a matter of minutes. They also excel at moist-heat cooking methods such as steaming. You can also sauté in a microwave oven. The only things you can't do are bake and roast, because there is no dry heat.

If you're in the market for a new microwave oven, look for at least a 700-watt model. The higher the wattage, the faster the cooking. If you plan to microwave often, you may want to get a 1,000-watt model for increased speed. Most recipes are developed using 700-watt microwave ovens. If you use a 1,000-watt model, decrease the cooking time by 10 to 20 seconds for each minute called for in the recipe. If you have an older 500- or 600-watt model, increase the cooking time by the same amount.

When microwaving individual pieces of food, arrange them in a spoke pattern for the most efficient and even heating. Microwave ovens cook hotter on the edges than in the center, so put the thickest or toughest portion of the food toward the outside. When microwaving cut-up foods, use small, uniform-size pieces (preferably no bigger than 3-inch cubes) for the fastest results, since the radio waves penetrate only about 1 inch into foods.

To speed microwave cooking even further, tightly cover the food to trap steam. Use microwaveable plastic wrap or waxed paper. If possible, try to keep the cover from touching the food.

It also helps to turn the food often for quick, even cooking. Most microwave ovens come with a carousel to turn the food. If yours doesn't, buy an after-market carousel or stop the cooking every minute or two to rotate the food. For casseroles, rice, and other mixed dishes, it also speeds things along to stir the food often.

Give in to the pressure. If you're considering just one new small appliance purchase this year, make it a pressure cooker. These simple, tight-lidded pots turn out tender, flavorful foods in 25 to 50 percent less time than is possible with traditional cooking methods. Let's say, for example, that you love the taste of risotto but hate the constant stirring and long cooking time. You'll swoon over the tender, creamy risotto that emerges from your pressure cooker in just 5 minutes with no stirring whatsoever. Seriously!

Pressure cookers also make quick work of preparing dishes like soups, stews, braises, and chili, which traditionally need time to simmer. Make a double batch of these simmered dishes and your pressure cooker can also help you fill the freezer with ready-made meals for those busy nights when you just don't have time to cook.

These ingenious pots work very simply. A locked-down, airtight lid forces the buildup of pressure inside. As the pressure builds and the liquid heats up, the trapped steam actually raises the boiling point of liquids from 212°F to about 250°F. The higher boiling point quickly breaks down the fibers in foods, causing flavors to mingle quickly and foods to cook faster. Tough cuts of meat are especially well-suited to pressure cooking because they become just as juicy and tender without the wait.

Older pressure cookers were noisy, hissed loudly, and sometimes exploded with improper use. But new, second-generation models operate quietly and have several safety features that prevent explosions, no matter how unskilled in the kitchen you may be. Good, reliable brands of new, second-generation pressure cookers include Kuhn Rikon, Magefesa, and Cuisinart.

Buy at least a 6-quart pressure cooker. It may sound like a lot, but you can fill a pressure cooker only two-thirds full, because you have to allow room for steam pressure to build up. If you often cook in quantity, you may even prefer an 8-quart model. Remember: You can always prepare less food in a large cooker, but you can't prepare more food in a small cooker. And the price difference between a 6-quart and an 8-quart cooker is negligible.

To adapt your favorite stovetop recipes for pressure cooking, reduce the cooking time by 25 to 30 percent. Reduce the liquid by about the same amount, because very little liquid is lost in a pressure cooker. The high heat of this method also tends to weaken the flavors of herbs and spices, so use about 50 percent more seasonings. Otherwise, follow the manufacturer's instructions, and pressure cook your way to lightning-fast meals night after night.

Or take it slow. In contrast to pressure cookers, slow cookers (also known by the popular brand name Crock-Pots) don't cook quickly. But they do offer the invaluable convenience of slow *unattended* cooking. You can start a meal in the morning before work, leave the slow cooker on low heat all day, then come home to a hot meal with no extra effort. This small appliance is a godsend during the cooler months when we crave hot, homemade meals but can't always devote the time to making them.

Buy a large (6-quart) or small (2-quart) slow cooker according to how much stewing and braising you do. If you love to make pot roast or beef stew in quantity or you have a large family, buy the larger model. For occasional unattended slow cooking for a family of four, a medium-size, 4-quart cooker would be ideal.

Almost any stew or braised dish that would gently simmer for a few hours can be adapted for a slow cooker. For every 2 to 4 hours of traditional stovetop simmering or braising, cook the same dish in the slow cooker for 8 to 10 hours on low heat or 4 to 5 hours on high heat. For instance, if your favorite pot roast recipe gently simmers on the stovetop for 2 to 3 hours, cook it in the slow cooker on low power for 8 hours.

Two ovens are better than one. Unless you simply must witness your perfectly toasted morning bread popping up out of a conventional toaster, buy a toaster oven instead of a toaster. A toaster oven does double duty: It toasts bread adequately, and it also serves as a small oven, which is a huge advantage for the quick cook. A standard 30-inch-wide oven takes about 10 to 15 minutes to heat up. Toaster ovens preheat in 2 minutes or less. Plus some baking jobs are just too small for the standard-size oven. Need to quickly melt the cheese on a tuna melt? Melt it in the toaster oven. Want to broil a single-serving steak? Quickly broil it in the toaster oven. Need to toast pine nuts for pasta or a salad? Toast them in the toaster oven. Use the toaster oven for quick baking, broiling, and toasting jobs or when you don't want to heat up the entire kitchen for a small piece of food.

All hail the food processor. In 1973, Carl G. Sontheimer changed the face of America's home kitchens by introducing the food processor under the brand name Cuisinart. He modeled it after an industrial blender he had seen at a food trade show. Food processors have since become the MVPs of the modern home kitchen. They chop, slice, shred, grind, blend, and puree in a fraction of the time it would take to perform these tasks by hand. Food processors also make it easy to knead heavy bread doughs, cut butter into flour, and grate large amounts of cheese.

The recipes in this book use many prechopped ingredients, but you'll still find a food processor to be invaluable for speeding along the odd shredding or pureeing job. And if you're choosing between a blender and a food processor, buy the processor. It can do more. About the only thing it can't do is puree large amounts of liquids at once. But you can use a stick blender for that.

If you don't already have a food processor, look for one that includes a mini bowl that rests in the larger bowl. The mini bowl does a better job with small quantities like mincing a couple cloves of garlic. A mini bowl also cleans up faster than a large bowl. And it's cheaper than buying two processors: a large standard one and a minichopper. Try to get a food processor with at least a 7-cup bowl. If you chop, slice, shred, and puree very often, buy a 10- or 12-cup model. A larger work bowl is especially handy for pureeing liquids in quantity. And if it comes with a mini bowl, you don't have to worry about the bowl being too large for small jobs.

Like all prep equipment, food processors take time to clean. Fortunately, you can speed cleanup by spraying a little cooking spray onto the work bowl and blades or slicing/shredding disk before using. That thin coating of oil prevents foods from sticking to the blades, which is especially important when chopping sticky foods such as dried fruit. For easy cleanup after you use the processor, squirt some dish soap into the work bowl and add a small amount of water. Blend the soapy water in the bowl for a few seconds, then rinse under running water. Simple. Or you can soak the dirty bowl in warm, soapy water as you would any other mixing bowl. To keep the soaking water from draining out through the center hole of the work bowl, plug the hole with a large cork (such as a champagne cork) or a rubber sink plug.

Get on the stick. Are you thinking about buying a conventional countertop blender? Consider a stick blender instead—especially if you already own a food processor. Also known as immersion blenders, stick blenders have one chief advantage over countertop blenders: portability. For this reason, busy restaurant chefs swear by them. Instead of pouring ingredients into the pitcher of a countertop blender, you immerse a stick blender directly into the bowl, pot, or pan containing the ingredients. That means faster blending and one less thing to clean. You save time by eliminating the need to transfer hot mixtures, such as soup, for pureeing. These handy tools also make smooth sauces right in the pan and superfast smoothies and milkshakes. They free up precious counter space, too.

Look for a stick blender with a stainless steel or other solid metal shaft. Metal shafts are more durable and easier to keep clean than plastic shafts. A removable shaft is another big plus. You can remove the dirty shaft and pop it into the dishwasher without worrying about the motor getting wet or wrestling with the cord at the sink. Speaking of cords, if at all possible, buy a cordless stick blender. When pureeing hot mixtures directly in the pan, a cordless model eliminates worries of burning the cord over the stovetop. You might also find extra attachments worth the minor expense. Some stick blenders are available with attachable whisks and even mini chopping bowls, which expedite countless prep jobs.

Bakers love stand mixers. Countertop mixers are space hogs, but if you bake often and have the room, it may be worth your while to keep a stand mixer in your kitchen. Why? Because it will free up your hands to do other things. While your stand mixer blends ingredients in the bowl, you can prep other ingredients or clean the countertop, cutting down on your total work time.

When buying a stand mixer, look for at least a 250-watt motor and a 4- to 6-quart mixing bowl. Some models come with a tilt-head mechanism to lift the beaters up and away from the mixing bowl. Others have a mechanism that lifts the bowl up to a stationary mixing head. The supersturdy bowl-lift model is inspired by commercial mixers and appropriate for heavy use. If you plan to knead heavy bread doughs often, go for the bowl-lift model. In that case, you might also want a bit more wattage in the motor—500 watts or more.

Most serious home bakers will prefer a stand mixer, but it's also a good idea to keep a handheld mixer in your cupboard. If you need to mix anything over the stovetop (such as Italian meringue), the hand mixer will be portable, whereas the stand mixer is not. Of course, if your handy stick blender comes with a beater or whisk attachment, you may just be able to use that in place of a handheld mixer.

Pots and Pans

Good-quality cookware can save time and frustration for the cook. After your knives, your pots and pans are the most often used equipment in the kitchen. Why fuss with cheap pans that warp and heat unevenly, turning out less than adequate food? A reliable sauté pan will deliver fast and fabulous meals year after year. And not all good pans are expensive. Silicone bakeware is the best thing to happen to bakers since stand mixers. Not only is it affordable, silicone bakeware is nonstick, flexible, and heatproof. Here are a few other smart picks among pots and pans.

Invest in heavy metal. Heavy-gauge cookware provides more-efficient heating, less burning, and better durability. Go for the heaviest pots and pans you can afford, such as 18/10 stainless steel. Heavy pans will sound a dull thud instead of a light, sustained ping when rapped with your knuckles. Among metals, the best all-around choice for home cooks is stainless steel with an aluminum or copper core, which provides quick and even heating along with a nonreactive, easy-to-clean, stainless steel cooking surface.

You don't necessarily have to buy an elaborate and expensive matched set of pots and pans. Most home cooks use only three essential pieces: a large skillet or sauté pan, a medium to large saucepan, and a large stockpot. Buy these pieces separately to save money. Use the skillet or sauté pan to sear meats, sauté vegetables, cook pancakes, and make stovetop skillet dishes. Use the saucepan for soups, stews, and sauces. And pull out the stockpot for boiling pasta water or making big batches of soups and sauces. If you frequently steam foods, consider buying a fitted steamer insert basket for the saucepan. And if you make a lot of stovetop or skillet dishes, you may want a small- or medium-size sauté pan in addition to the large one.

Definitely get lids for all of your pots and pans. Putting a lid on a pan traps heat so that water boils faster and sauces cook more quickly.

If you can, buy skillets or sauté pans with heatproof (solid metal) handles. Many dishes, such as braised dishes and frittatas, are cooked in this type of pan and then finished in the oven. A heatproof handle makes this cooking process easier. But if your pan has a plastic handle, don't worry. You can still put it into the oven. Just wrap it first with several layers of heavy-duty foil to protect it from the heat.

Size matters. Once you build up a stock of cookware, here's an easy way to save on cooking time with it: Choose the right pan for the job at hand. If you're preparing 8 ounces of pasta, use a 4-quart saucepan rather than a large 8-quart one. The water will boil faster, and you'll be eating sooner.

To speed heating even further, consider that liquids will boil fastest when the most surface area is exposed to the heat. That means choosing the widest pan you own for cooking liquidy foods, so that the liquid spreads out and covers a larger surface area on the bottom of the pan. For instance, tomato sauces will simmer more quickly in a sauté pan with a wide bottom than in a saucepan with a smaller, more narrow bottom. In the wide sauté pan, more of the liquid is exposed to the heat.

A superwide shallow pan, however, isn't the best choice when it comes to searing or braising meats. When searing or braising, you want the pan to be just big enough that pieces of food fit in it without touching each other or the sides of the pan. If the pieces of food touch each other in a small pan, cooking will be delayed because heat won't be able to get around the edges. If the pieces of food are too far apart in a large pan, the empty areas of the pan will scorch.

The same principle applies to roasting. Always choose a shallow roasting pan that fits the pieces of food without them touching each other or the sides of the pan. That way, the heat of the oven will be conveyed directly to the surface of the food, and the food will roast faster and more evenly. If the pieces of food are put into a deep or too-small roasting pan, are touching the sides of the pan, or are touching each other, the cooking may slow down and the food may steam rather than roast, because the raw heat of the oven will not be conveyed directly over the surface of the food.

Stock a nonstick pan or two. While you're stocking up on pans, keep in mind that at least one good-quality, nonstick skillet or sauté pan should be in every cook's kitchen, especially if you prefer to cook lower-calorie foods. Nonstick pans allow you to cook with fewer added calories by using less cooking fat. A heavy-gauge nonstick pan also makes it easy to pan roast or to sear meats on the stovetop and finish cooking them in the oven, a quick and nifty technique often used by restaurant chefs. See page 58 for more information on pan roasting.

One drawback: Nonstick pans are not as good as conventional metal pans for making pan sauces. If you plan to sauté meat in your pan and then remove the meat and deglaze the pan to make a sauce, a conventional metal pan is the better choice. Conventional metal pans create more brown bits, which are the flavorful by-products used to create a sauce. To learn more about deglazing and pan sauces, see page 57.

Bakers swoon over silicone. Many commercial bakeries swear by silicone bakeware. Home bakers are also discovering the joys of this revolutionary material. Silicone is inexpensive, flexible, nonstick, even-heating, freezable down to -58°F, and heatproof up to 675°F. This slick rubbery material is molded into many traditional baking-pan shapes, such as round cake layers and muffin cups. And silicone offers two distinct advantages over traditional metal bakeware: faster removal of baked goods and easier cleanup. Since silicone is flexible, you simply invert the pan and twist to quickly remove muffins or other individual baked goods. The nonstick surface eliminates the need for added cooking spray and makes cleanup a snap. You can even put silicone bakeware into the dishwasher. Silicone can also be folded, so it takes up less space than traditional metal or nonstick bakeware. These are all big bonuses for the harried home cook and baker.

Essential Gadgets and Utensils

Little cooking tools come in handy, but choose gadgets wisely. If you load your kitchen drawers with every gadget imaginable, you'll never find what you're looking for. Go for essentials like a garlic press, kitchen scissors, and, of course, some good-quality knives. A zesting tool also makes quick work of removing the flavorful zest from fresh lemons, limes, oranges, and other citrus fruits. Here's a quick overview of the top gadgets and how to choose each one.

Knives. The recipes in this book don't require much chopping, but you'll still need a few good knives for slicing grilled meats or loaves of fresh bread. Plan to stock at least three basic knives: an 8-inch or 10-inch chef's knife, a 3-inch or 4-inch paring knife, and a serrated knife for bread and tomatoes. All three should be fully forged (full-tang), meaning that a single piece of forged metal extends from the blade all the way through the handle, where it is riveted in place. For durability and ease of use, look for knives made of high-carbon stainless steel. Buy the best knives you can afford. They are the most often used kitchen utensil. To keep them from dulling, avoid storing them in a drawer. Instead, store them in a cutlery block or on a magnetic wall strip. To sharpen your knives quickly, invest in an electric knife sharpener rather than fussing with sharpening stones and steels.

Kitchen scissors. You'll use this utensil so often that you may want to keep it conveniently stored in a kitchen drawer. Just think about today's convenience foods such as premarinated meats, pres-liced cheeses and deli meats, refrigerated stuffed pasta, frozen preseasoned vegetables, prepared pizza crusts, and prepared cake mixes. They all come sealed in plastic rather than in cans. When cooking for speed and cutting open these ingredients, keep your kitchen scissors nearby at all times. In a utility or gadget drawer near the prep area is an ideal spot. Or, if you use a magnetic wall strip for your knives, you could store the scissors there. Also use the scissors to quickly snip chives and other herbs or to slice precut baby carrots.

Can opener. Many convenience foods, such as precooked beans and prechopped tomatoes, still come in cans. Store a sturdy hand-cranked can opener in your gadget drawer. Don't bother with electric openers. They take up valuable space in the prep area and will undoubtedly break before a good-quality handheld model will fail. Many electric openers are annoyingly slow as well. Look for a manual opener with solid metal construction and comfortable grips, such as the Oxo Good Grips can opener. Many companies make smooth-edge models that promise to eliminate worries over sharp edges, but cooks often complain that these smooth-edge openers do a less efficient job than traditional old-fashioned openers do.

Garlic press. If you're someone who prefers fresh over preminced garlic, a garlic press will save you loads of prep time. You don't even have to peel the garlic. Just pop an unpeeled clove into the chamber of the press, close it, and squeeze. Scrape the garlic paste from the holes and you're good to go. Using this no-peel method, the garlic skin usually pulls away any leftover garlic paste from the holes of the press. However, if any garlic does happen to get clogged in the holes, you can easily poke it out with the hole cleaners that come with most of today's garlic presses. If your garlic press has no hole cleaner, poke out any excess garlic with a toothpick, or run the chamber under warm water. As with most kitchen tools, look for solid metal construction for durability and ease of use.

Citrus reamer. Fresh citrus juice perks up marinades, sauces, drinks, and even plain steamed vegetables. Keep an inexpensive, handheld plastic citrus reamer in your kitchen for fresh citrus juice in seconds. Cut a lemon, lime, or orange in half, twist the cut side over the reamer, and out pours the best-tasting juice you'll find anywhere. To get the most juice from any citrus fruit, let it come to room temperature and roll it on your countertop to break the juice sacs before cutting into the fruit. A quick twist on the citrus reamer will extract the largest quantity of juice faster than hand-squeezing or using a fork.

Vegetable peeler. Here's some terrific news: None of the recipes in this book require you to peel vegetables or fruits—not even the Deep-Dish Golden Delicious Apple Pie (page 336)! So don't buy a vegetable peeler to make the recipes on the following pages. Still, it's a good idea to keep an inexpensive peeler on hand in case you happen to find yourself with a fresh vegetable that needs peeling.

Apple corer. The aforementioned apple pie doesn't require you to peel apples, but it does call for coring them. And an apple corer does it in seconds. Look for a sturdy metal corer with comfortable grips. The Oxo Good Grips corer is a very functional, durable, comfortable, and inexpensive model.

If you frequently make apple crisp, pie, and other desserts in the fall when fresh apples and pears are in season, consider investing in a peeling-coring-slicing machine. These metal contraptions attach to the edge of your countertop and cut your prep time in half for fresh apples, pears, and even potatoes.

Box grater. For big grating and shredding jobs, use the grating or shredding disk of your food processor. Otherwise, grate small amounts of cheese or carrot on a sturdy metal box grater found in most cookware shops and grocery stores.

Chimney starter. Here's an essential gadget for the grill if you're a devoted charcoal griller. Of course, using a gas grill saves even more time, but some folks prefer the smoke flavor of charcoal and the primal joy of tending embers instead of twisting a propane knob. If that's you, pick up a chimney starter at your local hardware store or home improvement center. This $15 contraption looks like tall coffee can with a divider near the bottom, holes in the sides, and a handle. You add some crumpled newspaper or paraffin lighter cubes in the bottom, arrange the charcoal (lump or briquettes) in the top, and light the bottom. The upward draft of oxygen helps to light the coals faster. Typically, you get hot, ashy coals ready for grilling in about 15 minutes—half the time it takes using the old-fashioned method of stacking the coals in a pyramid. Just pour the hot coals out of the chimney starter, spread 'em evenly, and you're ready to grill.

Sharpie and masking tape. Quick cooking almost always involves freezing things ahead. To freeze without confusion, always label and date freezer containers with a permanent marker such as a Sharpie. Use masking tape (or Scotch tape or a blank self-adhesive address label) so you can remove the label and reuse the container. If using foil as a covering, put the tape on the foil before laying the foil over the food. It also helps to jot down a "use by" date and any cooking or reheating instructions such as "Thaw; bake at 350°F for 30 minutes" or "Microwave for 5 minutes covered with plastic wrap." You and your family will appreciate these notes on busy nights when you pull the container from the freezer and expect a fuss-free meal.

Resealable bags. Buy freezer-quality zipper-lock bags. They help to prevent freezer burn and make marinating in the refrigerator a cinch. Spring for "easy zipper" types that close quickly and seal without worries.

CHAPTER 3

AN A-Z GUIDE TO INGREDIENTS

Walk into any supermarket and notice a storewide trend: Ninety percent of the ingredients are designed to save time in the kitchen. That's because food producers know that home cooks are busy people who want help. We're talking about everything from old standbys like canned beans and dried pasta to new products like concentrated broth bases, jarred Asian sauces, refrigerated doughs, preseasoned shredded cheeses, sun-dried tomato paste in a tube, precut produce, and pre-marinated meats.

Precut produce and premarinated meats are the most significant product developments in recent years. These foods traditionally have the longest prep times, but now they come ready to cook. Prechopped onions top the list. You can find refrigerated prechopped onions in tubs in the produce aisle along with prechopped peppers. Or look for frozen prechopped onions in bags. Items like these take the time-consuming prep work out of home cooking so you and your family can enjoy homemade meals without the hassle.

Here's a guide to all the ingredients that make quick cooking easy and delicious. Some products are new to supermarket shelves, but others are fairly traditional items used in innovative ways. Always be on the lookout for the hidden flavor potential in a plain old box of cereal or jar of salsa. Savvy cooks think of all prepared foods as "ingredients" on which to build bigger, better, faster meals.

Alfredo sauce. This popular pasta condiment is nothing more than a classic white sauce (flour-thickened milk) flavored with Parmesan cheese. It's traditionally used as a sauce to make fettuccine Alfredo, but why stop there? Use it as the sauce for a full-flavored lasagna. Or spread it on a pizza crust with broccoli florets to create a white pizza. Get a jump start on creamy vegetable soups by using Alfredo sauce as the base. Or enjoy it in Creamed Salmon on Crisp Potato Cakes (page 233). The French don't call white sauce a "mother" sauce for nothing. Alfredo sauce has endless uses, and it's sitting in your grocery store right now. As with most prepared sauces, both jarred and refrigerated versions are available. Refrigerated sauces tend to taste better because they are less processed.

Anchovy paste. If you like to add bold-flavored anchovies to pasta sauces, dips, and spreads, don't bother with canned anchovies. Pick up some anchovy paste in a tube. The tubes keep longer in the fridge and are more convenient to use. Simply squeeze out as much as you need, then pop the tube back into the fridge for a few months. Anchovy paste is available near the canned anchovies in most grocery stores.

Artichokes. One of today's most time-saving convenience foods, prepared artichokes eliminate the need to trim, cook, trim again, and finally get to the heart of the matter: tender artichoke hearts and bottoms. The bottoms tend to have slightly better flavor, but artichoke hearts are more commonly available. The hearts come whole, halved, quartered, and chopped. They can be marinated in a jar, canned in brine, or frozen. Whole artichokes (without the leaves) are also sold canned and frozen. Quartered, marinated artichoke hearts in jars are the most convenient, ready-to-use, and most widely available. They can be added to countless sauces, dips, spreads, and fillings. Or puree them to flavor a creamy soup. Keep in mind that the oil-and-vinegar marinade does impart a vaguely Italian flavor. If you want unflavored artichokes, go for frozen. They taste closer to fresh artichokes than do the jarred variety.

Asian noodles. Most Asian noodles cook faster than dried Italian pasta does and make speedy stir-fries, salads, and brothy noodle dishes. There are three main types: wheat noodles, rice noodles, and bean thread noodles. Japanese wheat noodles have three subtypes. Soba noodles are gray, nutty-tasting strands made with wheat and buckwheat. Somen noodles are thin, delicate strands, while udon noodles are thick, flat ribbons. All three are made with wheat, which makes them similar to dried Italian pastas. Once boiled, they are essentially interchangeable with pasta strands or ribbons of a similar size and shape.

The real time-savers among Asian noodles are the rice noodles (rice sticks and rice vermicelli) and bean thread noodles (cellophane noodles). Rice sticks are thin, opaque or white strands or ribbons. Rice vermicelli is similar but comes in the form of thin strands packaged in nests. Both types do not require boiling. Just soak in hot tap water for 10 minutes, then drain. Add the soaked noodles to a stir-fry or soupy broth to finish cooking. Bean thread or cellophane noodles are also soaked instead of boiled. These thin, translucent, slippery strands save both cooking and cleanup time. Just put the noodles in a heatproof bowl and add hot tap water. No further cooking is necessary. See bean threads work their magic in Thai Chicken-Noodle Salad (page 244).

Bacon. A concentrated source of salty pork flavor, bacon seems to have endless uses in the kitchen. And quick cooks save time by using precooked bacon. This recent convenience food needs only to be reheated. Look for precooked and crumbled real bacon in packs near the sliced bacon in your grocery store. Hormel is a reliable brand, and this real crumbled bacon tastes far better than crumbled bacon bits in a jar.

Baking mixes. The speedy baker's best friends, these boxed shortcuts include brownie, cake, cookie, gingerbread, cornbread, muffin, and bread mixes. They're excellent time-savers because they combine all the dry ingredients for you, saving on mixing and cleanup. While perfectly acceptable for their intended purpose, savvy cooks think of baking mixes as ingredients on which to build more-elaborate desserts or custom-flavored breads that come together in no time. If you like to bake bread, do it quickly in a bread machine with ready-made mixes for sourdough bread, wheat bread, and country white bread. Pick up some Italian herb bread-machine mix and transform it into Cheese-Herb-Pepper Bread (page 310). Keep brownie mix on hand to make impressive, no-fuss desserts such as Chocolate-Almond Torte with Orange Sauce (page 326). Even plain old yellow cake mix can become the base for a simple snack bar topped with creamy icing such as Banana Bars with Fudge Frosting (page 317). And cornbread mix can be used to make lightning-fast biscotti or cornmeal cake.

A word on brownie mix: Some mixes are good, and some are great. If you want the best-tasting brownie mix that's widely available, look for Ghiradelli Double Chocolate brownie mix. Chocolate chips in the mix help to boost flavor. But the real advantage of this mix over others is the higher quality of the chocolate used.

Barbecue sauce. This sauce is essentially spiced-up ketchup with a smoky aroma. It has built-in flavor, so use it to enrich the taste of any recipe in which you would normally use ketchup. It can be substituted one for one and adds big flavor without having to pull out half your spice drawer.

Barley. Quick-cooking barley is a nice change of pace from plain old rice. It makes a terrific risotto and cooks in about 20 minutes.

Beans. Canned beans are a mainstay of the quick kitchen. Who has time to soak beans overnight, then cook them for an hour the next day? Canned beans may be used right from the can. But some lesser-quality beans have an unpleasant mushy texture. If you dislike mushy beans, stick with canned chickpeas, which stand up to the canning process better than most other beans. Or try Goya, one of the better-quality brands available. To save more time, seek out preseasoned varieties of beans such as pinto beans with chili powder, black beans with lime and cilantro, and garlic-flavored refried black beans. Use them to jump-start black bean soup, dip, chili, stew, or any other bean dish.

Instant dried beans are even more convenient. Sold as a powder, instant beans are often pre-seasoned and designed to be rehydrated with water to make dips. But you can also use the powder to thicken bean soups and sauces. Or try them mixed into a dry spice rub to create a crust on sautéed or grilled fish, chicken, or pork. Instant chickpeas (falafel mix), black beans (refried bean mix), and pinto beans (chili bean mix) are commonly stocked by supermarkets.

Beef. The quickest cooking cuts of beef are ground chuck, flank steak, and tenderloin. For fast meals, keep these cuts in your kitchen along with frozen precooked meatballs and preseasoned hamburger patties. If you like steak, save time by buying barbecue sauce-marinated rib eye steaks, available in many grocery stores. You can also find tubs of completely prepared beef meals such as beef tips in gravy. These heat-and-eat meals taste a bit lackluster on their own, but you can use them to get a head start on a beef stew or stir-fry. Some markets also carry marinated teriyaki beef kebabs and spice-rubbed steaks. Look for them in the butcher's fresh meat case.

Berries. Fresh berries are best, but frozen are a close second when fresh berries are out of season. Keep frozen raspberries, strawberries, and blueberries in your freezer to make quick, refreshing smoothies with yogurt and bananas. When thawed, berries lose some of their juice and soften in texture, which makes them ideal in cooked fruit desserts such a crisps, crumbles, and compotes. Or puree thawed berries with a little sugar to make a simple coulis (fresh fruit sauce) to dress up pound cake, brownies, or other desserts.

Black bean sauce. This pungent Asian condiment is made from fermented black beans and garlic sometimes seasoned with star anise. Spicy "hot" black bean sauce also includes chile paste, toasted sesame oil, and sugar. Use black bean sauce to inject bold flavor into stir-fries, marinade, sauces, soups, and stews that have an Asian flavor profile.

Bread and croutons. Commercial bread bakers have stepped up their offerings in recent years. Most grocery-store bread sections now carry sliced "farmhouse" style sourdough and buttermilk breads as well as nutty, firm breads such as 12-grain and flaxseed bread. For people without a reliable bread baker in town, these grocery-store breads make flavorful meals just that much easier.

When it comes to croutons and stuffing cubes, definitely stick with fresh rather than dried. The flavor of fresh bread cubes is light years ahead of rock-hard stuffing cubes. Look for bags of fresh bread cubes in your grocery store's bakery section for stuffings and bread puddings.

Broccoli. One of the healthiest vegetables out there, fresh broccoli is now available precut, pre-washed, and ready to use. Bags of broccoli florets may cost more than whole heads of fresh broccoli, but once you factor in the large broccoli stem, which most people pay for and then throw away, the cost is nearly the same. Frozen broccoli remains an option, but fresh broccoli tastes much better and is now just as easy (if not easier!) to use. Shredded broccoli, made from the sweet stems, is also available for salads and cole slaws.

Broth. Options abound among supermarket broths—from canned and boxed to bouillon and concentrated broth base. Take a tip from restaurant chefs and use concentrated broth bases for the best flavor and most convenience. They taste richer than bouillon and canned broth, have less salt, and last for months in the refrigerator. Sold in 8-ounce jars by widely available brands such as Better Than Bouillon, concentrated bases come in several flavors so you can have good-tasting beef, chicken, and vegetable broth on hand anytime. Just add a little water for a strong flavor or a lot of water for a gentle flavor. These concentrated broths are terrific added to pan drippings to enrich a simple pan sauce.

If using canned or boxed broths, stick with low-sodium versions, which allow you to control how much salt you add in. Low salt content is especially important when you are reducing (boiling down) the broth because as you boil off water, the salt flavor becomes stronger and more concentrated. Reducing regular canned or boxed broth in this manner would result in an overly salty sauce.

The last resort among premade broths is powdered bouillon. Knorr and Herb-Ox both make long-keeping bouillon cubes with decent flavor, especially for fish and seafood broths that are otherwise unavailable in convenient forms (unless you make the broth from scratch!).

Bruschetta. Once upon a time, bruschetta referred to grilled Italian toast rubbed with garlic and topped with a simple relish, the most popular of which was tomato relish. Now the flavorful topping is so popular that bruschetta refers to the tomato relish itself, a combination of chopped tomatoes, onions, garlic, basil, and olive oil. These ingredients are so central to Italian cooking that prepared tomato bruschetta has endless uses. Keep some refrigerated or jarred bruschetta on hand for an instant pasta sauce, pizza topping, or sandwich spread.

Cabbage. Shredding a head of fresh cabbage isn't difficult, but it does take time. Preshredded green and red cabbage slashes prep time significantly. Often packaged with shredded carrots or broccoli for cole slaw and other salads, preshredded cabbage is a worthy staple if you cook often with cabbage.

Cakes. Most grocery store bakery sections carry prepared angel food cake and pound cake. Use these quick-start simple desserts that you can dress up with sorbet, ice cream, or fresh fruit. Try grilling thick slices of pound cake and top with caramel sauce and bananas. Fill the center of angel food cake with berries marinated in sugar and champagne. Or use these ready-made cakes to create your favorite desserts.

Capers. Packed in brine, these little flavor boosters are the unopened flower buds of a Mediterranean shrub. Use capers like olives to add a salty snap to pasta dishes, salads, and sauces. Capers have a particular affinity for lemon juice and seafood.

Caponata. This Italian eggplant relish comes jarred or canned. It's terrific for making flavorful dips in no time. Or use it as an instant chunky sandwich spread.

Carrots. Canned and frozen carrots suffer from a loss of flavor and texture. Stick with fresh carrots. Convenient forms are now available in grocery stores across America. Look for carrot sticks, shredded carrots, diced carrots, sliced carrots, and machine-cut "baby" carrots. If you can't find diced carrots, use the baby carrots to get a head start on reducing the carrots to bite-size pieces. For quick carrot soups, look for bottled or canned carrot juice near the V8 and other vegetable juices.

Cauliflower. Like broccoli, cauliflower is now available as washed, trimmed, ready-to-use florets in bags. No more trimming and throwing away the stem.

Celery. Even celery is sold prechopped or cut into sticks in the refrigerated produce section of most grocery stores. In the age of precut produce, cooking with fresh vegetables has never been easier.

Cereal. Break out of the rut and consider the cooking potential in a box of cereal. Crushed cornflakes have long been used as a breading for crispy fried chicken. Use Rice Krispies or Grape-Nuts the same way. Add crisp cereals to cookies or spice cakes for extra crunch. Use granola as the topping for a fruit crisp. The possibilities are endless.

Cheese. Purists will want to stick with block-style cheeses for the best flavor. Cheese sold in a solid block has stronger flavor because it is not subject to the air corruption or preservatives in preshredded and precrumbled cheeses. However, most harried cooks will cut a few corners to save time. And preshredded cheeses will save big on prep time. Look also for precubed cheeses, such as Cheddar, Swiss, and American. You won't even have to pull out a knife at mealtime.

Preshredded mozzarella is a must for quick homemade pizzas, but for the most flavor and convenience, look for shredded cheese blends rather than a single cheese, such as mozzarella-Asiago-provolone for pizza and Italian dishes and Cheddar-Monterey Jack for Mexican dishes. Some brands, such as Sargento, now make preshredded and *preflavored* cheese blends, such as Cheddar, tomato, and jalapeño with chili powder for Mexican dishes and mozzarella, sun-dried tomato, and basil for Italian dishes. These eliminate the extra step of adding herbs and spices, because the seasonings are already mixed right into the cheese.

Many preshredded cheeses are available finely shredded or coarsely shredded. Use finely shredded when you want the cheese to melt quickly, as on pizza. Also, when using preshredded cheese in a sauce, avoid overcooking the cheese as it may separate more easily than freshly shredded cheese.

A word on pregrated Parmesan. Most stores now sell *real* Parmesan cheese that is grated or shredded and sold in tubs. This Parmesan cheese tastes worlds apart (much better!) than the stuff you find in green canisters. Stick with real preshredded Parmesan cheese whenever possible.

To save time with other cheeses, look for precrumbled feta and blue cheese. And make use of preflavored soft cheeses, like ricotta mixed with mozzarella and Parmesan. These premixed cheese blends translate into superfast lasagna, stuffed shells, and similar pasta dishes. Also keep a supply of flavored cream cheese on hand, whether it is garlic and herb, salmon, vegetable, chive, scallion, cinnamon, strawberry, or blueberry flavored. Mix savory varieties of preflavored cream cheese into sauces to add creamy texture in an instant. Use flavored cream cheese to stuff chicken breasts for simple yet sophisticated entrées. Or try salmon cream cheese when making a quick lunch or breakfast-to-go, such as Dilly Egg and Salmon Wrap (page 69). You can even turn sweet varieties of flavored cream cheese into mousses, puddings, and cake icings. Available full-fat and reduced-fat, flavored cream cheese should be in every quick cook's kitchen.

While you're stocking up, throw some goat cheese into the cart as well. Unaged fresh goat cheeses (chèvre) are a classy form of cream cheese made with goat's milk instead of cow's milk. They have a drier texture and tangier flavor than cream cheese and a lot more panache. Use goat cheese anywhere you might use cream cheese. Again, make use of preflavored varieties such as cracked pepper, garlic, and herb-flavored to save time.

Chicken. This popular bird continues to reign as America's most frequently eaten meat. It's quick, easy, versatile, and healthy—exactly what today's busy cooks need. Rotisserie chickens offer the whole bird, prepared to be eaten as is or used however the cook sees fit. It is so convenient, in fact, that rotisserie chickens are called for in several recipes in this book, such as quick Chicken Pot Pie with Biscuits (page 216), made also with prepared refrigerated biscuits. To save time on flavoring the bird, look for honey, barbecue, or other flavors of rotisserie chicken as necessary. You can also find rotisserie chicken sold as breast-only or with pieces, depending upon your needs.

Chicken breast remains the most popular cut and is now available preflavored as teriyaki, lemon-pepper, honey-mustard, and garlic-herb boneless, skinless chicken breasts. These premarinated chicken breasts make quick weeknight meals a real cinch. Or look for chicken breasts precut into

QUICKEST COOKING CUTS

In general, tender and lean meats cook faster than tough, fatty, well-marbled cuts. When cooking a tough cut of meat, such as a beef brisket, it takes a long time (up to 12 hours!) for the fat to render out and the meat to become tender. But leaner, more tender cuts, such as beef tenderloin, cook and become juicy in a matter of minutes. Here's a roundup of the quickest cooking cuts of meat, poultry, and seafood to keep on hand for fast and fabulous meals.

BEEF

Ground chuck

Cubed chuck or stew meat

Flank steak

Tenderloin

PORK

Boneless loin chops

Ham

LAMB

Loin chops

Cubed leg meat or stew meat

POULTRY

Boneless, skinless chicken breasts

Boneless chicken thighs

Boneless, skinless turkey breasts

Turkey tenderloin

Ground turkey or chicken

SEAFOOD

Fish fillets

Scallops

Shrimp

Crabmeat

Clams

Mussels

strips for stir-frying or precut into cutlets for sautéing. Tenders or tenderloins are also quick and easy to use for stir-fries and sautés.

Boneless, skinless chicken thighs are moister than breast meat, so consider using them in place of chicken breast halves in your favorite recipes. Fully roasted chicken thighs and drumsticks are available preflavored and simply need to be reheated. Fully cooked chicken wings are also sold in many grocery stores. And for sausage lovers, pick up some chicken sausage in flavors ranging from apple and thyme to roasted pepper and pesto.

Chili-garlic sauce. A staple condiment in southeast Asian cooking, chili-garlic sauce is simply crushed fresh chiles and garlic packed with vinegar and salt. Use it to speed up spicy stir-fry sauces or any other fiery preparation in which chiles and garlic are combined—even Mexican dishes such as enchiladas, burritos, and fajitas.

Chutney. Combining sweet, hot, salty, and pungent flavors and chewy, tender, and smooth textures, chutneys have a lot to offer the busy cook. A dollop of jarred mango chutney can nicely finish a Caribbean-flavored broiled fish fillet. Or use peach-ginger chutney as the sauce for grilled chicken breasts. Find your favorite flavors. Chutney can round out a simple curry dish or be spread on bread to make exotic-tasting sandwiches. Use it to create a pan sauce or to make an instant chunky glaze over roasted meats.

Coconut milk. Canned coconut milk lends instant and interesting flavors to a variety of dishes. When boiling rice, replace half of the water with coconut milk to make coconut rice. Mix it with Thai curry paste for a simple two-ingredient sauce, as in Thai Catfish Curry with Green Beans and Rice (page 184). Or add some coconut milk to chicken broth to make a coconut-flavored chicken soup. You can even use it in desserts like coconut cake, pudding, and flan. Both full-fat and reduced-fat versions are available in the Asian or international section of most grocery stores. After opening, unused canned coconut milk can be frozen in plastic containers for up to 1 year.

Cooking spray. This convenience product saves both time and calories. Just a quick spray and your sauté pans are ready to go with a thin layer of oil on the surface. When baking, skip the painstaking greasing of baking pans and muffin cups with oil and a paper towel. A simple shot of cooking spray does the job quickly and efficiently, especially in pans with lots of nooks and crannies, like waffle irons. Many flavors are available, including canola oil, olive oil, and butter. Frequent bakers may also want to stock one of the baker's sprays such as Baker's Joy or Pam For Baking. These sprays blend flour and oil together in the can. A short spray takes the place of fussing with buttering and flouring cake pans or other baking pans. Look for baker's sprays in the baking aisle of your grocery store or near the other oils.

Corn. In the off-season, frozen corn makes a handy addition to stews, soups, chili, cornbread, or other dishes that incorporate fresh corn kernels. Most stores also sell whole frozen corncobs or cobs that have been halved or quartered. For posole and other Southwestern dishes, use canned hominy, which is simply dried white or yellow corn kernels that have been treated with an alkali to remove the hull.

Couscous. Boxed mixes of flavored couscous offer near-instant side dishes. They can also be turned into more-filling meals simply by adding vegetables and meats. Sauté vegetables or meat in a pan, add boiling water along with the couscous and flavor pouch that comes in the box, and cover. Five minutes later, a satisfying meal emerges from the pan. Flavors range from Italian to Mexican and Indian.

Cucumber. Many recipes instruct you to peel and seed cucumbers before using. That's because American garden cucumbers tend to have thick, bitter-tasting skins and lots of large seeds. To skip peeling and seeding, use English or hothouse cucumbers. These long, skinny cucumbers are often sold wrapped in plastic. Most English cucumbers have few or very small seeds, and the skins tend to be relatively thin and taste less bitter.

Curry paste. Sold in small jars and large envelopes, Thai curry paste usually includes chiles, garlic, lime, lemongrass, shrimp paste, coriander, and turmeric. That's a lot of flavor in a little jar. The jarred variety is often labeled "curry paste," while the envelope may be called "curry base." Despite the different names, these two forms of curry paste can be used interchangeably. And they both keep for months in the refrigerator. Keep some on hand to mix with coconut milk for quick and easy exotic meals anytime.

Deli meats. Why wait in the deli line for sliced meat? Look in the refrigerated case for presliced, prewrapped meats. Many shoppers are familiar with presliced salami and pepperoni. But did you know that now you can get good-quality presliced prosciutto, mortadella, bresaola, and pancetta as well? Look for Fiorucci brand, Italy's number one seller of specialty meat, which now has very wide distribution in American grocery stores.

Demi-glace. This concentrated brown sauce is made from poultry or veal. It's expensive but worth it for the quick cook. Restaurant chefs regularly use demi-glace to give pan sauces a professional finish at the last minute. Add a tablespoon of demi-glace concentrate to the pan with some water to create a glistening, silken sauce in seconds. It's available online and in many gourmet shops.

Dips. Sour cream–based veggie dips can be used to jump-start a sauce for goulash or flavor a Mexican taco salad. Think of these dips as flavored sour cream and use them anywhere you might use regular sour cream in a main dish.

Dough. Along with premarinated meats, refrigerated and frozen prepared doughs are among the best shortcut foods in your supermarket. It takes hours to mix, knead, and raise pizza dough the traditional way. With refrigerated pizza dough, just pop open the canister, unroll the dough, and shape it however you wish. Refrigerated pizza dough is more versatile than fully cooked pizza crusts because you can form them how you like, fill them to create calzones and strombolis, top them to make focaccia, or fry them in little pieces to make the Italian donuts known as zeppolis. Look for refrigerated pizza dough near the dairy section along with other ready-to-go doughs such as biscuit dough and crescent roll dough.

Make simple yet impressive appetizers by filling crescent roll dough with chopped ham and herbed cream cheese, crab and Cajun seasoning, or other fillings before baking. Use biscuit dough to top off a quick pot pie.

Don't forget to stock refrigerated cookie dough. Prepared chocolate chip, peanut butter, and sugar cookie doughs give you a head start on fabulous desserts like Fudgy Chocolate-Peanut Butter Torte (page 328) and Chocolate-Hazelnut Bar Cookies (page 316).

You can also find time-saving doughs in the freezer section. Thaw frozen bread dough, then fill with marinated artichoke hearts, roasted peppers, and provolone and bake it into a quick and satisfying warm picnic loaf. Frozen puff pastry comes in the form of sheets or shells so you can make elegant restaurant-quality appetizers, main dishes, and desserts anytime. To save time with phyllo dough, buy preshaped and prelayered frozen phyllo shells and fill them with your favorite savory or sweet fillings before baking. These time-savers are widely available in the frozen bread section of most grocery stores. See also the listing for piecrust on page 41.

Edamame. Another newcomer to the frozen section is edamame (EH-DUH-MOM-AY), which is a Japanese term for green or uncooked soybeans. Sold both in the shell and preshelled, frozen edamame makes a delicious and healthy snack. Just boil in-shell edamame for 5 minutes, then toss with salt and a touch of sesame oil for a wonderful Japanese appetizer. Preshelled edamame boils even faster and can be dressed up as a side dish, tossed into a stir-fry or pasta dish, or made into a salad that's rich in healthful soy protein.

Eggplant. If you like eggplant Parmesan and eggplant lasagna, pick up some frozen eggplant "cutlets" (breaded frozen eggplant slices) to cut your prep time in half. Eggplant lovers can also find pureed eggplant in the form of baba ghanouj, a Middle Eastern eggplant dip. Use pureed eggplant to flavor and thicken sauces without a whisper of extra work. Caponata is a third form of eggplant that's explained on page 29.

Eggs. Convenience foods are guaranteed to keep coming to your grocery store, and one of the newest is refrigerated pre-hard-cooked eggs. Deviled eggs in minutes? Superfast spinach salad with sliced hard-cooked eggs? These traditional dishes can now be prepared in no time using refrigerated pre-hard-cooked eggs. Look for these little gems in the produce or egg section of your grocery store.

To save time when using scrambled eggs, keep some refrigerated liquid eggs on hand, which are prescrambled. Liquid eggs are also pasteurized, which eliminates worries of bacterial contamination when the eggs will not be fully cooked, as in recipes for homemade mayonnaise, Caesar salad dressing, and Italian meringue. Frozen liquid eggs or low-fat liquid egg substitute can be used in a similar way.

Enchilada sauce. Use canned enchilada sauce as a no-fuss marinade for Mexican-flavored chicken, beef, or pork. Or employ it as intended to streamline the preparation of baked enchiladas. Available in mild and hot flavors, enchilada sauce makes a good taco sauce and chip dip as well. Find it near the canned jalapeños in the Mexican or international section of your supermarket.

Espresso powder. Here's the quickest way to rich coffee flavor. Keep some instant espresso powder on hand to infuse a mocha flavor into chocolate fondues, mousses, puddings, and sauces. You can even add espresso powder to your favorite spice rub to create bold-flavored grilled beef or pork.

Fish and seafood. Canned fish keeps for months and makes it easy to reap the health benefits of fish and seafood. Don't stop at canned tuna. Look also for canned salmon, whole baby clams, and smoked oysters to make easy salads, sandwiches, soups, stews, and paella.

Frozen fish now makes it incredibly convenient to eat seafood meals regularly. Most supermarkets stock good-quality frozen shrimp that's already peeled and deveined, as well as whitefish fillets such as flounder, catfish, and tilapia. You can even find frozen yellowfin tuna steaks. Many of these products are flash frozen before a ship even hits the docks, so their freshness is guaranteed. Considering that most "fresh" fish sold on ice in the seafood case has also been frozen and thawed, it makes good sense to buy some frozen fish to keep in your freezer for fast, fresh-tasting seafood meals whenever you like.

When cooking with fresh fish, buy it preflavored to save time. Many stores sell preflavored fresh fish such as teriyaki salmon steaks, crab-stuffed flounder, garlic-herb cod fillets, or Cajun catfish fillets that are ready to be baked, broiled, or pan-fried, saving you all the prep time.

Fish sauce. Here's another concentrated Asian flavoring that's now widely available in American markets. Also known as nam pla, Thai fish sauce is made from fermented salted fish and has a pungent briny aroma. Add a bit to soups and sauces to give them a signature Asian flavor.

Frozen breakfast items. Fill your freezer with ready-made pancakes, waffles, and French toast for instant breakfasts and brunches. Then you can put your effort into the sauces or side dishes. Or treat frozen breakfast items as ingredients to make knockout brunch and dessert dishes like Pineapple-Stuffed French Toast (page 76).

Frozen vegetables. Some vegetables, including corn and peas, taste better when frozen than when canned. Frozen vegetable mixes also speed prep time. Use a mix of stir-fry vegetables or braising vegetables to whip up quick, healthy meals anytime.

Fruit. The best-tasting option among convenience products here is precut fresh fruit sold in tubs in the refrigerated produce case. Precored and peeled fresh pineapple tastes as close to fresh as possible (short of preparing the fruit yourself!). You can also find handy precut fresh fruit mixes, such as blends of watermelon, cantaloupe, and honeydew melon, that make salads and frozen fruit desserts quick to prepare. Or use fresh fruit mixes to make fruit soups and homemade fruit salsas.

The second-best choice among whole fruit is jarred fruit packed in fruit juice or light syrup, which is sold near the canned fruit in most grocery stores. Jarred fruit retains a bit more flavor than canned fruit because it is not as heavily processed. Use jarred fruit to make simple desserts, or try it also in savory dishes like Caribbean Seafood-and-Black-Bean Salad (page 130).

Among fruit juices, frozen juice concentrates are the most convenient. Just take out a spoonful, dilute it with water, put the lid back on the container, and store it in the freezer for months. Frozen lemon and lime juice concentrates can be reconstituted in seconds to make juice. Plus, they taste better than the preconstituted juices sold near the whole lemons and limes in the produce section. You can also skip the dilution and use juice concentrates full-strength to enliven a marinade, sauce, or fruit soup. Slather full-strength orange juice concentrate over a grilled salmon fillet or full-strength lemon juice concentrate over sautéed chicken. Cranberry, pineapple, and mixed-fruit flavors are widely available and ready to infuse lively fruit flavor into fast-fixing meals.

Of course, purists will want to stick with fresh lemons for the best flavor. On the plus side, they keep for weeks in the fridge and need only be squeezed to release their flavorful juice. For more fruit options, see also individual listings of fruit.

Garlic. Preminced jarred garlic has made flavorful food prep pure joy. But some brands use so much citric acid that you get a bitter aftertaste and much of the garlic flavor leaches out into the packing liquid. For the best-tasting preminced garlic, buy minced garlic in oil. It retains more garlic flavor, and when the garlic is all gone, you can use the garlic-flavored oil as well.

Better yet, pop a clove of fresh garlic—peel and all—into a garlic press and squeeze. Instant mashed garlic.

For roasted garlic, look for roasted garlic paste, available in tubes near the fresh garlic in some grocery stores. These tubes offer the ultimate in convenience and flavor: Just squeeze out as much as you need, then put the tube back into the refrigerator where it will last for months.

Ginger. As with minced fresh garlic, preminced or pregrated fresh ginger shortens kitchen time for busy cooks who demand good flavor. Look for it in jars near the minced garlic in your grocery's produce section or in the Asian foods section. Some brands are labeled "preground" fresh ginger, but rest assured, it is the same product as pregrated fresh ginger. Some stores also sell a mix of preminced ginger and garlic in oil. This jarred product doubles your time savings when making Asian stir-fries, marinades, or any dish that combines fresh ginger and garlic. If you can't find either product, here's the fastest way to peel a knob of fresh ginger: Use the side of a plain old teaspoon to scrape off the peel.

Greens. Bagged salad and cooking greens have revolutionized the produce department. Most

---

USE THE SALAD BAR WISELY

The grocery store salad bar (even fast-food restaurant salad bars) can be a source of precut ingredients that slash your prep time in the kitchen. But shop smart. Salad bar ingredients typically cost $4 to $7 a pound. Sliced cucumbers and sliced onions may be worth the high price tag if you can't get them elsewhere. But shredded carrots, broccoli florets, mixed salad greens, shredded cabbage, chopped onions, and sliced peppers are now available in bags or plastic tubs in the produce aisle for much less money. Use the salad bar only for precut produce or salads that you can't get in the produce aisle.

---

stores now have huge sections devoted to prewashed and pretrimmed spinach, arugula, kale, and collards, not to mention endless varieties of lettuce mixes such as hearts of romaine mix, preshredded iceberg and carrot mix, and tender, leafy green mixes featuring once-exotic greens for salads. Smart cooks make full use of these prepared bagged greens for salads as well as for cooking. Hint: Baby greens such as spinach and arugula tend to cook the fastest and need no chopping into bite-size pieces. It also saves time to buy cooking greens such as spinach in a microwaveable bag. Why dirty another pan if you don't have to?

Guacamole. This Mexican dip of mashed avocado, onion, lime, and cilantro can now be enjoyed any time. Prepared refrigerated guacamole is sold in tubs and dramatically cuts prep time for layered Mexican salads and other dishes employing mashed avocado. Or use it as a creamy and healthful sandwich spread. For the best flavor and texture, look for prepared guacamole made without vegetable gums and thickeners. Calavo is a reliable brand.

Herbs. For the quick cook, dried herbs are the most convenient option. They simply last longer than fresh herbs and come in premixed blends that save prep time. Keep a few basic herb blends on hand, such as poultry seasoning, Greek seasoning, and Italian seasoning.

However, fresh herbs can't be beat for last-minute flavor in salads, sauces, and other dishes. To make fresh herbs last longest, refrigerate them stem-down in a glass of water. A plastic bag loosely draped over the herbs extends shelf life even further. Refill the water as the herbs drink it up through their stems.

Hoisin sauce. This jarred Chinese seasoning sauce is made from fermented soybeans. It's thick, sweet, dark brown, and redolent of aromatic Chinese five-spice flavors. Use hoisin sauce to enhance stir-fry sauces, glaze grilled or roasted meats, or flavor roasted vegetables in an instant.

Hummus. No longer a fringy health food, hummus is now recognized as a tasty, convenient, and versatile dip or spread. Made from pureed chickpeas, garlic, sesame paste, lemon juice, and oil, hummus is usually stocked in the refrigerated case near the refrigerated cheese or produce. It's sold in dozens of flavors, from scallion and roasted red pepper to herbed and olive. Instead of limiting hummus to a veggie or chip dip, think of it as exotic mayonnaise. Use it as a spread on sandwiches (especially wraps) or as a thickener for sauces. Hummus also makes a nifty hot dip when heated with Brie cheese in the microwave oven.

Ketchup. A longtime friend of the quick cook, ketchup now comes in a variety of flavors—and colors! Look for spicy ketchup, barbecue-flavored ketchup, green ketchup, and organic ketchup. Like most sauces, ketchup offers built-in flavor that slashes prep time.

Lamb. Some markets carry boneless premarinated leg of lamb roast in flavors such as garlic and herb. These make Sunday dinners a cinch. Or ask your grocery store butcher for a boned, butterflied, fat-trimmed leg of lamb. This cut is excellent for effortless roasting. Just shake on a spice rub and roast for about an hour. It's perfect for impressing a crowd without taking all day to pull it off.

Lentils. One of the fastest-cooking legumes around, lentils do not need to be presoaked like many beans. Look for boxed lentil mixes sold with seasoning packs that keep kitchen time to a minimum. Flavors range from Italian to Mexican and Indian and put tasty side dishes or main dishes within easy reach of the harried home cook.

Mango. One of the trickiest fruits to peel and chop, mangoes are now available in quick-frozen slices. Upon thawing, the fruit softens a bit and loses some juice, but it's still excellent for smoothies, frozen fruit desserts, pies, cobblers, crisps, and sauces. When buying frozen mango, feel the bag to make sure the fruit is still in individual pieces. If you feel uneven or large chunks, the fruit probably thawed during shipping and was frozen again, which translates into inferior-quality fruit.

Marinades. If you can't find premarinated meats, premixed marinades and fresh cuts of meat are the next quickest thing. Flavors ranging from garlic-herb to lemon-pepper and mango-lime are typically sold near the bottled salad dressings, ketchup, and hot sauces in supermarkets. Fresh marinades tend to taste a bit better and are stocked in the refrigerated case of the produce section near the refrigerated salad dressings.

Keep in mind that marinades have a more concentrated flavor than salad dressings and sauces because they are intended to penetrate tough meats and to be discarded after use. If using a bottled or refrigerated marinade as a sauce, dilute the marinade with liquid such as wine, broth, juice, water, milk, or cream.

Mushrooms. Presliced button mushrooms have been available for years, but now you can also get presliced cremini (Italian brown) mushrooms and pretrimmed, precleaned portobello mushroom caps. Or take advantage of the many gourmet mushroom mixes now on supermarket shelves, featuring mushrooms such as shiitake, oyster, and enoki. Even more convenient are dried mushrooms such as dried porcini. Dried mushrooms keep indefinitely at room temperature and need only to be rehydrated in hot water. Dried mushrooms are best for soups, stews, and sauces, because the soaking liquid retains much of the mushroom flavor. Alternatively, pulverize dried mushrooms and mix the mushroom powder into flour to coat poultry, beef, or pork before sautéing. You can also mix mushroom powder into your favorite spice rub for a subtle mushroom flavor on grilled meats.

Mustard. Take a look at the mustard shelf in your grocery store, and you'll notice something. It's grown! Plain old mustard has now given way to preflavored mustards such as honey mustard, horse-radish mustard, and hot chile mustard in varieties that include grainy, yellow, brown, and Dijon. With flavor built right into the mustard, home cooks now have one less ingredient to add.

Nuts. Preshelled and prechopped nuts will of course save time. But quick cooks go one step further and buy preflavored nuts. Honey-roasted peanuts can be chopped as a sweet garnish for an iced chocolate cake, used to jump-start a crisp or crumble topping, or made into peanut brittle. Spiced nut mixes can speed the preparation of nut crusts for fish fillets. And chopped smoked almonds make a terrific topping for a side dish of steamed green beans. Look for flavored nuts near the other chopped nuts in the snack aisle of your grocery store.

Olives. If your market has an olive bar or Mediterranean bar, make full use of it. Prepitted kala-mata and niçoise olives and prestuffed Greek, Spanish, and Italian olives are terrific time-savers with multiple uses in the kitchen. Many olive bars also sell prepared tapenade (olive and anchovy spread), which makes a terrific dip, sauce, sandwich spread, or wet paste for grilled and roasted meats and fish. For the ultimate in convenience, use olive paste sold in tubes. Squeeze out as much olive paste as you need, then store the rest in the fridge for months. Another convenient newcomer is jarred olive salad, a mix of chopped olives, peppers, garlic, and herbs. It's also called muffuletta, after the classic New Orleans sandwich that it flavors. Olive salad can be added to sauces, soups, and stews for a quick shot of strong olive flavor. Check it out in the vegetarian Broccoli and Bell-Pepper Toss with Tortellini (page 178).

Onions. Chopping onions is perhaps the most tedious and dreaded kitchen prep job. Save yourself the tears by using refrigerated or frozen prechopped onions. Frozen tastes quite close to fresh, if a bit moister due to freezing and thawing. Both refrigerated and frozen prechopped onions are sold in bags or tubs in the refrigerated produce or frozen vegetable sections. You can also find frozen pearl onions, which eliminates peeling time.

Oyster sauce. Similar to hoisin sauce, this thick Asian condiment has a slightly more pungent, fishy flavor from oyster extract. Use it as you would use hoisin sauce in stir-fries and sauces.

Pasta. Refrigerated pasta cooks faster than dried, tastes fresher, and is available in a wider array of flavors when stuffed. Look for refrigerated stuffed spinach-cheese tortellini, chicken-and-prosciutto ravioli, or simple refrigerated pasta strands such as angel hair and fettuccine. Use stuffed mini ravioli to make quick appetizers like Crispy Fried Ravioli with Sicilian Caponata Dip (page 138).

Among dried pastas, save time by using no-boil lasagna noodles instead of traditional dried lasagna noodles. No-boil or "oven-ready" noodles can be layered directly in the pan with a little extra sauce. The noodles cook or rehydrate during baking, saving you one lengthy preparation step.

Peaches. Like frozen mango, quick-frozen peach slices speed prep time. Use them for quick-to-fix smoothies, pies, cobblers, crisps, sauces, and frozen fruit desserts.

Peanut sauce. Bottled Thai peanut sauce packs in loads of exotic flavor from coconut milk, peanuts, fish sauce, garlic, ginger, coriander, lemongrass, and chiles. Keep some Thai peanut sauce on hand to use as an instant nutty-flavored dipping sauce or marinade and to enrich Asian-flavored sauces, soups, and stir-fries.

Peppers. To trim prep time, buy tubs of prechopped or presliced bell peppers from the produce section. Prepared tricolor bell pepper mixes are now available right alongside prechopped mixed onions and peppers. Considering how often fresh bell peppers are used in cooking, it pays to stock them prechopped. Or look for ready-cut frozen bell peppers in the freezer section. See also the listing for roasted peppers on page 43.

Pesto. As with most sauces, refrigerated pesto tends to taste better than jarred. But if you can't find refrigerated, a good jarred brand that's widely available is Sacla. This brand uses fresh basil in its jarred sauce, while many other jarred pestos use dried basil that just can't match the flavor of fresh. The dried pesto mixes sold in envelopes are not recommended, because they also use dried basil and other dried seasonings, which have weak flavor. Take advantage of the many flavors of jarred and refrigerated pesto, including parsley, cilantro, sun-dried tomato, roasted red pepper, and artichoke pestos. Or use pesto in a tube, sold in some gourmet supermarkets. It will last the longest in the refrigerator.

Piecrust. Nothing satisfies quite like a homemade pie. But who has time to mix and roll out piecrust? Newly available sheets of refrigerated pie dough have made homemade pies simple once again. Unroll the dough to create savory galettes and quiches or sweet pies and turnovers with homemade flavor in a fraction of the time. Look for sheets of pie dough near the refrigerated "poppin' fresh" doughs. Refrigerated pie dough tastes closer to fresh than frozen preformed piecrusts do. See it at work in French Mixed-Fruit Galette (page 322).

You can also find prepared graham cracker, vanilla wafer cookie, and Oreo cookie piecrusts in the baking aisles of grocery stores. Combine one of these with your favorite flavor of instant pudding mix for lightning-fast homemade pies.

Polenta. Most Americans love Italian food, and polenta (Italian cornmeal mush) is now widely available in a convenient form. Prepared polenta is sold in a tube shape in the refrigerated produce sections of most supermarkets. Look for flavors such as green chile and cilantro, mushroom, and basil and garlic. It's supereasy to use. Just slice and bake, grill, or brown the polenta in a skillet. Add a sauce, and the meal is done. Prepared polenta is also handy for making polenta stacks with sautéed veggies, cheese, and sauce layered between rounds of the reheated polenta.

Pomegranates. These have a wonderful tropical flavor but are very time-consuming to prepare and juice. Luckily, refrigerated bottled pomegranate juice has recently made its way to grocery store produce sections. It speeds the prep time for any dish, including fresh pomegranate juice. Blend bottled pomegranate juice with a little frozen orange juice concentrate to make an outstanding two-ingredient sauce for pork. Or blend it with other juices and fresh fruit to make smoothies and frozen fruit desserts. Now that good-quality bottled pomegranate juice is available, you can add panache to homemade meals in a fraction of the time it would take with fresh pomegranates.

Pork. Sales of pork continue to climb, and producers have expanded their supermarket offerings for busy cooks. Look for premarinated cuts such as pork tenderloins, chops, spareribs, and sirloin roasts in flavors ranging from teriyaki and barbecue to peppercorn and garlic and herb. Even ham steaks are more convenient to use with flavors such as maple-glazed and honey-glazed. Hormel makes fully prepared tubs of heat-and-eat pork in gravy or barbecue sauce, too. Use these to get a jump on creating a stew, stir-fry, or quick skillet dinner.

Note that some premarinated pork is sold as pork "fillet" or "scaloppini," a thinner cut from the sirloin area. See how delicious a premarinated honey-mustard pork fillet can be when grilled and topped with Swiss cheese in the ultraeasy Cuban Pork Sandwich (page 165). For more pork products, see the listing for sausage on page 44.

Potatoes. One of the most popular foods on the planet, potatoes are now more convenient than ever. Eliminate peeling and prep time by using frozen shredded hash browns, frozen twice-baked potatoes, refrigerated mashed potatoes, and oven-ready seasoned potato wedges. Prepared mashed potatoes can be used to make a savory pie, cream sauce, or soup in minutes. See just how easy dinner can be using prepared mashed potatoes in Basque Shepherd's Pie (page 222). Or pull together an easy weekend breakfast with seasoned diced red potatoes in Frittata with Rosemary Potatoes, Tomatoes, and Feta (page 73).

Among fresh potatoes, small new potatoes are the most convenient. They often don't need scrubbing or peeling because the skins are so thin and they are scrubbed prior to sale. Peeled new potatoes are also available in cans, but canned potatoes have a slightly moister texture and are best cooked with dry heat methods such as grilling, broiling, roasting, or sautéing.

Pudding. Instant pudding mixes give you a great head start on desserts that feature creamy mousses and custards. Use instant pudding to fill frozen puff pastry shells or to make a cold custard dessert such as Clementine Tart with White Chocolate–Macadamia Cookie Crust (page 320). Prepared custard or curd in a jar also speeds prep time for desserts such as lemon meringue pie. Find jarred lemon curd, lime curd, and orange curd near the pie fillings in your grocery store's baking aisle.

Pumpkin. Here's one of the few foods that actually improves upon canning. The canning process breaks down the tough fibers of pumpkin and makes it creamier. Choose solid-pack pumpkin puree for pumpkin pies, custards, and other pumpkin dishes. Pure canned pumpkin puree has no added ingredients and tastes better than flavored pumpkin pie filling.

Rice. Boxed rice mixes can really streamline your meal prep. Seasoned with herbs, spices, and nuts in ethnic flavors ranging from Italian and Mexican to Indian and Spanish, boxed rice mixes make it supersimple to create a main-dish paella, jambalaya, curry, or stir-fry.

Roasted peppers. Roasted pepper paste is now available in tubes. Like other tubed pastes such as sun-dried tomato paste, anchovy paste, and olive paste, roasted pepper paste is the most convenient form of the prepared food. It lasts the longest and can be stirred into sauces, soups, dips, and spreads for on-the-spot flavor. Of course, roasted peppers in jars are also quite convenient.

Salad dressing. The salad dressing offerings continue to grow. In the center aisles of the grocery store, look for sophisticated new flavors of salad dressings, such as sesame ginger. Avoid cooking with these shelf-stable dressings, as they tend to separate upon heating. For the best flavor among creamy dressings, use refrigerated versions sold in the produce section of grocery stores. Blue cheese dressing can be stirred into a creamy soup or used as the base for a summer vegetable tart.

Salsa. Tomato salsa is now more popular than ketchup. Most of it gets used for chips and dip, but you can also use salsa as a convenience ingredient anytime you need chopped tomatoes, onions, bell peppers, and chile peppers. Salsa could be the start of a Caribbean seafood stew or an Asian stir-fry. Look for flavors that match the dish you are making. Perhaps green salsa made with tomatillos, fruit salsa made with mangoes, or black bean salsa made with corn can quick-start your dish and be used as a filling or flavor enhancer. Refrigerated salsa tastes closest to freshly made, but it's also more watery. When substituting refrigerated salsa for jarred, drain the refrigerated salsa before using.

Sauces. See individual listings.

Sauerkraut. Nothing new here, but refrigerated sauerkraut in bags often tastes fresher than canned.

Sausage. Made with a variety of meats in a wide range of flavors, sausage is making a big come-back. Healthy options abound in chicken sausage made with apples and nutmeg, turkey sausage, and low-fat kielbasa. You'll also find spicy andouille and chorizo, hot Italian sausage, and sausages sold in both small and large links. Bold-flavored and easy to use, sausage is a boon to the quick cook. Use kielbasa to add rich smoky flavor to dishes like Chicken-and-Smoked-Sausage Paella (page 204).

Seafood. See fish and seafood (page 35).

Sesame oil. Toasted sesame oil is a mainstay of Asian cooking. Mix it with soy sauce and rice vinegar for a basic stir-fry sauce. Drizzle it onto sautéed greens for a subtly nutty flavor. No matter how you use it, toasted sesame oil adds a distinctive Asian flavor to foods with no extra work from the cook.

Soy sauce. Keep some soy sauce on hand to quickly add salty, savory flavor to stir-fries, marinades, and sauces. Tamari is dark Japanese soy sauce with a very deep, rich flavor. Chinese and Thai soy sauces tend to be lighter in body and taste. Use whichever soy sauce matches the dish that you are making.

Spice mixes. Once upon a time, chili powder was something new in the spice aisle. Today, you can find ancho chile powder, chipotle chile powder, and different chili powder blends for making homemade chili taste mild or blazingly hot. You'll also see a few similar blends sold as fajita seasoning or Southwest seasoning. Keep at least one Mexican chili powder in your spice rack. Also have on hand at least one curry powder blend (whether Madras, garam masala, or plain curry powder), one Cajun or Creole seasoning blend, an Asian blend (such as Chinese five-spice, Szechwan, or Thai seasoning), and a lemon-pepper seasoning. These spice blends save mixing time. Use crab boil seasoning such as Old Bay to quickly flavor seafood. Other good spice blends to have on hand include blackening seasoning and at least one spice rub for grilling or roasting meats.

To quickly flavor sweet pies, puddings, crisps, and crumbles, keep a pumpkin pie spice or apple pie spice blend on hand.

Bear in mind that ground dried spices generally begin to lose flavor after about 6 months. Restock your pantry as necessary.

Sun-dried tomatoes. The concentrated flavor of sun-dried tomatoes makes it easy to enrich sauces, spreads, and dips. They're widely available dried, but for more convenience, use the sliced, halved, or chopped versions that are packed in oil. Or use sun-dried tomato paste in a tube. If you can't find either, sun-dried tomato pesto makes a good substitute.

Tea bags. Think of these little pouches as dried herb and spice blends. Tea bags can be easily added to any hot liquid to create a flavorful infusion for rice, a poaching liquid for fish or poultry, or a deceptively simple dessert sauce. Jasmine tea makes exotic, floral-scented rice. Mint or orange tea creates an aromatic poaching liquid for chicken breasts, fish fillets, and shrimp or scallops. Earl Grey tea can deepen the flavor of a savory sauce to be served with pork or poultry. Use tea bags just like you would use any other bouquet garni or herb and spice mix.

Teriyaki sauce. This is the classic Japanese blend of soy sauce, rice vinegar, ginger, garlic, and sugar. Bottled teriyaki sauce simplifies any dish in which you would combine these ingredients. Use it to marinate meats and fish, to make stir-fry sauces, or as a dipping sauce with a chopped scallion garnish. Most bottles labeled "stir-fry sauce" are very similar to teriyaki sauce, and the two can be used interchangeably.

Tofu. Extra-firm tofu has the most appealing texture for most American palates. Softer tofu tends to taste mushy. Many recipes call for draining, pressing, and then cooking tofu to firm it up even further and release excess moisture. You can skip these steps by using premarinated, baked, or smoked tofu, all of which have a firm texture and can be added directly to stir-fries or other tofu dishes. Smoked tofu is particularly chewy and delicious, with a subtle smoky aroma. It's perfect for kebabs or baking with hoisin sauce and vegetables. Some manufacturers make ready-to-eat tofu that's already cut into triangles or cubes and marinated in lemon-pepper or sesame-ginger seasoning. Use these prepared tofu products to cut down on the time it takes to make healthy, vegetarian meals.

Tomato paste. Tomato paste packaged in a tube is longer-keeping than the canned version and very convenient to use. Just squeeze out as much as you need and return the rest to the fridge, where it keeps for months. No more wasting half a can of tomato paste when you need only 1 tablespoon!

Tomato sauce. Jarred spaghetti sauces generally come in two forms: marinara or ragu. Marinara is light, fresh, and thin or sometimes mixed with vegetables. Ragu is thick and rich and usually includes meat. Marinara is more versatile and fresher-tasting for most quick-to-fix pasta meals. For flavor that's closest to homemade, choose refrigerated marinara, usually stocked with the other sauces near the refrigerated produce, cheese, or hummus.

Tomatoes. Think of canned tomatoes as partially cooked tomatoes. They give you a head start on any dish that includes cooked tomatoes, such as sauces, soups, stews, and braises. Canned fire-roasted tomatoes from Muir Glen have a wonderful smoky flavor, and many grocery stores now carry this brand. Or look for flavored diced tomatoes, such as Italian-seasoned or Mexican-flavored, to save time. These have built-in flavor so the cook has fewer ingredients to add to the dish. Use canned stewed tomatoes for long-cooking dishes like soups and stews, and canned crushed tomatoes for smooth tomato sauces.

To save time with fresh tomatoes, use grape tomatoes. Their smaller size means less chopping, and they can often be added whole to pasta sauces and salads. See also sun-dried tomatoes on page 44 and tomato paste and tomato sauce on page 45.

Turkey. The fastest cooking cut of turkey is boneless, skinless breasts. When sliced through the side into cutlets, boneless turkey breast cooks even faster. Try superfast turkey cutlets in Turkey Scaloppine and Broccoli in Creamy Pan Gravy (page 179).

You can also find the breast sold as turkey London broil, which is a whole boneless butterflied turkey breast. This cut is perfect for marinating and grilling to feed a crowd.

Other quick-cooking cuts include turkey tenders, tenderloins, and ground turkey. Like chicken tenders, turkey tenders make a great addition to fast-fixing stir-fries and sautés. And turkey tenderloin comes premarinated in a variety of flavors such as teriyaki, peppercorn, and lemon garlic. Ground turkey can be made into burgers or meatballs or used anywhere you would use ground beef. Turkey sausage comes in a wide range of flavors and makes a healthier alternative to pork sausages.

V8 juice. This vegetable juice blend makes a more flavorful substitute for tomato juice. Use low-sodium V8 to start up a soup, sauce, gravy, or braising liquid.

Vegetarian products. Grocery stores are filled with vegetarian options in the refrigerator and freezer sections. You can find everything from vegetarian hot dogs, burgers, sausages, bacon, and "chick'n" patties to phony bologna and pepperoni. If you cook vegetarian often, these frozen and refrigerated convenience foods can help you pull together sandwiches, pizzas, and main dishes in no time.

Vinegar. Vinegars capture flavor and acidity in a bottle. Go beyond apple cider vinegar and distilled white vinegar. Stock a good-quality red wine vinegar, white wine vinegar, well-aged balsamic vinegar, sherry vinegar, raspberry vinegar (or other fruit vinegar), and tarragon or other herb vinegar. Whenever you need to perk up a salad, poultry dish, vegetable side dish, or sauce, your flavored vinegar will be ready to help.

Wasabi. Prepared wasabi paste in a tube is easier to use than wasabi powder, which must be rehydrated. Think of wasabi paste as a seasoning and use it as you would chopped ginger, garlic, or prepared horseradish. Mix it into a dipping sauce, marinade, soup, stew, or prepared wet spice paste to be spread over grilled seafood or meat. Look for the words "100 percent grated hon-wasabi" on the tube's label. Lesser quality imitation wasabi paste is made only with horseradish, mustard, and colorings such as spinach powder.

Wonton wrappers. These Asian convenience foods are essentially the same as fresh pasta. If you like to make your own ravioli fillings but don't have time to mix, roll, and cut fresh pasta, use wonton wrappers as a time-saving substitute. Wonton wrappers also allow you to make quick-fixing dumplings and empanadas using the fillings of your choice.

CHAPTER 4

MASTERING QUICK-COOKING
TECHNIQUES

So you've got your quick-cooking equipment and ingredients on hand. Now what do you do with them? Fortunately, most quick-cooking techniques are quite simple. This chapter covers the basics of microwave cooking, pressure cooking, grilling, broiling, sautéing, and stir-frying. For pure speed, these are the fastest cooking methods available, cooking most foods in less than 20 minutes. Deep-frying is another quick-cooking method, but harried home cooks usually avoid this method because it's messy, tricky, and excessively caloric. It takes time for the frying fat to heat up, cool down, and be cleaned up. It's also difficult to maintain a consistent and even temperature in the frying oil, even if you use an electric deep fryer. For these reasons and the decline of deep-frying in home kitchens, only the other quick-cooking techniques are covered below.

Microwave Cooking

Most people use their microwave ovens just to reheat leftovers. But quick cooks take full advantage of this appliance to quickly melt butter or steam vegetables and seafood. The fact is that microwave cooking is the number one fastest cooking method. The high-frequency radio waves generated by a microwave oven cause the water in foods to vibrate so rapidly that the water heats up in seconds, quickly spreading heat throughout food and cooking it in minutes. Because it is a moist-heat cooking method, use the microwave oven only to speed along traditional moist-heat methods such as steaming and sweating. You can't bake or roast in a microwave oven because there is no dry heat to brown the surface of foods.

Steam faster. The microwave oven excels at quickly steaming foods such as vegetables and seafood. Simply put the food into a ceramic, glass, or microwave-safe plastic container that fits the food snugly. Or, if you're steaming bagged spinach or other foods in a microwave-safe package, follow the package directions. (They usually tell you to vent the plastic wrap.)

Keep in mind that microwave ovens cook hotter on the edges than in the center, so put the thickest or toughest portion of the food toward the outside. For vegetables such as broccoli and cauliflower, put the tough stems toward the edges and the tender florets toward the center. For fish fillets and steaks, put the thicker or wider ends toward the edges of the plate and the thinner or narrower ends toward the middle. It also helps to arrange pieces of food in a circular or spoke pattern for the most efficient heating. Or when microwaving cut-up vegetables and seafood, use small, uniform-size pieces that are no bigger than 3-inch cubes to ensure fast, even cooking.

Season the food with spices, garlic, onions, or herbs, then cover the plate or cooking vessel to trap steam and speed cooking even further. Use microwave-safe plastic wrap or waxed paper, and try to keep the cover from touching the food. It also helps to turn and stir foods often for more-efficient heating. If your microwave oven doesn't include a carousel to turn the food, buy an after-market carousel or stop the cooking every minute or two to rotate the food.

In most cases, you just push "start" to microwave foods on high power. Change to medium power if directed by a recipe. Plan on about 30 seconds to 1 minute of cooking for every 4 ounces of vegetables, and 1 to 2 minutes of cooking for every 4 ounces of seafood. For instance, a single 4-ounce fish fillet will cook in about 1 minute. That's much faster than you can steam a fish fillet over simmering water! Avoid overcooking vegetables and seafood, as the residual heat will continue to cook microwaved foods after they are removed from the oven.

Sweat vegetables in seconds. "Sweating" is a form of sautéing that uses lower heat to develop the flavors of vegetables without browning the surface. Many long-cooking dishes, such as soups, stews, and sauces, begin by sweating vegetables before adding meats, liquids, and seasonings. To quickly sweat vegetables, skip the stovetop and head for the microwave oven. Toss each cup of vegetables with about 2 teaspoons of oil, ⅛ teaspoon salt, and a pinch of black pepper directly in a 1-quart microwave-safe container. Cook, uncovered, until the vegetables are tender, 1 to 2 minutes.

Nuke it to get a head start. Use the microwave oven to precook foods so that they can be roasted, baked, or grilled faster. The microwave oven quickly heats up the interior of food; then the grill or conventional oven takes over by browning the surface and finishing the cooking. For chicken parts and pork spareribs, toss every 2 pounds of meat with about ½ cup of your favorite sauce (barbecue sauce or other sauce) right in a microwaveable baking dish. Microwave, uncovered, for 8 to 10 minutes. Meanwhile, preheat your oven or grill, then baste the meat with a little more sauce before transferring it to the oven or grill (if grilling, remove the food from the dish, of course). The meat should brown and finish cooking in about 5 minutes–less than half the time it would take if you began and finished cooking the food in the oven or on the grill.

Melt foods in record time. Butter and chocolate melt in a matter of seconds in the microwave oven. Cut butter into tablespoon-size pieces and microwave in 30-second increments until just melted. To melt chocolate, cut the chocolate into tablespoon-size pieces (or use chips) and microwave for 1 minute. Stop and stir, then continue microwaving in 30-second increments until the chocolate is just soft enough to be stirred into a smooth liquid. When melting chocolate and butter together, add the cut-up butter to the chocolate during the last 30 seconds to 1 minute of cooking.

Keep in mind the cardinal rule of microwaving chocolate: Your bowls and utensils must be bone dry before adding or stirring the chocolate. Even a drop of water on the bowl or the spoon can cause chocolate to seize into a stiff mass. If your chocolate seizes up, unseize it by adding a generous 2 teaspoons of vegetable oil or shortening for every 2 ounces of chocolate. Stir constantly until the chocolate regains its smooth texture.

Pressure Cooking

Science explains why pressure cooking has scores of home cooks singing its praises. Under normal cooking circumstances, liquid boils at about 212°F. But in the airtight environment of a pressure cooker, heat is trapped and pressure builds up, effectively raising the boiling point of liquids to about 250°F. This higher boiling point causes the fibers in foods to break down more quickly, resulting in soups, stews, braises, and chili that cook 25 to 50 percent faster than is possible with traditional cooking methods. Tough cuts of meat are perfect for pressure cooking because they transform into juicy, tender meals in a fraction of the time it would normally take.

With new "second generation" pressure cookers, pressure cooking is far safer and easier than it was in the days of jiggle-top cookers. Simply sauté or combine foods in the cooker, lock on the lid, and bring up the pressure over high heat. New cookers have a "high-pressure line" to clearly indicate exactly when high pressure is reached. Then you lower the heat just enough to maintain high pressure throughout the recommended cooking time. At the end of the cooking time, release the pressure with the cooker's release valve or, for some recipes, remove the cooker from the heat and let the pressure come down naturally. (You can also lower the pressure by leaving the lid on and running the cooker under cold water.) Remove the lid, and that's it. Total cooking time for most pressure-cooked dishes—even those including meat? Less than 15 minutes.

Most cookers come with detailed directions, and the recipes in this book, such as Chunky Mesquite-Pork-and-Beans Chili (page 200), include all the instructions you need. Nonetheless, here are a few quick tips so you can experiment with your cooker and make full use of it for superfast meals.

Leave some headroom. Fill your cooker only one-half to two-thirds full to allow room for pressure to build up. Look for the maximum fill line inside your cooker and stay below it.

Brown meat as usual. To make a pot roast or other braised dish in a pressure cooker, brown the meat in the cooker, uncovered, in a small amount of oil, just as you normally would when sautéing in a conventional pan. Add vegetables, seasonings, and liquids, and then lock on the lid and heat to high pressure. Adjust the heat to maintain high pressure, and cook for the allotted time. Let the pressure come down naturally off the heat, then release the pressure and serve.

Add just enough liquid for gravy. When adding liquid to the cooker along with meat, add the exact amount of liquid you want to create the same amount of sauce or gravy. For instance, if you want 1 cup of gravy when cooking a pot roast, add 1 cup of liquid to the pan. Almost no liquid is lost during pressure cooking.

Cut cooking time by up to 30 percent. When adapting stovetop recipes for pressure cooking, reduce the cooking time by 25 to 30 percent. Liquids should also be reduced by about 25 percent due to the lack of moisture loss in the enclosed environment of the pressure cooker. Increase herbs and seasonings by up to 50 percent, because the high heat of the cooker weakens these flavors.

Broiling and Grilling

These two methods are the oldest and simplest ways to cook food. They're also among the fastest, because the food and heat are close together and there is nothing (such as a pan) between them to slow down the cooking. The intense, direct heat of a broiler or grill quickly browns the surface of food, caramelizing the food's natural sugars, and creates an exterior crust that's full of complex flavor. This is what most people love about the taste of broiled or grilled foods. And inside, the food remains moist and juicy—so long as it isn't overcooked. Thanks to the high heat, the actual cooking time of broiled or grilled foods is typically less than 20 minutes.

Keep in mind that, for the most part, broiling and grilling are mirror images of each other: Broiling cooks by direct, dry heat that is located above the food, while grilling cooks by direct, dry heat that is located below the food. Whether your heat is above or below, the goal is to quickly brown the food's surface for that richly flavored crust while keeping the interior moist and juicy. In many cases, the two techniques are interchangeable. Here's how to master each one.

Choose somewhat thin foods. You can't properly broil or grill a piece of meat that's 3 inches thick. The high heat will burn the exterior before the interior is done. Choose foods that are an inch thick or less.

Keep the food close to the heat. Adjust the height of your grill rack or oven rack for optimum grilling and broiling. Most foods should be broiled or grilled 3 to 4 inches from the heat. Very thin foods such as $\frac{1}{4}$-inch- to $\frac{1}{2}$-inch-thick fish fillets can get as close as 2 inches from the heat. Thicker foods such as 2-inch-thick steaks work best 5 to 6 inches from the heat. Foods that are 3 or more inches thick should be broiled or grilled as far as 10 inches from the heat to prevent burning. And for huge pieces of meat, such as a spit-roasted whole goat or pig, 2 to 4 feet from the heat is best. But this "indirect" grilling method is really closer to roasting than strict high-heat grilling. (See page 53 to learn more about indirect grilling.)

Let foods come to room temperature. Here's an axiom for cooking with dry heat: Warm meat sears better than cold meat. For the best crust on broiled and grilled foods, let them come to room temperature first, about 20 minutes out of the refrigerator, before cooking.

Preheat the grill or broiler. Preheating is most important when grilling, because the grill rack rests between the food and the heat. The rack should get very hot to help create a quick sear on the food and to prevent sticking. Preheat your grill for at least 10 minutes to let the rack get good and hot before adding the food.

When broiling, you can get away with less preheating time or none at all, because the broiler rack is not between the heat and the food. For instance, if you are broiling foods that will cook for more than 5 minutes, such as steaks, you can skip the preheating step and just add 1 more minute to the total cooking time.

Trim excess fat. The close, high heat of broiling and grilling causes fat to quickly melt out of food and drip away, sometimes igniting on the broiler's or grill's heat source. These flare-ups can burn your food and give it an acrid aftertaste. Avoid flare-ups by trimming excess fat from meats before cooking. It also helps to use a drip pan beneath a roasting rack when broiling. On a grill, you can get foods out of the flare-up zone by moving them momentarily to an unheated part of the grill.

But keep lean foods oiled. Broiling and grilling both use high, dry heat. If the food is also very lean (read: dry), it may become overly dry after cooking or stick to your grill rack or broiling pan. When broiling or grilling very lean food such as skinless chicken breasts or vegetables, brush or spray the food with oil or a basting sauce that includes some fat to prevent dryness.

Avoid steam. Creating a perfectly crisp crust requires a dry cooking environment. To prevent steam buildup in a grill or broiler, keep the lid off or the oven door ajar to allow steaming juices to escape.

Let foods cool down. The intense heat of broiling and grilling brings a food's juices quickly to the surface. After cooking, let the food rest for 5 to 10 minutes so that the flavorful juices can redistribute throughout the food. This minor resting period results in moister, better-tasting grilled and broiled meats.

Brush and oil your grill rack. For the best results when grilling, brush and oil the rack just before adding the food. Scrape the preheated rack with a stiff wire grill brush. Then wad up a paper towel, dip it into oil with tongs, and wipe the oily towel over the hot rack. An oily paper towel does double duty here: It lubes up the metal bars of the rack and cleans off any remaining residue from your last grilling session. You could also spray the rack with cooking spray after brushing it, but first remove the rack from the hot grill to avoid flare-ups.

Use indirect grilling for bigger, tougher foods. Thus far, we've been discussing direct grilling, the most common form. To successfully grill tough foods or foods that are more than 1 inch thick, use a method known as indirect grilling. Instead of putting food directly over the heat, you keep the food away from the heat and keep the heat on medium-low to low so that the food cooks more slowly. This method coaxes great flavor out of big or tough cuts of meat like beef brisket or whole tenderloin, pork shoulder or loin roasts, whole chickens and turkeys, and bone-in poultry parts.

Let's assume you're using a gas grill. If you really want homemade flavor in half the time, it is undeniably faster to grill with gas than with charcoal. To do indirect grilling on a gas grill, just fire up some of the burners while leaving the others off. If your gas grill has two burners, light one and put your food over the unlit burner. If your grill has three or more burners, fire up the outside burners and put the food over the middle unlit burner(s). Unlike the method for fast, direct grilling, when indirect grilling, you want to keep the grill lid down, because heat escapes every time you lift the lid, which lowers the overall temperature and lengthens the already-slow cooking time. It also helps to put a disposable aluminum pan of water (or other liquid) on another part of the grill rack to provide steam, which keeps long-cooking foods from drying out.

Grill with wood chips for smoky flavor. While gas grilling is convenient, it doesn't provide the signature smoke flavor of food grilled over a wood or charcoal fire. For both flavor and convenience, use wood chips on a gas grill. Wood chips soaked in water (or other liquids) slowly smolder, infusing smoke flavor into foods. Because this flavor infusion intensifies over time, wood chips are best suited to indirect grilling rather than direct grilling, because the food has more time to absorb the smoky aromas from the smoldering wood.

NO-COOK SAUCES

Perhaps the most famous no-cook sauce is pesto. A blend of fresh basil, garlic, olive oil, pine nuts, and Parmesan cheese, pesto makes a fabulous pasta sauce that requires absolutely no cooking. Here are a few other uncooked sauces that cut down on kitchen time.

Avocado Sauce: Mash half a ripe avocado with ½ cup Italian salad dressing. Dollop onto grilled poultry or fish. Makes about 1 cup.

Mustard Tarragon Sauce: Combine ¼ cup mayonnaise, 2 tablespoons extra-virgin olive oil, 1 tablespoon white wine vinegar, 1 tablespoon sour cream, 1 tablespoon Dijon mustard, 1 tablespoon chopped fresh tarragon, ¾ teaspoon salt, and ⅛ teaspoon ground black pepper. Dollop onto grilled or broiled chicken or seafood. Makes about ½ cup.

Horseradish Dill Sauce: Combine ½ cup plain yogurt, ½ cup sour cream, 1 finely chopped scallion, 1 tablespoon prepared horseradish, 2 tablespoons minced fresh dill,

½ teaspoon salt, and ¼ teaspoon ground black pepper. Dollop onto grilled fish and serve with lemon wedges for squeezing. Makes about 1 cup.

Fresh Tomato-Tuna Sauce: Toss together ¼ cup extra-virgin olive oil, 1½ tablespoons balsamic vinegar, 3 chopped large ripe tomatoes, 3 tablespoons pitted kalamata olives, 3 tablespoons chopped fresh basil, 1 chopped scallion, 2 minced garlic cloves, ½ teaspoon salt, and ⅛ teaspoon ground black pepper. Gently fold in 1 can (6 ounces) oil-packed tuna along with its canning liquid, leaving the tuna in large chunks. Toss with hot cooked pasta. Makes about 4 cups.

Most backyard grillers use all-purpose hickory or oak chips, but try others as well. Pair alder wood chips with poultry and seafood; apple wood chips with pork, vegetables, and seafood; cherry wood chips with poultry; mesquite with beef; and pecan with pork and vegetables. To make sure the chips smoke instead of incinerate, soak them in cold water for about 30 minutes. The longer you soak them, the longer they'll smolder before burning up.

How do you add wood chips to a gas grill? Some high-end models have a smoker box and dedicated burner for wood chips. If your grill has a smoker box, put a thick layer of soaked wood chips right into the box. If your grill doesn't have a smoker box, use a foil cooking bag as a pouch, or make a pouch by wrapping the wood chips in foil. Poke holes in the foil so smoke can escape. Put the foil-wrapped chips right over one of the hot burners and crank the burner (or your dedicated smoker box burner) to high until you see lots of smoke. Then turn the heat to whatever temperature is right for the food you're cooking. The rich, smoky flavor you get from wood chips is really worth this little bit of fuss on a gas grill. For the best results, keep the lid down to trap the smoke.

Sautéing

Proper sautéing is accomplished in a matter of minutes, making it one of the fastest and most popular cooking techniques. It's also one of the easiest: Heat some fat in a pan, add food, and cook, turning or stirring a few times, until the food is nicely browned all over. Technically speaking, sautéing is in the same genre as grilling and broiling. It's a high-heat, dry-heat cooking method that rapidly browns the surface of food, creating a delicious crust. The two major differences are the pan and the added fat. Both help to keep sautéed food from drying out as it cooks. The leftover juices in the pan also give you a head start on creating a simple sauce.

Sautéing is often done as an initial cooking step to brown the surface of foods before finishing the cooking with another method such as braising or roasting. In fact, "browning" is a synonym for sautéing. If you ever read a recipe that directs you to "brown" foods in a pan, you will essentially be sautéing. No matter what you call it, here's how to get the technique right every time.

Choose thin foods for stand-alone sautéing. Most sautéing is done in 10 minutes or less. To use this technique on its own (as opposed to sautéing in combination with another cooking method), choose foods that are an inch thick or less, such as fish fillets or boneless chicken breasts, so that the interior of the food cooks before the exterior burns.

Or combine sautéing with another method. For foods that are thicker than 1 inch, begin by sautéing and browning the surface of the food, then finish the cooking with another method such as roasting (in which you transfer the food—in the pan—to a 450°F oven) or braising (in which you add a small amount of liquid to the pan, cover it, and finish cooking slowly over low heat).

Preheat the pan and fat. The biggest mistake made with sautéing is using a pan or oil that's not hot enough. Hot fat performs two functions in a sauté. It browns the surface of the food, and it prevents it from sticking to the pan. Even if you use a nonstick pan, include a small amount of oil or cooking spray to facilitate browning. Here's the easiest way regardless of the pan you use: Put the pan over high or medium-high heat and let it preheat for 1 minute. Then add the fat until it melts and shimmers, about another 30 seconds to 1 minute. The fat should be hot enough so that the food hops around a bit when added to the pan.

Use just enough fat. How much fat is the right amount? It depends on the type of pan you use, the size of the pan, and the amount of food added to it. Plan on adding at least enough fat to create a thin film (about $\frac{1}{16}$ inch) over the entire bottom of the pan. For a 10-inch cast-iron or stainless steel pan, 1 to 3 teaspoons of fat should do it. However, you could use up to 2 tablespoons if you'll be sautéing several cups of food or using the fat to create a sauce after sautéing. In a 10-inch non-stick pan, you can get away with as little as $\frac{1}{2}$ teaspoon of fat. When in doubt, add a little more fat rather than a little less, because hot fat is crucial to a good sauté. Before adding the food, swirl the hot fat so that it covers the entire bottom of the pan.

Use dry foods at room temperature. Wet or cold ingredients will steam in a hot pan rather than sauté. And steaming inhibits browning. For the best, most flavorful browning, bring foods to room temperature before adding them to the pan. It also helps to keep the food dry. Pat excess moisture from foods or add juicy vegetables to the pan right after they are cut and before they release lots of moisture. To create a dry surface on moist foods such as thin pieces of fish, poultry, or meat, dust the food with seasoned flour, bread crumbs, or a ground spice mix.

Give the food some room. Leave some space around sautéing food so that heat can circulate freely. Overcrowding the pan will trap steam and inhibit proper browning. Again, sautéing is really a dry-heat cooking method, and moist steam derails the process.

Choose a 6-inch or 8-inch sauté pan for sautéing 1 cup of food or less. A 10-inch or 12-inch pan nicely handles 3 to 5 cups of food. The food should remain in a single layer, and you should be able to see the bottom of the pan between pieces of the food. Don't use a huge pan for sautéing a small amount of food, however. The unused areas of the pan will scorch and create a burnt flavor in a sauce made in the pan after the food is sautéed.

Saute in batches if necessary. For large amounts or several pieces of food (such as multiple chicken breasts or pork chops), sauté the food in continuous batches, removing pieces as they are done. This allows the remaining pieces to cook more quickly.

Don't stir right away. To facilitate browning, let foods cook a minute or two in the pan before stirring. Once the food begins to turn light brown, frequently stir cut-up foods like vegetables to prevent burning. Stirring cut-up foods also speeds along the cooking by allowing heat to constantly penetrate all surfaces of the food.

Let bigger, thicker, or uncut foods like chicken breasts brown a bit longer, turning them only once or twice after the food has browned. Resist the temptation to constantly turn thicker, flat foods.

Make a pan sauce. Here's the major advantage of sautéing for quick cooks: You can easily make a flavorful sauce in the same pan after the food is sautéed. Simply sauté your food, and then remove it to a plate to keep warm near the stove. Then add liquid to the hot pan. Add double the amount of liquid that you'd like to end up with as sauce. For instance, add 1 cup of liquid to end up with ½ cup of sauce. Use wine, vermouth, sherry, port, stock, milk, cream, vegetable juice, or another liquid of your choice. The liquid will bubble when added to the pan, at which point you scrape the leftover brown bits from the bottom of the pan and stir them into the liquid (known as deglazing). Gently boil the liquid over medium-high to high heat until the browned bits dissolve and the liquid reduces in volume by about half (also known as reduction). Stir in a small amount of butter for a silky texture, or thicken the sauce with a little cornstarch that's been dissolved in cold water.

Get creative. The basic pan-sauce procedure described above has endless possibilities—from the liquids used to the aromatic seasonings added. For extra flavor, toss some vegetables like shallots or mushrooms into the leftover hot fat in the pan before adding the liquid. Or create complex flavors by using a combination of liquids, such as wine and stock or sherry and cream. For the best-tasting "layered" flavor, add liquids separately as described above, reducing each one in volume before adding the next. You can also add chopped fresh herbs, ground spices, prepared chutney, flavored oil, flavored vinegar, pesto, or almost any other flavorful ingredient to the sauce. One caution: Add strong-flavored seasonings—especially salt—toward the end of cooking, because the flavors will concentrate as the liquid reduces in volume. And if you want a supersmooth texture for your sauce, strain it through a fine-mesh sieve after cooking is complete.

Pan Searing

Sautéing in nonstick pans has given way to two modified forms of the technique: pan searing (or pan grilling) and pan roasting. Both methods are like sautéing in that they create an extra-crisp and browned crust on seafood, poultry, and meat. The major difference is that no fat is added to the pan. Otherwise, the technique follows the same path: You add food to a hot pan and cook it quickly over high heat.

Use pan searing for thin, moist foods. Sea scallops, pounded boneless chicken breasts, and thin steaks and chops are great choices for pan searing. This method is also tailor-made for foods that you want to cook the surface of but keep raw or rare in the center, such as seared tuna steaks or lamb chops.

Here's how: First, turn on a fan or open the windows, because pan searing creates smoke. If you don't like smoke, don't pan sear. Next, heat a heavy nonstick pan over high heat until very hot. Your hand should get warm pretty quickly when held a few inches from the pan's bottom. Add the food to the hot pan and let it brown without turning. When the food is nicely seared and browned on the bottom (1 to 2 minutes), turn and brown the other side. Simple. Because the foods used are thin (or intended to be rare inside), they will finish cooking in less than 5 minutes in the pan.

Use pan roasting for thicker foods. Pan searing is so quick that it doesn't give thick foods time to cook through. For thicker steaks and chops, take the technique one step further by finishing the cooking in a hot oven—known as pan roasting. Before you start, preheat your oven to about 500°F. Then pan sear the food as directed above. Sear the food until the bottom is lightly browned, then quickly turn the food and transfer the entire pan with the food in it to the hot oven to finish the cooking. Close the oven door to contain the smoke and the heat. The food should finish cooking all the way through in less than 10 minutes and still retain a wonderfully crisp crust.

Use this method only in a pan with heatproof (solid metal) handles, because the handle will get smoking-hot in the oven. Of course, you'll also need oven mitts or a folded kitchen towel to remove the hot pan from the oven. But you'll be rewarded with a supercrisp, restaurant-quality crust on your food.

Stir-Frying

Second only to microwave cooking, stir-frying is incredibly fast. Actual cooking time is usually less than 5 minutes. The process is similar to sautéing except that the food is constantly stirred over very high heat and liquid is usually added to the food during cooking. Here's how to make perfect stir-fries at home.

Prep everything ahead. Once you start stir-frying, you'll have no time for last-minute prep. Everything from slicing meats and chopping vegetables to gathering spices and mixing sauces should be done before the cooking begins. To facilitate quick and even cooking, cut food into thin strips or other small, uniform pieces. Create the signature tender-crisp texture of stir-fried vegetables by cutting long vegetables (such as carrots, celery, and asparagus) on the diagonal. A diagonal cut exposes more of the food's surface area to the heat and fosters a tender-crisp texture. No matter what you stir-fry, keep it simple. Choose one meat or seafood and just one or two vegetables. Classic combinations include beef with broccoli, chicken with mushrooms, and shrimp with asparagus. Let additional flavor come from the stir-fry sauce and aromatic ingredients such as scallions, ginger, garlic, and chiles.

Choose the right pan. Woks are traditional for stir-fries but made for tall flames that reach up and around the curved exterior of the pan. Most home stovetops can't create this sort of flame, so the best pan choice is a deep, heavy skillet or sauté pan with sloping sides. Avoid nonstick pans for stir-frying because they slow down the cooking and inhibit browning.

Preheat the pan and fat. Put your dry pan over maximum high heat. This cooking method starts and ends with the pan over the highest possible heat, which is how it's done so quickly. When the pan is hot, add an oil that has a high smoke point, such as peanut, canola, or soybean oil. Swirl the oil around the hot pan until it shimmers but doesn't smoke (10 to 15 seconds). The oil should be hot enough so that a drop of water evaporates instantly in the pan.

Add tough foods first. Keep the heat on maximum high and add foods in order of toughness: first, meats such as sliced beef (30 seconds to 1 minute); then, fibrous vegetables such as broccoli (30 seconds); then, soft vegetables or seafoods such as bell peppers or shrimp (30 seconds); and finally, aromatics such as scallions, ginger, and garlic (15 to 30 seconds). As foods are added and while they cook, stir constantly to promote quick, even browning.

To speed the cooking of very fibrous or thick foods such as cauliflower, precook them in the preheated pan by adding a small amount of water and covering the food, lifting the lid to stir every 10 to 15 seconds. The steam will help to quickly soften the food's tough fibers. Remove the food from the pan, continue stir-frying the other ingredients, then add the precooked food back into the pan along with the aromatics and seasonings.

Sauces go in last. Just before cooking is complete, add soy sauce, hoisin sauce, oyster sauce, or other liquids (prepared teriyaki or stir-fry sauces are quickest). The sauce will sputter and reduce slightly in the hot pan, at which point you can remove the pan from the heat. Serve the stir-fry with this somewhat thin sauce (the fastest, easiest, and purest way), or thicken the sauce by keeping the pan over the heat and adding a small amount of cornstarch that has been dissolved in water. To do

GUIDELINES FOR ADJUSTING RECIPES

Recipes are typically designed as precise formulas. Yet sometimes you may want to double or triple the recipe to increase its yield or halve it to decrease the yield.

The Ground Rules: Follow these basic guidelines when altering any recipe.

■ When increasing the recipe, try to multiply by an even number.

■ When decreasing the recipe, try to divide by an even number.

■ Increase or decrease measurements proportionally. The one exception: salt and other seasonings, which you should hold back on increasing proportionally. You can always add more salt later if necessary.

■ Look at the lowest common denominator. Some recipes don't divide in half neatly. For instance, you don't want to end up halving an egg.

■ For clarity, rewrite the recipe with the changed amounts. Or write the new amounts in the margin and follow them religiously.

■ Timing can often change when altering a recipe, so it's more important to focus on visual cues and/or internal temperatures to determine doneness.

Doubling with Ease: Some foods double up with very few complications. For example, if you want to make an extra pound of pasta, simply increase the amount of cooking water. To make twice the standard amount of rice, double the water and use a wider, deeper pan.

Other recipes are a bit more tricky. The additional volume of food may mean that you'll need to add to the cooking time. For instance, you may want to double a cookie recipe and place two baking sheets in the oven when the recipe calls for one sheet. In this case, it's best to increase the total baking time slightly (and possibly reduce the oven temperature by 25°F for more delicate cookies). Also, place the sheets above and below on different oven racks, and rotate the sheets halfway through to ensure even baking.

To double a batch of food for sautéing, it's easy enough to use a larger sauté pan and increase the sautéing time slightly. But be careful not to use a pan so large that it heats unevenly on your burner. And if the amount

this, push the food to the sides of the pan and stir the cornstarch mixture into the liquid in the center of the pan until the sauce thickens.

Garnish as necessary. A sprinkling of sesame seeds, peanuts, cashews, or chopped fresh herbs finishes a stir-fry nicely.

of food will crowd the pan that you're using, sauté in batches instead. When doubling a recipe for a sauté, it's not necessary to add twice the amount of oil or butter to the pan at the start. Begin with the amount specified for one batch, and add more oil as needed.

The one caveat of doubling is this: Avoid doubling recipes for eggs in the same pan. When making scrambled eggs or omelettes, for example, too many eggs in one pan will take too long to cook and will turn rubbery. For the best results, cook the eggs in batches.

Reducing Amounts: Most recipes can be halved easily. Keep in mind that less food will cook in less time; you may need to reduce the total cooking time to avoid overcooking the smaller amount of food. For a sauté, there are fewer ingredients absorbing heat from the pan. Pull the food from the pan sooner, or cook it at a lower temperature or in a smaller pan to avoid overcooking. For cookies, make sure that the pan has no significant vacancies, or it may overheat and burn the cookie bottoms. For muffins or cupcakes, if you aren't filling all of the cups in the muffin pan,

add 1" or so of water to each empty cup to prevent the pan from overheating.

Baking by the Book: Altering baking-related recipes is decidedly more risky than altering any other recipe. Whenever possible, follow a baking recipe to the letter. Amounts of leavener, flour, sugar, liquid, and other ingredients are specifically calculated for balanced results in the crucible of the oven. Change the amounts, and the results can be drastically different. Cakes, for instance, are very temperamental. If you want to double the yield of a cake recipe, make one cake, then follow the recipe again to make another cake while the first one bakes in the oven. Or look for a cake recipe that is specifically written for a large cake. Likewise, with piecrusts for a two-crust pie, it's best to make one crust according to the recipe, then make another one as the first crust chills to avoid overworking a large amount of pie dough (which results in tough, chewy pastry). Cookies, on the other hand, are generally more amenable to increasing or decreasing yields. That's yet another reason why cookies are so popular and versatile.

BROCCOLI AND SUN-DRIED TOMATO QUICHE *page 80*

CHAPTER 5

FASTER THAN THE DINER—
GREAT BREAKFASTS FOR
FAMILIES ON THE GO

Looking for a way to break your cold cereal rut? Start your day off on the right foot with one of these easy-to-prepare breakfasts. Many can be assembled the night before so your mornings are as stressfree as possible. Several are so satisfying, you may even prefer to have them at night.

Peanut-Butter Banana-Raisin Waffle Sandwiches

Egg-Cheddar-Chutney Muffin Sandwich

English Muffins with Cinnamon Cream-Cheese and Apricots

Dilly Egg and Salmon Wrap

Mexican Eggs

Scrambled Eggs and Baby Shrimp

Hot Links Hash

Frittata with Rosemary Potatoes, Tomatoes, and Feta

Baked German Apple Pancake with Lemon Curd

Pineapple-Stuffed French Toast

Oats Pudding with Dates and Walnuts

Sonoma Baked Eggs

Broccoli and Sun-Dried Tomato Quiche

Ginger-Granola Breakfast Bars

Tutti-Frutti Smoothie

PEANUT-BUTTER BANANA-RAISIN WAFFLE SANDWICHES

Five Ingredients or Less!

Replacing ordinary bread with frozen waffles adds fun to these classic sandwich elements. For a variation, you can drizzle 1 teaspoon of honey or jelly over the filling. Or, for a nutritional boost, top with 1 teaspoon of toasted wheat germ.

Hands-On Time: 5 minutes

Total Time: 5 minutes

Makes 4 servings

8　frozen whole-grain or regular waffles

½　cup creamy or crunchy peanut butter

4　tablespoons raisins

2　medium bananas, halved and sliced lengthwise

Preheat the oven to 400°F. Line a small baking sheet with aluminum foil.

Lay the waffles on the baking sheet. Spread the peanut butter over the waffle tops. Sprinkle half of the waffles with the raisins. Top with the banana slices and the remaining waffles, peanut butter sides down. Bake for 2 to 3 minutes, turning once, or until the waffles are crispy. Cut in halves diagonally.

MAKE AHEAD FOR THE REFRIGERATOR: The sandwiches can be assembled the night before serving. Place on a small baking sheet lined with aluminum foil. Cover tightly with plastic wrap. Refrigerate. In the morning, remove the plastic wrap and bake.

EGG-CHEDDAR-CHUTNEY MUFFIN SANDWICH

Five Ingredients or Less!

Aged Cheddar cheese is one of the glories of the traditional English breakfast table, often paired with hot-and-sweet fruit chutney. Here these classic flavors get your day going with egg in a portable muffin sandwich.

Hands-On Time: 2 minutes

Total Time: 6 minutes

Makes 1 serving

1 multigrain English muffin, split

1 tablespoon fruit chutney, such as peach-ginger

1 pre-hard-cooked egg, sliced

2 slices (2 ounces) sharp Cheddar cheese

Open the muffin and place, split sides up, on a 6" long piece of aluminum foil. Spread both sides with the chutney. Top with the egg and cheese. Broil 6" from the heat source for about 4 minutes, or until the cheese is bubbling. Fold the foil to bring the halves together into a sandwich.

QUICK TIP: To get a head start the night before, slice the egg and refrigerate it in a zipper-lock bag. Split the muffin and wrap it in the aluminum foil.

ENGLISH MUFFINS WITH CINNAMON CREAM-CHEESE AND APRICOTS

Five Ingredients or Less!

Simple and quick, these toasts
are an agreeable convergence
of crunchy, creamy, and fruity.
The apricot spread can easily
be doubled and refrigerated for
up to a week so you can make
a single-serving breakfast or
snack in an instant.

Hands-On Time: 5 minutes

Total Time: 5 minutes

Makes 4 servings

⅓ cup (4 halves) drained jarred or canned apricot halves in light syrup, patted dry

2 tablespoons all-fruit apricot spread

1 teaspoon lemon juice

4 multigrain English muffins, split and toasted

4 tablespoons cinnamon-brown sugar whipped cream cheese

In a bowl, combine the apricots, apricot spread, and lemon juice. With a fork, tear apart and coarsely mash the apricots. Lay the muffins, split sides up, on a work surface. Spread the cream cheese on all the muffin halves. Spoon the apricot mixture over the top.

DILLY EGG AND SALMON WRAP

Five Ingredients or Less!

*This tasty breakfast-to-go won't
get soggy if you make it up the
night before. Wrap it in plastic
wrap or aluminum foil before
refrigerating.*

Hands-On Time: 2 minutes
Total Time: 2 minutes

Makes 1 serving

1 (8"-wide) regular or whole wheat flour tortilla

3 tablespoons salmon cream-cheese spread

1 pre-hard-cooked egg, sliced

¼ teaspoon dried dillweed

 Ground black pepper (optional)

3 leaves baby spinach

Place the tortilla on a paper towel or a piece of waxed paper.
Spread with the cream cheese. Top with the egg and dill. Season to taste with pepper, if desired. Top with the spinach. Roll
into a tube.

—————— *Double-Duty Gadgets* ——————

MELON BALLER

Most cooks pull out their melon ballers only when making fruit salad. But these sharp-edged
spoons have many other uses. Need to quickly seed a cucumber that's halved lengthwise? Scoot
out the seeds with a quick swipe of the melon baller. Or use a melon baller to easily remove the
core from a whole apple or pear that will be baked or poached. You can also use it to easily and
accurately portion out teaspoon- or tablespoon-size balls of cookie dough onto a baking sheet.

MEXICAN EGGS

Five Ingredients or Less!

Serve with warm tortillas to complete this fast, but satisfying, rendition of huevos rancheros, or "ranch-style eggs."

Hands-On Time: 5 minutes

Total Time: 5 minutes

Makes 4 servings

1 can (15 ounces) vegetarian refried beans

³/₄ cup refrigerated or jarred salsa, divided

8 eggs

Chili powder

¹/₄ cup sour cream

Coat a large nonstick skillet with cooking spray. Add the beans and ¹/₂ cup of the salsa. Stir to mix. Cook over medium-high heat for 2 minutes, or until the mixture is bubbling hot. Spoon the beans onto 4 plates.

Wipe the skillet with a paper towel. Coat with cooking spray. Set over medium heat. Add the eggs. Season to taste with chili powder. Cover and cook for about 6 minutes, or until the eggs are cooked to the desired doneness (see note).

With the side of a spatula, cut the eggs into 4 servings. Place the eggs on the reserved plates. Garnish each serving with 1 tablespoon of the reserved salsa and 1 tablespoon of the sour cream.

NOTE: The USDA recommends that unpasteurized eggs be cooked until the yolks are firm, or to a temperature of 160°F. If in-shell pasteurized eggs are available, they can safely be cooked just until the white is opaque and the yolk is set but still runny.

SCRAMBLED EGGS AND BABY SHRIMP

It's a good idea to keep some frozen baby shrimp on hand for quick salads and dips. Here they're mixed into scrambled eggs for a no-fuss brunch dish.

Hands-On Time: 10 minutes

Total Time: 10 minutes

Makes 4 servings

6 eggs

1 tablespoon water

1 teaspoon hot-pepper sauce

1/2 teaspoon salt

1/4 teaspoon ground black pepper

2 tablespoons vegetable oil

1 cup cleaned and shelled bagged frozen baby shrimp, thawed

3 scallions, sliced

1/2 teaspoon preminced oil-packed garlic

In a medium bowl, beat the eggs, water, hot-pepper sauce, salt, and pepper until blended.

Heat the oil in a wok or large skillet over medium-high heat. Add the shrimp, scallions, and garlic, and stir-fry for 30 seconds. Reduce the heat to medium-low and add the egg mixture. As the mixture begins to set on the bottom of the pan, scrape up with a spatula until all the egg is set.

TIP: For a tasty garnish, sprinkle 1 to 2 tablespoons of shredded Cheddar cheese over each serving.

HOT LINKS HASH

This country-style dish is hearty enough as a breakfast on its own. It's also good as a side for eggs.

Hands-On Time: 3 minutes
Total Time: 13 minutes

Makes 4 to 6 servings

- 2 tablespoons vegetable oil
- ½ cup prechopped onion
- ½ cup tricolored prechopped bell pepper
- 1 package (5 ounces) fully cooked breakfast sausage links, cut into ½" chunks
- 2 cups (8 ounces) frozen potato wedges
- 2 tablespoons chopped fresh parsley (optional)

In a large skillet, heat the oil over medium-high heat. Add the onion and bell pepper. Cover and cook, stirring occasionally, for 4 minutes, or until browned. Add the sausage, potatoes, and 2 tablespoons of water. Cover and cook, stirring occasionally, for 8 minutes, or until the potatoes are hot. With the back of a spatula, smash some of the potatoes. Sprinkle with the parsley, if using.

QUICK TIP: Prepare the Hot Links Hash and cool completely. Spoon into a plastic storage container and refrigerate for up to 5 days. To reheat, place 1 serving on a microwaveable plate. Cover with waxed paper. Microwave on medium-high power for 2 minutes.

FRITTATA WITH ROSEMARY POTATOES, TOMATOES, AND FETA

A frittata is an Italian-style open-faced omelet. Equally delicious served warm or at room temperature, it's a fantastic one-dish breakfast.

Hands-On Time: 5 minutes

Total Time: 15 minutes

Makes 4 to 6 servings

2 tablespoons olive oil

$\frac{1}{2}$ bag (16 ounces) refrigerated rosemary and roasted-garlic diced red potatoes

1 can (14 ounces) diced tomatoes with zucchini, bell pepper, and carrots, drained and patted dry

6 eggs

$\frac{1}{4}$ cup water

$\frac{1}{2}$ teaspoon ground black pepper

$\frac{1}{2}$ cup (2 ounces) precrumbled feta cheese

In a large nonstick skillet, heat the oil over medium-high heat. Add the potatoes and tomatoes. Cook for 3 minutes, stirring occasionally, or until heated through.

In a bowl, beat the eggs, water, and pepper. Pour into the skillet. Cook for 1 minute, or until the edges start to set. With a spatula, carefully lift up the edge to let the uncooked egg run underneath. Sprinkle on the cheese. Cover and reduce the heat to low. Cook for 2 minutes, or until the eggs are cooked through.

BAKED GERMAN APPLE PANCAKE
WITH CHERRY PRESERVES

If you don't have cherry preserves on hand, you can replace it with strawberry jam, maple syrup, or black currant jelly.

Hands-On Time: 4 minutes
Total Time: 40–45 minutes

Makes 6 to 8 servings

2 Golden Delicious apples, cored and sliced in the food processor

¼ cup butter

¼ cup packed brown sugar

1 cup whole milk

4 eggs

1 cup biscuit baking mix

½ teaspoon ground cinnamon

Confectioners' sugar

½ cup jarred cherry preserves

Preheat the oven to 400°F. Coat a 9" deep-dish pie plate with cooking spray.

Place the apples, butter, and brown sugar in the dish. Stir to combine. Cover with plastic wrap, leaving a corner vent. Microwave on high power, stirring once, for 6 minutes, or until partially cooked.

Meanwhile, measure the milk in a large measuring cup. Add the eggs. Beat with a fork until smooth. Add the baking mix and cinnamon. Mix just until no longer dry. Pour the batter over the apple mixture.

Bake for 30 to 35 minutes, or until puffed and golden. Dust with confectioners' sugar. Dollop some of the cherry preserves on each serving.

PINEAPPLE-STUFFED FRENCH TOAST

Hands-On Time: 10 minutes
Total Time: 10 minutes

Makes 4 servings

8 slices (³/₄" thick) Hawaiian sweet bread

4 tablespoons pineapple cream cheese

4 eggs

1 cup milk

2 tablespoons butter

¹/₂ cup maple syrup (optional)

Arrange the bread in four stacks so that equal-size slices are on top of each other. Evenly spread 1 tablespoon of cream cheese over 1 slice in each stack, leaving a ¹/₄" border. Top each stack with the remaining slice, and press gently to seal.

In a large shallow bowl or pie plate, combine the eggs and milk, whisking until smooth.

Melt 1 tablespoon of butter in a large nonstick skillet over medium high heat. Working in batches, quickly dip both sides of each sandwich into the egg mixture (do not soak). Transfer to the skillet and cook for 2 to 3 minutes on each side, or until golden brown. Repeat with the remaining butter and sandwiches. Serve warm. If desired, serve with syrup.

OATS PUDDING WITH DATES AND WALNUTS

Modeled after old-fashioned British steamed puddings, this morning meal can be prepared on an evening or weekend to have on hand. It's tasty and satisfying served hot, accompanied by milk, or cold, with sliced fruit.

Hands-On Time: 5 minutes

Total Time: 1 hour and 5 minutes

Makes 6 to 8 servings

1½ cups quick oats

3 cups vanilla soy milk

½ cup (3 ounces) prechopped dates

½ cup (3 ounces) prechopped walnuts

¼ teaspoon apple pie spice

Preheat the oven to 325°F. Coat an 8" × 8" glass or ceramic baking dish with cooking spray. Place the oats, milk, dates, walnuts, and spice in the dish. Stir to mix. Cover with aluminum foil. Bake for about 1 hour, or until thickened and bubbling. Let stand for 10 minutes.

QUICK TIP: Prepare Oats Pudding with Dates and Walnuts and cool completely. Cover with plastic wrap and refrigerate. To reheat, place 1 serving on a microwaveable plate. Cover with waxed paper. Microwave on medium power for 2 minutes.

SONOMA BAKED EGGS

This easy entrée is great for a weekend brunch. It also makes a wonderful weeknight supper that can be assembled the night before or in the morning.

Hands-On Time: 6 minutes

Total Time: 1 hour

Makes 4 to 6 servings

1 dozen eggs

½ package (4 ounces) sliced Canadian bacon, cut into 1" pieces

1½ cups (3 ounces) bagged Parmesan-ranch croutons

1 cup whole milk

1 cup (4 ounces) bagged Cheddar-Jack cheese chunks

½ cup sliced scallions, white and light green part

Preheat the oven to 325°F. Coat a 12" × 8" glass or ceramic baking dish with cooking spray.

Break the eggs into the dish. Beat with a fork until smooth. Add the bacon, croutons, milk, cheese, and scallions. Stir with a fork to combine. Press the croutons into the milk mixture to moisten. Bake for 45 minutes, or until the eggs are set and golden. Let stand for 10 minutes.

MAKE AHEAD FOR THE REFRIGERATOR: This dish may be assembled the night before serving. Cover tightly with plastic wrap. Refrigerate. In the morning, remove the plastic wrap and bake according to the recipe directions.

BROCCOLI AND SUN-DRIED TOMATO QUICHE

A traditional broccoli quiche would require making a pie shell from scratch, washing broccoli florets and blanching them, grating cheese by hand, and lightly frying onion in a skillet. This streamlined variation requires almost 50 minutes less of hands-on preparation time but tastes fabulous.

Before 1 hour 45 minutes

After 58 minutes

Time Saved 47 minutes

Makes 4 to 6 servings

Photo on page 62

1 (9"-wide) deep-dish frozen pie shell

5 ounces (2 cups) bagged broccoli florets, coarsely chopped in the food processor

$\frac{1}{2}$ cup prechopped onion

3 tablespoons olive oil

$\frac{1}{2}$ teaspoon salt

$\frac{1}{2}$ teaspoon ground black pepper

$\frac{1}{2}$ teaspoon ground paprika

1 cup half-and-half

$\frac{1}{4}$ cup prechopped oil-packed sun-dried tomatoes

1 cup (4 ounces) preshredded Parmesan-Romano-Asiago cheese blend, divided

3 eggs

Preheat the oven to 400°F. Bake the pie shell for 8 minutes, occasionally pricking with a fork to deflate any air bubbles, or until lightly colored. Remove the shell and set aside. Reduce the oven temperature to 350°F.

Meanwhile, in an 8" × 8" microwaveable baking dish, combine the broccoli, onion, oil, salt, pepper, and paprika. Cover with plastic wrap, leaving a small corner vent. Microwave on high power, stirring once, for 3 minutes, or until sizzling. Remove. Add the half-and-half, tomatoes, and $\frac{3}{4}$ cup of the cheese. Add the eggs, one at a time, beating with a fork after each addition. Pour the filling into the reserved pie shell. Sprinkle with the remaining $\frac{1}{4}$ cup of the cheese. Bake for about 35 minutes, or until set. Let stand for 15 minutes.

We Saved Time By

- Using a prepared frozen pie shell instead of mixing, chilling, and rolling dough into a shell from scratch

- Using precut, prewashed bagged broccoli florets instead of washing a head of broccoli and cutting it up

- Using prechopped onion instead of peeling and chopping an onion

- Using a microwaveable dish, which won't require scrubbing, instead of a skillet to sauté the onion and broccoli

- Using preshredded cheese instead of shredding it from a block

- Using prechopped sun-dried tomatoes instead of chopping whole sun-dried tomatoes

GINGER-GRANOLA BREAKFAST BARS

Five Ingredients or Less!

Like a cross between moist ginger muffins and packaged granola bars, these hearty, portable pastries are ideal to tuck into a backpack or briefcase.

Hands-On Time: 5 minutes

Total Time: 30 minutes

Makes 12 bars

1 egg

1¼ cups lukewarm water

1 box (14 ounces) gingerbread mix

3 cups reduced-fat granola cereal

Preheat the oven to 350°F. Coat a 12" × 8" baking pan with cooking spray. In a mixing bowl, combine the egg with the water. Beat with a fork until blended. Stir in the gingerbread mix just until moistened. Add the granola. Stir to combine. Pour into the prepared pan. Bake for about 25 minutes, or until the bars spring back when pressed with the fingertips. Cool in the pan on a rack.

QUICK TIP: For instant breakfasts, store the cooled bars in an airtight container for up to 4 days.

TUTTI-FRUTTI SMOOTHIE

Five Ingredients or Less!

This portable fruit bowl is refreshing, pure, and simple. For an extra-frosty frappe, slice the bananas onto a sheet of waxed paper and freeze them overnight.

Hands-On Time: 3 minutes
Total Time: 3 minutes

Makes 2 servings (1 cup per serving)

$\frac{1}{2}$ cup loose-pack mixed frozen berries or strawberries

$\frac{1}{2}$ cup canned crushed pineapple in juice

$\frac{1}{2}$ cup plain yogurt

$\frac{1}{2}$ cup sliced ripe banana

$\frac{1}{2}$ cup orange juice

In a food processor fitted with the metal blade, in a blender, or in a large measuring cup with an immersion blender, combine the berries, pineapple (with juice), yogurt, banana, and orange juice. Process for about 2 minutes, or until smooth.

PROVENÇAL SUB SANDWICH *page 98*

CHAPTER 6

ON THE LIGHTER SIDE—
SANDWICHES, SOUPS, AND SALADS

Celebrate seasonal, garden-fresh dishes without spending hours prepping vegetables; many ingredients are already prechopped at your grocery salad bar.

Minted Melon Soup

Gazpacho

Chilled Borscht

Chunky Broccoli-Spinach Soup

Italian Wedding Soup

Colorado Corn Bisque

New Mexico Bean-and-Green-Chile Stew

Spicy Black-Bean Soup with Bacon

Seven-Grain Veggie-Delight Sandwich

Teriyaki Tuna Roll-Up

Chicken Caesar Sandwich

Provençal Sub Sandwich

Bacon-and-Egg Salad

Bacon-Tomato-Pesto Sandwich

Hot-Beef Sandwich with Horseradish and Provolone

Cajun Potato Salad

Quick Carrot Slaw

Blue Cheese–Walnut Cabbage Salad

Sicilian Cauliflower-Olive Salad

Spring Greens, Chickpeas, and Tomatoes with Feta Dressing

Spinach Salad with Hot Bacon Dressing

MINTED MELON SOUP

Melons are one of summer's supreme pleasures. Why not get creative with them? Here's a fun way to enjoy melons—in a refreshing soup that cools even the most intense summer heat.

Hands-On Time: 5 minutes

Total Time: 5 minutes (plus 1 hour chilling time)

Makes 4 servings

7   cups cubed honeydew melon or cantaloupe

$\frac{1}{4}$ cup lemon or lime juice

8   fresh mint leaves

1   tablespoon honey

$\frac{1}{8}$ teaspoon almond extract

$\frac{1}{4}$ teaspoon ground nutmeg

Pinch of salt

Puree the melon or cantaloupe, juice, mint, honey, almond, nutmeg, and salt in a large food processor or blender. Refrigerate for at least 1 hour or as long as 2 days.

GAZPACHO

By combining good-quality canned tomatoes and a few selected fresh prepared ingredients, this refreshing soup truly rivals the made-from-scratch fresh tomato standard.

Hands-On Time: 5 minutes

Total Time: 5 minutes (plus 1 hour chilling time)

Makes 4 to 6 servings (6 cups)

1   red bell pepper, quartered

$\frac{1}{3}$ English cucumber (15 ounces)

2   cans (15 ounces each) diced tomatoes

$\frac{1}{2}$ cup refrigerated or jarred tomato salsa

1   bunch scallions, white and light green parts, sliced

1   teaspoon ground black pepper

1   cup ice water

In a food processor fitted with the shredding blade, shred the bell pepper. Without emptying the work bowl, shred the cucumber. Add the tomatoes (with juice), salsa, scallions, and pepper. Pulse 12 times, or until coarsely chopped. Add the water. Refrigerate for 1 hour or as long as 2 days.

QUICK TIP: Store unopened canned tomatoes in the refrigerator to eliminate the chilling time for the soup.

CHILLED BORSCHT

Five Ingredients or Less!

Lovers of this colorful potage had to go through quite a mess to prepare it. Beet roots had to be scrubbed and either boiled or baked until tender. The beets had to cool before peeling, a process that colored the cook's hands magenta. The beets then had to be shredded by hand, seasoned, and chilled. This modern rendition beats the clock.

Before 2 hours

After 1 hour and 5 minutes (1 hour chilling time)

Time Saved 55 minutes

Makes 4 to 6 servings (4 cups)

2 jars (16 ounces each) sliced pickled beets, drained (reserve juice)

2 dill pickles, quartered

2-3 tablespoons pickle brine

1 bunch scallions, white and light green parts, sliced ($\frac{1}{3}$ cup)

$\frac{1}{4}$ cup sour cream

In the bowl of a food processor fitted with a metal blade or in a blender, combine the beets and pickles. Process for about 1 minute, or until coarsely chopped. Add the beet juice and 2 tablespoons of the pickle brine. Pulse to combine. Refrigerate for about 1 hour to chill. Taste and add up to 1 tablespoon of pickle brine, if needed. Top each serving with scallions and a dollop of sour cream.

QUICK TIP: Store the pickled beets in the refrigerator beforehand to eliminate the chilling time for the soup.

———————————— *We Saved Time By* ————————————

- Using precooked, canned beets instead of cooking fresh beets

- Using a food processor to save time on chopping and cleanup

- Using natural juices from the canning and pickling process to thin the soup instead of making stock and using additional seasonings

CHUNKY BROCCOLI-SPINACH SOUP

With its intense color, this mellow soup could be the signature dish of the Emerald City of Oz.

Hands-On Time: 4 minutes
Total Time: 12 minutes

Makes 4 to 6 servings (6 cups)

¼ cup butter

1 cup prechopped onion

¼ cup flour

5 cups vegetable broth

1 bag (5 ounces) baby spinach (5 cups)

1 bag (8 ounces) broccoli florets, finely chopped in the food processor

½ teaspoon salt

½ teaspoon ground black pepper

In a large saucepan, cook the butter and onion over medium heat for 3 minutes, or until softened. Add the flour. Stir to combine with the onion mixture. Add the broth. Cook, stirring constantly, for 3 minutes, or until simmering briskly. Add the spinach, broccoli, salt, and pepper. Stir. Cook for 8 minutes, or until the broccoli is crisp-cooked.

ITALIAN WEDDING SOUP

One legend has it that this delightful soup takes its name from the harmonious marriage of ingredients.

Hands-On Time: 4 minutes
Total Time: 12 minutes

Makes 4 to 6 servings (7 cups)

1 tablespoon olive oil

$\frac{1}{2}$ cup prechopped onion

8 cups chicken broth

3 ounces thin spaghetti, broken in half

$\frac{3}{4}$ teaspoon ground black pepper

3 ounces (about 1 cup) precooked cocktail-size meatballs, quartered

$1\frac{1}{2}$ cups baby spinach, shredded

In a large pot, combine the oil and onion. Cook over medium heat for 1 minute, or until sizzling. Add the broth, pasta, and pepper. Bring to a boil. Cook, stirring, for 5 minutes. Add the meatballs and spinach. Reduce the heat to low. Cook for 5 minutes, or until the pasta is tender.

COLORADO CORN BISQUE

This brightly hued, spicy soup comes together in a snap from ingredients in the pantry and refrigerator. If prepared guacamole isn't on hand, replace it with a dollop of sour cream or plain yogurt.

Hands-On Time: 5 minutes
Total Time: 12 minutes

Makes 4 to 6 servings (4 cups)

2 tablespoons olive oil

½ cup prechopped onion

½ teaspoon poultry seasoning

½ teaspoon chili powder

2 cans (15 ounces each) cream-style corn

½ cup jarred roasted red bell peppers, drained, torn into chunks

¾ cup vegetable broth or water

1 teaspoon hot-pepper sauce

4-6 tablespoons prepared guacamole

In a large saucepan, combine the oil, onion, poultry seasoning, and chili powder. Cook, stirring occasionally, over medium-high heat for 5 minutes, or until the onion is lightly browned. Add the corn, bell peppers, broth or water, and hot-pepper sauce. Bring to a brisk simmer. Reduce the heat to medium-low. Simmer for 5 minutes. Serve each portion with a dollop of the guacamole.

NEW MEXICO BEAN-AND-GREEN-CHILE STEW

Convenient canned pumpkin puree takes the place of hard-shell squash, a vegetable that requires a great deal of time and effort to peel and cook. Satisfying and flavorful, this superfast main dish is also a nutritional powerhouse packed with vitamin A and fiber. But that can be the cook's secret.

Hands-On Time: 5 minutes
Total Time: 15 minutes

Makes 4 to 6 servings

¼ cup vegetable oil

1 cup prechopped onion

2 tablespoons preminced oil-packed garlic

1 tablespoon ground cumin

1 teaspoon salt

2 cans (15 ounces each) great Northern beans, rinsed and drained

1 cup frozen corn kernels

1 can (15 ounces) pumpkin puree

1½ cups vegetable broth or water, divided

½ cup mild, medium, or hot refrigerated or jarred green salsa

2 teaspoons sherry wine vinegar or red wine vinegar

¼ cup minced fresh parsley or cilantro (optional)

In a large skillet, combine the oil, onion, garlic, cumin, and salt over medium heat. Cook, stirring occasionally, for 5 minutes, or until the onion is softened. Add the beans and corn. Stir to coat with the seasonings. Add the pumpkin, 1 cup of the broth or water, and the salsa. Bring to a simmer. Reduce the heat to medium-low. Simmer for 5 minutes. Stir in the vinegar and more broth or water if the stew is too thick. Sprinkle with the parsley or cilantro, if using.

SPICY BLACK-BEAN SOUP WITH BACON

*Dried, or "instant," black beans
are usually turned into black
bean dip. But you can also
rehydrate them with chicken or
vegetable broth to make a soup
base. This easy soup gets to the
table in less than 10 minutes.
Look for instant black beans
near the beans or boxed rice
mixes in your grocery store.*

Hands-On Time: 5 minutes

Total Time: 10 minutes

Makes 4 servings

4 cups chicken or vegetable broth

1 box (7 ounces) instant black beans

1 can (15 ounces) black beans, rinsed and drained

1 cup chunky salsa

¼ cup (1 ounce) bagged crumbled bacon

¼ teaspoon salt

⅛ teaspoon ground black pepper

Bring the broth to a boil in a medium saucepan. Stir in the
instant black beans, canned black beans, and salsa. Simmer for
5 minutes. Stir in the bacon, salt, and pepper and heat through.

SEVEN-GRAIN VEGGIE-DELIGHT SANDWICH

This pleasant alternative to delicatessen meat sandwiches boasts colorful, crunchy ingredients.

Hands-On Time: 2 minutes
Total Time: 2 minutes

Makes 1 sandwich

2 slices seven-grain sandwich bread, toasted

2 teaspoons stone-ground mustard

2 slices (2 ounces) sharp Cheddar cheese

¼ cup thinly sliced cucumber

2 tablespoons preshredded carrots

¼ cup alfalfa sprouts

Place the bread on a work surface. Spread the mustard on the top sides. On top of 1 slice, layer the cheese, cucumber, carrots, sprouts, and the other bread slice. Cut diagonally.

TERIYAKI TUNA ROLL-UP

Exotic restaurant-style wrap sandwiches are as close as your cupboard. With this Far East–inspired sandwich, tuna fish experiences a welcome makeover from the mundane.

Hands-On Time: 2 minutes

Total Time: 2 minutes

Makes 2 servings (2 rolls each)

1   large (10"-wide) burrito-style tortilla

2   tablespoons teriyaki baste-and-glaze sauce

1   can (6 ounces) water-packed tuna, drained

1   cup shredded lettuce leaves

2   radishes, thinly sliced

Place the tortilla on a work surface. Spread with the sauce. Scatter the tuna, lettuce, and radishes over the tortilla. Roll it into a tube. Cut diagonally into 4 pieces.

CHICKEN CAESAR SANDWICH

The salad that's taken the country by storm is every bit as good (perhaps better!) when captured between two layers of rustic bread.

Hands-On Time: 5 minutes
Total Time: 5 minutes

Makes 6 servings

1 loaf (1 pound) pain rustique or ciabatta bread

1 cup bottled Caesar salad dressing

1 rotisserie chicken breast, removed from the bone, sliced, or 1 pound sliced roasted chicken breast

3 cups bagged hearts of romaine

¼ cup preshredded Parmesan cheese

Ground black pepper (optional)

Split the bread in half lengthwise. Spread the dressing over both cut sides. Pile the chicken on half of the loaf. Top with the romaine and the cheese. Season to taste with pepper, if desired. Top with the top half of the bread. With a serrated knife, cut diagonally into 6 portions.

PROVENÇAL SUB SANDWICH

In the south of France, this classic sandwich, known there as pan bagnat, is the first choice for many an impromptu summer lunch under a big shade tree.

Hands-On Time: 5 minutes

Total Time: 5 minutes

Makes 6 servings

Photo on page 84

2 cans (6 ounces each) olive oil–packed tuna

1 loaf (1 pound) pain rustique or ciabatta bread

1 cup refrigerated tomato bruschetta topping

1 cup drained roasted red bell peppers

2 cups bagged spring greens mix

2 pre-hard-cooked eggs, sliced

Ground black pepper

Drain the tuna, reserving 2 tablespoons of the oil. Discard the remaining oil. Slice the bread in half lengthwise. Drizzle both cut sides with the reserved oil. Spread the bruschetta topping over both cut sides. Pile the peppers, tuna, greens, and eggs on the bottom half of the loaf. Season to taste with pepper. Cover with the top half of the loaf. With a serrated knife, cut into 6 portions.

BACON-AND-EGG SALAD

Breakfast for lunch! Tuck this souped-up egg salad into pita pockets, or serve it on lettuce leaves for a satisfying midday meal.

Hands-On Time: 5 minutes
Total Time: 5 minutes

Makes 4 servings

6 pre-hard-cooked eggs, chopped

$\frac{1}{3}$ cup mayonnaise

2 teaspoons Dijon mustard

$\frac{1}{4}$ teaspoon salt

Pinch of ground black pepper (optional)

$\frac{1}{3}$ cup (about $1\frac{1}{4}$ ounces) bagged crumbled bacon

In a medium bowl, combine the eggs, mayonnaise, mustard, salt, and pepper, if using. Stir in the bacon. Serve immediately or cover and refrigerate overnight for a smokier flavor. Refrigerate for up to 2 days.

BACON-TOMATO-PESTO SANDWICH

Five Ingredients or Less!

For people who say you can't improve on a good thing, here is the delectable proof. The time-honored BLT goes Italian in this rapid rendition, prepared with precooked bacon.

Hands-On Time: 5 minutes
Total Time: 5 minutes

Makes 1 sandwich

3   slices precooked bacon strips

2   slices multigrain bread, toasted

1   tablespoon refrigerated or jarred basil pesto

1   small (2 ounces) tomato, sliced

1   large leaf romaine lettuce

Place the bacon between 2 sheets of paper towels. Heat in the microwave oven according to the package directions. Toast the bread. Spread one slice with the pesto. Top with the tomato, bacon, and lettuce. Cover with the other slice of bread. Cut in half diagonally.

Shelf-Ready Shortcuts

V8

Vegetable juice makes a healthy alternative to soda and other sugary drinks. It also gives you a head start on anything that you might make with tomato juice or that uses onions, celery, and carrots as the flavor base. That includes most soups and stews, and many sauces. Use V8 to save time when making soups, braising liquids, tomato-based sauces, and gravies.

HOT-BEEF SANDWICH WITH HORSERADISH AND PROVOLONE

Five Ingredients or Less!

A hot sandwich doesn't have to be difficult. This one comes together in less than 10 minutes and really satisfies a hungry stomach.

Hands-On Time: 8 minutes

Total Time: 8 minutes

Makes 1 sandwich

¼ cup bottled barbecue sauce

¼ pound sliced deli roast beef

1 tablespoon prepared horseradish

1 soft Kaiser roll or hamburger bun

1 slice (about 1 ounce) provolone cheese

Bring the barbecue sauce to a simmer in a small saucepan over medium heat. Add the beef, stirring to coat with the sauce, and heat through for 5 minutes. Spread the horseradish over the top of the roll or bun, and lay a slice of provolone over the bottom. Using tongs, place the hot beef over the cheese on the roll or bun, and put on the top.

CAJUN POTATO SALAD

Your family will never complain about boring spuds salad again after a taste of this Louisiana specialty. Offer it with fried chicken, grilled catfish, or New Orleans Barbecued Shrimp (page 206).

Hands-On Time: 7 minutes

Total Time: 7 minutes (plus 1 hour chilling time)

Makes 4 to 6 servings

½ cup mayonnaise

1½ teaspoons Cajun seasoning mix

1 can (16 ounces) sweet potatoes or yams, rinsed and drained, patted dry

1 can (14 ounces) white potatoes, rinsed and drained, patted dry

⅓ cup prechopped tricolor bell pepper

⅓ cup prechopped celery

1 bunch scallions, white and light green parts, sliced (⅓ cup)

⅓ cup chopped fresh parsley

In a serving bowl, combine the mayonnaise and seasoning mix. Stir to mix well. Add the sweet potatoes or yams, white potatoes, pepper, celery, scallions, and parsley. Stir to coat thoroughly with the dressing. Cover and refrigerate for at least 1 hour or several hours to chill.

QUICK TIP: Store the sweet potatoes or yams and the white potatoes in the refrigerator to eliminate the chilling time for the salad.

QUICK CARROT SLAW

Honey in the dressing lends a sweet note to this simple slaw. Serve it as a refreshing side salad with sandwiches and roasted meats.

Hands-On Time: 5 minutes
Total Time: 5 minutes

Makes 4 servings

1 tablespoon honey

¼ cup olive oil

3 tablespoons red wine vinegar

¼ teaspoon salt

¼ teaspoon ground black pepper

3 cups preshredded carrots

½ cup prechopped onion

¼ cup golden raisins

3 tablespoons capers

In a medium bowl, whisk together the honey, oil, vinegar, salt, and pepper. Stir in the carrots, onion, raisins, and capers.

BLUE CHEESE-WALNUT CABBAGE SALAD

Five Ingredients or Less!

The mellowness of cheese and nuts marries beautifully with the sharpness of the shredded cabbage in this sophisticated slaw.

Hands-On Time: 4 minutes

Total Time: 4 minutes

Makes 6 servings

1 bag (1 pound) shredded cabbage or cole slaw mix

³/₄ cup refrigerated or bottled blue-cheese dressing

   Ground black pepper

¹/₄ cup chopped walnuts

In a serving bowl, combine the cabbage and dressing. Toss to coat. Season to taste with pepper. Sprinkle on the walnuts.

SICILIAN CAULIFLOWER-OLIVE SALAD

This change-of-pace salad, inspired by the rustic cooking of Sicily, is a natural with the Rigatoni with Chunky Meat Sauce (page 263).

Hands-On Time: 3 minutes

Total Time: 8 minutes

Makes 4 to 6 servings

1 cup water

2 bags (8 ounces each) cauliflower florets

¼ cup olive oil

1 tablespoon red or white wine vinegar

¼ teaspoon red-pepper flakes

3 tablespoons jarred green olive salad

Bring the water to a boil in a covered saucepan. Add the cauliflower. Cover and cook for 5 minutes, or until a knife can be inserted. Drain and rinse with cold water. Cut the florets into thick slices and set aside.

Meanwhile, in a serving bowl, whisk the oil, vinegar, and pepper. Add the olive salad and the reserved cauliflower. Toss.

SPRING GREENS, CHICKPEAS, AND TOMATOES WITH FETA DRESSING

Five Ingredients or Less!

You can transform this salad into a complete meal by adding sliced hard-cooked egg, sliced grilled chicken, or cooked shrimp.

Hands-On Time: 4 minutes
Total Time: 4 minutes

Makes 4 to 6 servings

¼ cup bottled French vinaigrette dressing

⅓ cup precrumbled garlic-herb feta cheese

1 bag (5 ounces) mixed spring greens

⅔ cup canned chickpeas, rinsed and drained

¾ cup (4 ounces) cherry or grape tomatoes, halved

In a serving bowl, combine the dressing, cheese, greens, chickpeas, and tomatoes. Toss to mix.

SPINACH SALAD WITH HOT BACON DRESSING

Classic spinach bacon salad with cooked dressing is surprisingly time-consuming to prepare from scratch. This neo-classic version speeds the process and maintains the great taste.

Before 30 minutes

After 5 minutes

Time Saved 25 minutes

Makes 4 to 6 servings

1/4 cup olive oil

2 tablespoons sherry wine vinegar or white wine vinegar

1 tablespoon Dijon mustard

2 teaspoons sugar

1/2 teaspoon ground black pepper

1/4 teaspoon salt

2 pre-hard-cooked eggs

1 bag (6 ounces) baby spinach leaves (6 cups)

1 cup presliced fresh mushrooms

1 bunch scallions, white and light green parts, sliced (1/3 cup)

1/4 cup (1 ounce) bagged crumbled bacon

In a large microwaveable bowl, combine the oil, vinegar, mustard, sugar, pepper, and salt. Microwave on high power for 2 minutes, or until bubbling.

One at a time, place the eggs on an egg slicer. Slice once. Holding the slices together, turn the egg 90 degrees. Slice again to chop. Add the eggs, spinach, mushrooms, scallions, and bacon to the bowl. Toss to coat.

We Saved Time By

■ Using prewashed bagged baby spinach instead of washing, trimming, and drying spinach leaves

■ Using presliced mushrooms instead of washing, trimming, and slicing fresh mushrooms

■ Using pre-hard-cooked eggs instead of boiling and cooling eggs and then washing a pan

■ Using a microwaveable salad bowl for cooking the dressing instead of cooking in and then washing a pan

■ Using precooked, chopped bacon instead of frying, draining, and crumbling bacon and then washing a pan

■ Using an egg slicer to chop the egg instead of a knife and cutting board to wash

---

ROASTED PEPPERS

One of the best convenience foods out there, roasted peppers have a ton of uses. Put them in bruschetta. Layer them into lasagna or sandwiches. Or mix them into a sauce. Here are six more ideas, including three appetizers that dress them up to be enjoyed on their own before the main meal. Buy the best-quality roasted peppers you can find. Lengthwise quarters of pepper with plenty of blackened bits are usually better-tasting than small, limp pieces of perfectly clean peppers with no signs of charring.

1. **Marinated Roasted Peppers:** In a large, shallow dish, combine ⅓ cup olive oil, 1 tablespoon red wine vinegar, 1 tablespoon balsamic vinegar, ½ teaspoon salt, and ½ teaspoon ground black pepper. Toss with 3 cups roasted bell pepper strips (use various colors if possible). Cover and refrigerate for at least 2 hours or up to 2 days. Makes 8 appetizer servings.

2. **Roasted Red Peppers with Olives:** Toss together 1 chopped roasted red bell pepper, 2 cups green olives with their brine, 1 tablespoon white wine vinegar, 1 tablespoon preminced oil-packed garlic, and ⅛ teaspoon ground red pepper. Makes 8 appetizer servings.

3. **Roasted Red Peppers with Anchovies:** Toss 3 cups roasted red bell pepper strips with ½ teaspoon preminced oil-packed garlic, 6 julienned oil-packed anchovies, 1 tablespoon of the oil in which the anchovies were packed, a pinch of red-pepper flakes, and 1 teaspoon white wine vinegar. Makes 8 appetizer servings.

4. **Creamy Roasted Pepper Sauce:** In a mini food processor, combine 1 cup roasted red peppers, 2 tablespoons softened cream cheese, 1 teaspoon white wine vinegar, ½ teaspoon sugar, ¼ teaspoon salt, and ⅛ teaspoon ground red pepper. Blend until smooth, scraping down the sides once or twice. Refrigerate for up to 3 days. Makes 1 cup.

5. **Cream of Roasted Red Pepper and Tomato Soup:** In a food processor or blender, puree ¾ cup roasted red peppers, 1 container (32 ounces) ready-to-serve creamy tomato soup (not condensed), and ½ cup chicken broth. Pour into a saucepan and bring to a boil. Add ⅛ teaspoon dried basil, reduce the heat to medium-low, and simmer for 5 minutes. Makes about 4 servings.

6. **Roasted Red Pepper Pesto Pizza:** Preheat the oven to 400°F. Unroll one can (10 ounces) refrigerated pizza dough and cut in half. Pat and shape each half into two pizza shells, each about 10 inches in diameter, on a large greased baking sheet or two smaller sheets. Spread each pizza shell with 3 tablespoons prepared pesto and then top each with ¾ cup roasted red pepper strips, ¼ cup chopped canned tomatoes, and ½ cup precrumbled gorgonzola cheese. Bake for about 10 minutes, or until the cheese melts and the bottoms are nicely browned. Makes about 4 servings.

CRISPY FRIED RAVIOLI WITH SICILIAN CAPONATA DIP *page 138*

CHAPTER 7

SPEEDY SNACKS AND APPETIZERS

What do you do when friends drop by unannounced? You'll find dozens of great ideas in this chapter for quick snacks that you can whip up from ingredients you already have on hand.

Black Bean–Chipotle Dip with White Tortilla Chips

Sesame Breadsticks with Stone-Ground Mustard Dip

Crispy Fried-Onion Focaccia

Layered Eastern Mediterranean Dip with Vegetable Chips

Artichoke Dip Arrabiata

Creamy Clam Dip

Cajun-Roasted Chickpeas

Chicken-Olive Crostini

Bacon-Cheddar Pinwheels

Hummus-and-Camembert Phyllo Tartlets

Baked Brie with Peach-Zinfandel Chutney

Devilishly Delicious Eggs

Caribbean Seafood-and-Black-Bean Salad

Thai Chicken-Satay-and-Cucumber Salad

Chinese Sugar-Snap Peas and Tofu in Lettuce Cups

Chinese Chicken Wings with Hot Apricot Glaze

Spinach-Artichoke Squares

Spanikopita in Phyllo Shells

Crispy Fried Ravioli with Sicilian Caponata Dip

Meatball Pesto Pockets with Warm Tomato-Basil Sauce

BLACK BEAN–CHIPOTLE DIP
WITH WHITE TORTILLA CHIPS

Spicy, yet mellow, from the distinctive flavor of black beans and chipotle (smoked jalapeño) salsa. If chipotle salsa isn't available, substitute ½ cup mild tomato salsa mixed with 1 tablespoon bottled chipotle-pepper sauce.

Hands-On Time: 8 minutes
Total Time: 8 minutes

Makes 12 servings (3 appetizers per serving)

1   can (16 ounces) refried black beans

½   cup jarred chipotle salsa

1   container (1 pound) prepared guacamole

1   cup sour cream

½   cup (2 ounces) preshredded Mexican four-cheese blend

1   bunch scallions, all parts, sliced (½ cup)

   Bite-size white tortilla chips

Coat a 1-quart straight-sided glass or ceramic dish with cooking spray. Add the beans and salsa. Stir to mix. Spread on the guacamole and then the sour cream. Sprinkle with the cheese and scallions. Serve with the tortilla chips.

QUICK TIP: Black Bean–Chipotle Dip can be prepared up to 48 hours before serving. Cover with plastic wrap and refrigerate.

SESAME BREADSTICKS
WITH STONE-GROUND MUSTARD DIP

Five Ingredients or Less!

Kids will have fun helping to unroll and slice the dough into strips with a pizza cutter.

Hands-On Time: 8 minutes

Total Time: 18 minutes

Makes 16 servings

1 tube (11 ounces) refrigerated crusty French loaf dough

1 tablespoon sesame seeds

1 cup refrigerated ranch-veggie dip

3 tablespoons stone-ground mustard

Preheat the oven to 375° F. Coat a large baking sheet with cooking spray.

On a lightly floured surface, carefully unroll the dough into a rectangle. Fold one long side of the rectangle over to meet the other. Starting at one shorter side of the rectangle, cut the dough into 16 short strips. Place the strips on the prepared baking sheet. Coat the strips generously with cooking spray. Sprinkle with half of the sesame seeds. Flip the dough strips. Repeat with cooking spray and seeds. Bake for 10 minutes, or until browned.

Meanwhile, in a bowl, combine the dip and mustard. Stir to mix well. Serve the breadsticks with the mustard dip.

CRISPY FRIED-ONION FOCACCIA

Five Ingredients or Less!

Think of this Italian-style flat bread as a pizza without the tomato sauce. It can be varied in many ways by adding different herbs, such as oregano or rosemary, and varying the cheese blend.

Hands-On Time: 5 minutes
Total Time: 17 minutes

Makes 8 servings

1   tube (11 ounces) refrigerated crusty French loaf dough

½   cup canned French-fried onions

2   tablespoons preshredded Parmesan-Romano-Asiago cheese blend

½   teaspoon herbes des Provence

2   tablespoons olive oil

Preheat the oven to 375° F. Coat a large baking sheet with cooking spray.

On a lightly floured surface, carefully unroll the dough into a rectangle. Transfer the dough to the baking sheet.

Scatter the onions, cheese, and herbs over the dough. Let stand for 10 minutes.

Drizzle the focaccia with the oil. Bake for about 12 minutes, or until golden and sizzling.

LAYERED EASTERN MEDITERRANEAN DIP
WITH VEGETABLE CHIPS

Look for tubs of seasoned hummus—a versatile puree of cooked chickpeas, olive oil, and garlic—in the gourmet cheese case.

Hands-On Time: 4 minutes
Total Time: 4 minutes

Makes 12 servings

1 container (8 ounces) roasted garlic hummus

2 tablespoons kalamata olive spread or tapenade

½ cup jarred Peppadew or pimientos, drained and chopped

½ cup (2 ounces) precrumbled garlic-herb feta cheese, finely crumbled

1 bag (8 ounces) exotic vegetable chips

Spoon the hummus into a 3-cup glass bowl, preferably with straight sides. Cover with the olive spread or tapenade. Scatter on the Peppadew or pimientos and then the cheese. Serve with the chips for dipping.

QUICK TIP: The dip can be assembled, covered with plastic, and refrigerated for up to 2 days before serving.

ARTICHOKE DIP ARRABIATA

Inspired by the fiery Italian tomato-pancetta pasta sauce, this contemporary version of the traditional artichoke dip will win raves.

Hands-On Time: 6 minutes

Total Time: 36 minutes

Makes 12 servings (3 appetizers per serving)

3 tablespoons olive oil

¾ cup prechopped onion

¼ cup (1 ounce) bagged crumbled bacon

1 carton (15 ounces) part-skim ricotta cheese

1 can (14 ounces) artichoke hearts, rinsed, drained, and torn into chunks

½ cup canned petite-diced Roma tomatoes, drained

½ teaspoon red-pepper flakes

½ cup (2 ounces) preshredded Parmesan-Romano-Asiago cheese blend, divided

Sesame crackers or toasted pita wedges

Preheat the oven to 350°F.

In an 8" × 8" microwaveable baking dish, combine the oil, onion, and bacon. Cover with plastic wrap, leaving a small corner vent. Microwave on high power for 4 minutes, or until pale golden. Add the ricotta cheese, artichokes, tomatoes, red-pepper flakes, and ¼ cup of the cheese blend. Stir to mix thoroughly. Sprinkle with the remaining cheese blend.

Bake for 30 minutes, or until bubbling. Serve with the crackers or pita.

CREAMY CLAM DIP

Crisp crackers love this summery dip. You could also reduce the cream or half-and-half to 2 tablespoons and serve it atop melba toast or grilled bread as an appetizer.

Hands-On Time: 5 minutes
Total Time: 5 minutes

Makes about 1½ cups

1 package (8 ounces) garlic-and-herb-flavored cream cheese, softened to room temperature

¼ cup cream or half-and-half

1 tablespoon lemon juice

1 teaspoon Worcestershire sauce

1 teaspoon prepared horseradish

1 can (6½ ounces) minced clams, drained

½ teaspoon salt

Pinch of ground black pepper

In a small bowl, stir together the cream cheese and cream or half-and-half. Stir in the remaining ingredients. Serve immediately or refrigerate for up to 2 days. Bring to room temperature before serving.

CAJUN-ROASTED CHICKPEAS

Five Ingredients or Less!

These addictive nibbles can be made ahead and left out at room temperature for unexpected guests or snack attacks.

Hands-On Time: 5 minutes

Total Time: 40 minutes

Makes 8 appetizer servings

1 can (15 ounces) chickpeas, rinsed and drained

1 tablespoon olive oil

1½ teaspoons Cajun seasoning

Preheat the oven to 400°F.

In a medium bowl, toss the chickpeas with the oil and seasoning. Spread in a single layer on a baking sheet. Bake, shaking occasionally, until golden, about 35 minutes. Let cool before serving. Cover and keep at room temperature for up to 3 days.

CHICKEN-OLIVE CROSTINI

Select your favorite prepared olive spread for this nosh. Jarred kalamata olive spread, tapenade, pâté de olive, and bruschetta olive topping are all zesty options.

Hands-On Time: 10 minutes
Total Time: 10 minutes

Makes 12 servings (3 crostini per serving)

1 rotisserie chicken breast or 1 pound roasted boneless, skinless chicken breast

3 scallions, cut into 1" lengths

1 sprig fresh rosemary, about 1 teaspoon of leaves

½ cup mayonnaise

½ teaspoon ground black pepper

2 tablespoons prepared olive spread

1 box (3 ounces) mini toasts or 36 slices plain cocktail bread

Remove and discard the bones and skin from the chicken breast. Tear the chicken into chunks. Set aside.

In the bowl of a food processor fitted with a metal blade, combine the scallions and rosemary. Pulse about 12 times, or until minced. Add the mayonnaise, pepper, olive spread, and the reserved chicken. Pulse about 24 times, or until the chicken is minced and the ingredients are well mixed. Serve with the toasts or bread.

QUICK TIP: The chicken-olive spread can be prepared up to 3 days in advance. Refrigerate in a tightly covered container. Let stand at room temperature for 15 minutes before serving.

CHICKEN-OLIVE CROSTINI *opposite* and BACON-CHEDDAR PINWHEELS *page 124*

BACON-CHEDDAR PINWHEELS

Five Ingredients or Less!

These tasty pinwheels look impressive on an appetizer plate. And they couldn't be simpler to put together.

Hands-On Time: 10 minutes

Total Time: 25 minutes

Makes 30 pinwheels

Photo on page 123

2 tubes (8 ounces each) refrigerated crescent-roll dough

$3/4$ cup preshredded sharp Cheddar cheese

1 cup (4 ounces) bagged crumbled bacon

$1/2$ cup prechopped onion

1 teaspoon dried thyme

Preheat the oven to 375°F.

Separate the dough into 8 rectangles. Using your fingertips, push together the perforations in each rectangle to seal them up. Scatter on the cheese, bacon, onion, and thyme. Roll up each rectangle, starting at the short end. Cut each crosswise into 4 slices. Place the slices, cut side down, on a baking sheet and flatten slightly. Bake for 15 to 20 minutes, or until puffed and golden.

Shelf-Ready Shortcuts

PREPARED DOUGH

Prepared pizza, bread, pie, and dinner-roll dough saves loads of prep time. But don't limit these doughs to their intended purposes. Fill refrigerated pizza dough with your favorite fillings to create calzones and strombolis. Top it to make focaccia. Or fry it in small pieces to make the Italian donuts known as zeppolis.

Create simple yet impressive appetizers by filling crescent-roll dough with herbed cream cheese, crab, or other fillings, then slicing it crosswise before baking.

HUMMUS-AND-CAMEMBERT PHYLLO TARTLETS

Five Ingredients or Less!

Your guests will think you slaved over these hot hors d'oeuvres. In reality, they take just a few minutes of preparation. You can even assemble them ahead and bake them when you are ready for effortless entertaining.

Hands-On Time: 5 minutes

Total Time: 10 minutes

Makes 15 mini tartlets

Photo on page 137

1 container (8 ounces) scallion-flavored hummus

4 ounces Camembert or Brie cheese, rind removed, chopped (about $^2/_3$ cup)

1 box (2 ounces) frozen miniature phyllo dough shells (15 shells), thawed

$1^1/_2$ teaspoons sesame seeds

2 tablespoons chopped roasted red pepper

Preheat the oven to 350°F.

Put the hummus and cheese in a microwaveable bowl. Microwave on high power for 1 minute, or until the cheese melts and can be stirred into the hummus.

Put the phyllo shells on a baking sheet and spoon the hummus filling into them. Sprinkle with the sesame seeds and top with red pepper. Bake for 5 minutes, or until heated through.

BAKED BRIE WITH PEACH-ZINFANDEL CHUTNEY

Five Ingredients or Less!

This is so sophisticated yet so easy. Buttery brie baked with a sweet-hot fruit condiment will launch any party successfully. If chutney isn't available, use apricot preserves instead.

Hands-On Time: 2 minutes
Total Time: 32 minutes

Makes 12 servings

1 round (15 ounces) Brie cheese

1 jar (8 ounces) peach-zinfandel chutney

$\frac{1}{2}$ cup drained jarred or canned peaches in juice

$\frac{1}{4}$ cup raw slivered almonds

Plain or wheat crackers

Preheat the oven to 350°F. Line a 9" pie pan with aluminum foil. Coat with cooking spray.

Place the cheese in the pan. Top with the chutney, peaches, and almonds. Bake for 30 minutes, or until the chutney is bubbly and the cheese is heated through. With a large spatula, transfer the cheese to a serving dish. Spoon the sauce over the top. Serve with the crackers.

QUICK TIP: The dish can be assembled, covered with plastic wrap, and refrigerated, for up to 24 hours before baking.

DEVILISHLY DELICIOUS EGGS

Five Ingredients or Less!

A must for every potluck or outdoor picnic, this old-fashioned favorite used to require advance planning. While zapping the preparation time to a bare minimum, the flavor of the filling has also been zipped up.

Before 1 hour and 30 minutes

After 8 minutes

Time Saved 1 hour and 22 minutes

Makes 16 egg halves

8 pre-hard-cooked eggs, halved lengthwise

$\frac{1}{2}$ cup mayonnaise

$1\frac{1}{2}$ teaspoons Asian chili-garlic sauce

$\frac{1}{4}$ cup chopped fresh cilantro

Place the egg yolks in a bowl. Set the cooked egg whites on a serving platter.

Mash the yolks with a fork. Add the mayonnaise and chili-garlic sauce. Stir to mix well. Spoon the mixture into the reserved egg whites. Sprinkle with the cilantro.

MAKE AHEAD FOR THE REFRIGERATOR: The assembled eggs can be covered with plastic wrap and refrigerated for up to 24 hours before serving.

--- *We Saved Time By* ---

■ Using refrigerated purchased pre-hard-cooked eggs instead of waiting for water to boil, boiling the fresh eggs, taking the time to cool and then chill them, and washing a pan

■ Using a prepared sauce with complex flavors to season the filling instead of mincing, chopping, and measuring separate ingredients

CREAM CHEESE

Nowadays, cream cheese is sold in a variety of flavors from blueberry to scallion. Here are a few that you won't find on grocery store shelves, but they're easy to mix up at home. Mix these into your favorite sauces to add creamy texture and bold flavor in an instant. Or use these flavored cream cheeses to stuff pounded chicken breasts, then roll and bake. Of course, you could always spread them on bagels too. Each recipe makes about ½ cup.

1. **Arugula Cream Cheese:** Combine ½ cup softened cream cheese, ¼ cup finely chopped arugula leaves, 1 teaspoon lemon juice, ¼ teaspoon salt, and ¼ teaspoon ground black pepper.

2. **Dill Cream Cheese:** Combine ½ cup softened cream cheese, 2 to 3 tablespoons chopped fresh dill, 2 teaspoons lemon juice, ¼ teaspoon salt, and ¼ teaspoon ground black pepper.

3. **Mediterranean Cream Cheese:** Combine ½ cup softened cream cheese, 1½ tablespoons finely chopped canned anchovies, 2 tablespoons chopped fresh parsley, 1 tablespoon grated lemon zest, and 2 or 3 drops hot-pepper sauce (optional).

4. **Parsley Cream Cheese:** Combine ½ cup softened cream cheese, ¼ cup chopped fresh parsley, 2 teaspoons grated lemon zest, ¼ teaspoon salt, and ¼ teaspoon ground black pepper.

5. **Tarragon Cream Cheese:** Combine ½ cup softened cream cheese, 3 tablespoons chopped fresh tarragon, 1½ teaspoons orange juice, ¼ teaspoon salt, and ¼ teaspoon ground black pepper.

6. **Parmesan Cream Cheese:** Combine ½ cup softened cream cheese, ¼ cup pregrated Parmesan cheese, ½ teaspoon dried oregano, ¼ teaspoon salt, and ¼ teaspoon ground black pepper.

CARIBBEAN SEAFOOD-AND-BLACK-BEAN SALAD

This festive seafood dish will enliven any special occasion. At a more formal dinner, serve it as a plated appetizer on a bed of lettuce leaves. It also makes waves as part of an appetizer buffet, accompanied by soft pita wedges.

Hands-On Time: 10 minutes

Total Time: 10 minutes (plus 1 hour chilling time)

Makes 8 to 10 servings

3 tablespoons olive oil

½ pound peeled, deveined medium or large shrimp, cut into chunks

8 ounces bay scallops

1 tablespoon preminced oil-packed garlic

1 can (15 ounces) black beans, rinsed and drained

1 cup drained jarred tropical fruit in light syrup

¼ cup chopped fresh cilantro

3 tablespoons frozen lime juice concentrate

1 teaspoon hot-pepper sauce

½ teaspoon salt

Heat the oil in a medium skillet over medium-high heat. Add the shrimp, scallops, and garlic. Cook, stirring, for 2 minutes, or until the shrimp and scallops are opaque in the center. Remove to a bowl. Add the beans, fruit, cilantro, lime juice concentrate, hot-pepper sauce, and salt. Stir. Cover and refrigerate for 1 hour or as long as 24 hours.

THAI CHICKEN-SATAY-AND-CUCUMBER SALAD

The popular restaurant appetizer is condensed into its essential element in this ultrasimple hors d'oeuvre. It can be served as part of an appetizer buffet or plated on a bed of shredded lettuce. It's also wonderful stuffed and rolled into transparent rice paper wrappers (think Asian tortillas).

Hands-On Time: 4 minutes
Total Time: 4 minutes

Makes 10 servings

½ English cucumber (14 ounces), sliced in the food processor

½ bag (20 ounces) cooked chicken breast strips (2 cups)

¼ cup bottled Thai stir-fry and dipping peanut sauce

In a serving bowl, combine the cucumber, chicken, and dressing. Toss to coat.

Double-Duty Gadgets

PEELING FRESH GINGER

If you can't buy pregrated ginger, removing the peel from fresh ginger can be a time-consuming and frustrating alternative. Make it easy on yourself and scrape off the peel with the side of a teaspoon. If you're making a sauce, a hot mulled beverage, or any other liquid mixture, skip peeling altogether. Instead, thinly slice the unpeeled ginger and drop the slices into the hot mixture at the beginning of cooking. Let the ginger infuse the liquid with its flavor for as long as possible. Then remove the slices before serving or proceeding with the recipe.

CHINESE SUGAR-SNAP PEAS AND TOFU IN LETTUCE CUPS

The pale green colors of this starter are visually refreshing on a humid summer day. For even quicker preparation, you can serve the stir-fry mixture in a shallow bowl and invite everyone to fill their own lettuce leaves.

Hands-On Time: 10 minutes
Total Time: 10 minutes

Makes 14 servings

1 tablespoon vegetable oil

½ bag (8 ounces) stringless sugar-snap peas (1 cup), cut into thirds

1 bunch scallions, white and light green parts, sliced (⅓ cup)

1 teaspoon jarred pregrated fresh ginger

½ block (6 ounces) onion-garlic-seasoned firm tofu, cut into ¼" cubes

2 tablespoons Chinese oyster sauce

1 head (8 ounces) Boston lettuce

Heat the oil in a large skillet over high heat. Add the peas, scallions, and ginger. Cook, tossing constantly, for 1 minute, or until the peas are bright green. Add the tofu and sauce. Toss to combine. Let stand to cool.

Place 14 lettuce leaves, curved side up, on a large platter. Spoon the stir-fry mixture into the leaves.

QUICK TIP: The cooled stir-fry can be covered with plastic wrap and refrigerated for several hours before serving.

CHINESE CHICKEN WINGS
WITH HOT APRICOT GLAZE

Sizzling spicy wings are made-to-order for a casual get-together. They practically cook themselves while you join the party.

Hands-On Time: 10 minutes

Total Time: 1 hour and 10 minutes

Makes 6 servings (2 wings per serving)

¼ cup vegetable oil

¼ cup soy sauce

1 tablespoon jarred pregrated fresh ginger

3 pounds chicken wings (12 wings)

⅓ cup all-fruit apricot spread

2 teaspoons Asian chili-garlic sauce

In a large zipper-lock bag, combine the oil, soy sauce, and ginger. Massage the bag to mix. Add the wings. Close and massage the bag to coat the wings evenly. Refrigerate for 30 minutes.

Meanwhile, in a bowl, combine the apricot spread and the chili-garlic sauce. Set aside.

Preheat the oven to 425°F. Line a 17" × 11" baking pan or other large shallow baking pan with aluminum foil. Coat with cooking spray.

Place the wings in the pan. Discard the marinade. Bake for 25 minutes, or until browned and sizzling. Drizzle on the reserved apricot sauce. Turn the wings to coat. Bake for 5 minutes, or until the juices run clear.

SPINACH-ARTICHOKE SQUARES

Think of these as little frittatas. The combination of cheese and eggs makes them very satisfying—as an after-school snack, predinner appetizer, or midnight munchie.

Hands-On Time: 5 minutes
Total Time: 45 minutes

Makes 24 squares

5 eggs

1 box (10 ounces) frozen chopped spinach, thawed and squeezed dry

1 can (14 ounces) artichoke hearts, drained and chopped

1 package (8 ounces) shredded mozzarella cheese

1 teaspoon dried oregano

½ cup all-purpose flour

½ cup prechopped onion

½ cup pregrated Parmesan cheese

Preheat the oven to 350°F. Coat a 13" × 9" pan with cooking spray.

Beat the eggs in a large bowl and mix in the remaining ingredients. Scrape into the prepared pan and bake for about 40 minutes, or until a knife comes out clean. Cool slightly, then cut into 24 squares. Serve at room temperature.

SPANIKOPITA IN PHYLLO SHELLS

The filling for the beloved Greek spinach-feta cheese pie is often used as a stuffing for bite-size phyllo dough appetizers. While delicious, they're time-consuming to assemble because each triangle is created by multiple foldings of several long strips of phyllo dough brushed with melted butter. This speedy adaptation tastes fabulous but passes over all the tedious assembly.

Before 1 hour and 10 minutes

After 18 minutes

Time Saved 52 minutes

Makes 15 servings

1 box (2 ounces) frozen miniature phyllo dough shells (15 shells), thawed

1 tablespoon olive oil

2 tablespoons prechopped onion, minced

1 cup packed baby spinach

$\frac{1}{8}$ teaspoon dried dillweed

2 tablespoons precrumbled feta cheese

2 tablespoons refrigerated Alfredo sauce (see note)

$\frac{1}{8}$ teaspoon ground black pepper

Preheat the oven to 350° F. Place the shells on a baking sheet. Set aside.

In an 8" × 8" microwaveable baking dish, combine the oil and onion. Cover with plastic wrap, leaving a small corner vent. Microwave on high power for 2 minutes, or until softened. Add the spinach and dillweed. Stir to coat with the onion mixture. Cover with plastic wrap and microwave on high power for 1 minute, or until wilted. Stir in the cheese, sauce, and pepper. Fill the reserved shells with the spinach mixture. Bake for 10 minutes, or until heated through.

NOTE: Alfredo sauce can be frozen in small amounts to have on hand as a versatile addition to sauces, appetizers, and pasta dishes. To freeze, spoon the sauce in 2- or 4-tablespoon measures into zipper-lock bags. Be sure to label. Freeze for up to 3 months.

SPANIKOPITA IN PHYLLO SHELLS *opposite* and **HUMMUS-AND-CAMEMBERT PHYLLO TARTLETS** *page 125*

— *We Saved Time By* —

- Using prechopped onion instead of peeling by hand

- Using prewashed bagged baby spinach instead of trimming, washing, and drying spinach leaves by hand

- Using prepared Alfredo sauce instead of preparing a white sauce from scratch

- Using precrumbled feta cheese instead of grating a block by hand

- Using frozen prebaked phyllo dough shells instead of cutting, buttering, layering, and folding sheets of phyllo dough

CRISPY FRIED RAVIOLI
WITH SICILIAN CAPONATA DIP

Your guests will devour these irresistible morsels faster than you can prepare them. Cooking time is about 1 minute.

Hands-On Time: 10 minutes

Total Time: 10 minutes

Makes 8 to 10 servings (4 or 5 ravioli per serving)

Photo on page 112

¼ cup fresh parsley leaves

1 jar or can (10 ounces) caponata

2 tablespoons lemon juice

1½-2 cups vegetable oil

1 package (9 ounces) cheese- or chicken-stuffed ravioli

2 tablespoons (½ ounce) pregrated Parmesan cheese

Paprika

Place the parsley in the bowl of a food processor fitted with a metal blade. Pulse 6 times to chop. Add the caponata and lemon juice. Pulse about 12 times, or until the mixture is coarsely pureed. Transfer to a serving bowl.

Fill a large skillet with about 1" of oil. Place over medium-high heat for 2 to 3 minutes, or until hot enough for frying. Test by dropping 1 ravioli in the pan. If the oil bubbles and the ravioli browns, the oil is hot enough. Drop the ravioli in a single layer into the pan. (Fry in two batches if necessary.) Fry for about 1 minute, turning with a slotted spoon, or until golden on both sides. Remove to a paper towel–lined plate to drain. Transfer to a platter. Sprinkle with the cheese and paprika to taste. Serve right away with the caponata dip.

MAKE AHEAD FOR THE REFRIGERATOR: The prepared caponata dip can be refrigerated up to a week in advance.

MEATBALL PESTO POCKETS
WITH WARM TOMATO-BASIL SAUCE

Round up the family to help roll these tasty snacks. Prepare them during halftime, and they'll be ready to eat at the third quarter kick-off.

Hands-On Time: 10 minutes

Total Time: 25 minutes

Makes 8 servings (2 meatball pockets per serving)

2 tubes (8 ounces each) refrigerated crescent-roll dough

$\frac{1}{2}$ cup refrigerated basil pesto

$\frac{3}{4}$ cup (3 ounces) preshredded mozzarella and provolone cheese blend

8 precooked $1\frac{1}{4}$"-wide meatballs (about 6 ounces), halved

$1\frac{1}{2}$ cups refrigerated or jarred tomato-basil pasta sauce

Preheat the oven to 375° F.

Open the dough rolls and lay them flat on a work surface. Separate the dough triangles. Spread the top sides with the pesto. Scatter the cheese over the pesto. Place a meatball half, cut side down, at the wide base of each dough triangle. Starting at the meatball end, roll each dough triangle. Press the bottom and pinch the sides to seal. Press lightly between palms to make a domed disk. Place on a large baking sheet. Coat with olive oil cooking spray.

Bake for about 15 minutes, or until browned. Meanwhile, place the sauce in a microwaveable bowl. Cover with waxed paper. Cook on medium-high power, stirring once, for 5 minutes, or until steaming. Serve on the side for dipping.

QUICK NOTE: To make ahead, assemble the meatball pockets and place them on the baking sheet. Cover with plastic wrap and refrigerate for up to 2 hours. To serve, remove the plastic wrap and bake according to the recipe directions.

BRUSCHETTA TOPPINGS

Bruschetta makes a wonderful appetizer, and most of the toppings can be prepared ahead of time. To make bruschetta, slice a baguette into ½" thick slices and toast them under the broiler, on the grill, or in a 400°F oven. While the toast is warm, spray one side with olive oil cooking spray, then finish with one of the following toppings. Each recipe below makes enough to top one sliced baguette, or about 16 pieces total.

1. **Tomato, Mozzarella, and Arugula:** Place 1 thin slice fresh mozzarella cheese (16 slices total; about ½ pound) onto each hot toast. Add 1 arugula leaf (16 leaves total; about ⅓ cup packed) to each, and top with 1 thin slice plum tomato (about 4 tomatoes total). Sprinkle with a pinch of salt and a pinch of ground black pepper.

2. **Pesto, Tomato, and Provolone:** Preheat the oven to 400°F. Spread each toast with 1 teaspoon pesto (about ⅓ cup total). Top each with 1 slice plum tomato (about 4 tomatoes total) and 1 small, thin slice provolone cheese (16 slices total; about ½ pound). Bake in the top of the oven for 2 to 4 minutes, or until the cheese melts.

3. **Tomato-Anchovy:** Preheat the oven to 400°F. Place 1 slice plum tomato (about 4 tomatoes total) on each toast, and top with 1 anchovy fillet (or half if you are not a big fan). Sprinkle with ½ teaspoon grated Parmesan cheese per toast, and bake in the top of the oven for 2 to 4 minutes, or until the cheese melts and turns golden.

4. **Broccoli Rabe and Parmesan:** Drop 1 or 2 bunches broccoli rabe into a large pot of lightly salted boiling water over high heat. Cook for 2 to 3 minutes, or just until tender (it will shrink considerably). Drain well. While the broccoli rabe is cool-

ing, preheat the oven to 400°F. Coarsely chop the broccoli rabe when cool enough to handle. Spoon 2 to 3 tablespoons olive oil into a large skillet over medium heat. Add ½ to 1 teaspoon preminced oil-packed garlic and sauté for 20 to 30 seconds. Add the broccoli rabe and ½ teaspoon salt. Cook for 3 to 5 minutes. Sprinkle each piece of toast with ½ teaspoon pregrated Parmesan cheese and arrange on a baking sheet. Bake in the top of the oven for 2 to 4 minutes, or until the cheese is golden. Divide the reserved broccoli rabe topping among the toasts.

5. **Mushrooms and Parmesan:** Preheat the oven to 400°F. Thickly slice about 8 large white or brown (cremini) mushrooms (1 large mushroom slice for each toast). Coat a large skillet with olive oil and add the mushroom slices close together. Brown one side over medium-high heat, then stir and cook for 1 minute longer. Sprinkle with ½ teaspoon dried oregano and ¼ cup dry white wine and cook for 1 minute longer. Arrange 1 mushroom slice over each toast. Sprinkle with ½ teaspoon pregrated Parmesan cheese per toast and bake on a baking sheet for 2 to 4 minutes, or until the cheese is golden.

6. **Caramelized Onion:** Melt 2 tablespoons butter in a skillet over medium-high heat. Add 2 cups prechopped onion, 1 tablespoon sugar, and ½ teaspoon dried thyme. Sauté for about 10 minutes, stirring often. If dry, add 2 tablespoons water and continue cooking for about 5 minutes longer, or until the onions caramelize and turn medium brown. Stir in 1 tablespoon balsamic vinegar or sherry vinegar. Mound 1 tablespoon topping on each toast and serve warm.

SEASONED PEPPER TURKEY WITH PORTUGUESE TOMATOES page 160

CHAPTER 8

GREAT GRILLING

One of the oldest cooking methods, as well as one of the fastest, grilling is a sure-fire way to lock in great flavor. Whether you use a gas, stovetop, or contact grill, you'll find plenty of mouth-watering creations for all occasions.

TURKEY CRANBERRY CREAM-CHEESE SANDWICHES

At Thanksgiving time, you'll be grateful for leftover sliced turkey. This casual dish is especially tasty if you start with home-roasted fowl.

Hands-On Time: 12 minutes

Total Time: 12 minutes

Makes 4 to 6 servings

12 slices farmhouse-style white bread or challah bread

3 tablespoons softened butter, divided

$^3/_4$ cup chive-and-onion-flavored cream cheese spread

1 cup + 2 tablespoons canned whole-berry cranberry sauce

12 ounces sliced honey-roasted delicatessen turkey

Lay the bread slices in a single layer on a work surface. Lightly and evenly spread the butter over the top side of each slice. Flip all the slices. Spread 1 tablespoon of the cream cheese over each slice. Spread 1½ tablespoons of the cranberry sauce over each slice. Place the turkey, overlapping, on 6 of the slices. Flip the remaining bread slices onto the turkey.

Preheat a stovetop grill pan over medium-high heat. With a spatula, transfer the sandwiches to the pan. Cook, flipping once, for about 3 minutes total, or until golden.

Cut into halves diagonally.

FLAVORED MAYONNAISE

Quickly transform jarred mayonnaise into a flavored dip, spread, or sauce just by adding a few ingredients. Doctor your favorite mayonnaise, reduced-fat or regular, using the minirecipes below. Start with ¼ cup of mayonnaise and stir in the ingredients as directed. Serve flavored mayonnaise with any grilled food, such as grilled chicken breasts, or with pan-fried fish fillets, in sandwiches, or as a dip for precut vegetables.

1. **Sesame Mayonnaise:** Stir in 1 teaspoon toasted sesame oil and ½ teaspoon lemon juice, lime juice, or rice vinegar.

2. **Mediterranean Caper Mayonnaise:** Stir in 1 tablespoon drained and chopped capers, 1 teaspoon olive oil, and 1 teaspoon lemon juice.

3. **Anchovy Mayonnaise:** Stir in 2 to 3 teaspoons anchovy paste, 1 teaspoon olive oil, and 1 teaspoon lemon juice.

4. **Olive Mayonnaise:** Stir in 3 tablespoons finely minced pitted kalamata or niçoise olives and 1 tablespoon chopped fresh oregano.

5. **Cilantro Mayonnaise:** Stir in 2 tablespoons chopped fresh cilantro, 1 teaspoon olive oil, 1 teaspoon lemon or lime juice, ⅛ teaspoon ground cumin, and a pinch of freshly ground black pepper.

6. **Curried Mayonnaise:** Toast 1 teaspoon curry powder in a small dry skillet over medium heat until fragrant, and stir into mayonnaise along with 1 teaspoon honey.

SIZZLING GRILLED CHEDDAR-SALSA SANDWICHES

Five Ingredients or Less!
Vegetarian Dish

It's hard to believe that such a simple combination of ingredients makes such a tasty impact. Use the best sharp Cheddar you can find.

Hands-On Time: 5 minutes
Total Time: 10 minutes

Makes 4 servings

8 slices farmhouse-style nutty-oat bread

½ pound extra-sharp Cheddar cheese, sliced

½ cup drained refrigerated or jarred salsa

1 loose-packed cup bagged baby spinach

Preheat a stovetop griddle over medium heat or set a contact grill to medium.

Place 4 slices of the bread on a work surface. Coat with cooking spray. Flip. Top with the cheese, salsa, and spinach. Cover with the remaining slices of bread. Coat the tops with cooking spray. Cook on the griddle or grill, turning occasionally, for 5 minutes total, or until the cheese starts to melt and the bread is well browned. Reduce the heat if the bread is browning too quickly.

Double-Duty Gadgets
GRILL SCRAPER

The key to great grilling every time is a clean, hot grill rack. And the best tool for the job is a stiff wire grill brush. But these will wear out after repeated use. And sometimes, you may have to do without one, if you're using a public grill at a picnic, for instance. No problem. Just wad up some aluminum foil and use the ball of foil to scrape the grill rack clean.

Hint: A hot rack cleans easier than a cold rack. For the best results, preheat the grill to burn off any remnants of the last meal, then put on grill mitts and scrape the rack clean with your aluminum foil ball.

TOMATOES STUFFED WITH
CANNELLINI AND COUSCOUS

Vegetarian Dish

After the initial assembly, this dish takes care of itself. If you like, you can prepare and grill the tomatoes well ahead of serving. The flavors will get even better.

Hands-On Time: 12 minutes

Total Time: 57 minutes (plus 20 minutes standing time)

Makes 4 to 6 servings

1 box (6 ounces) roasted garlic with olive oil–couscous mix, divided

4 tablespoons olive oil (preferably extra-virgin), divided

½ cup prechopped onion, minced

6 large ripe but firm tomatoes (10 ounces each; about 4¾ pounds total)

1 can (15 ounces) cannellini beans, rinsed and drained

2 tablespoons chopped fresh parsley

1½ teaspoons Italian seasoning

½ teaspoon ground black pepper

Preheat the grill. Coat a 9" × 6" disposable foil pan with cooking spray. Measure ½ cup of the couscous and 1 tablespoon of the seasoning packet from the mix. Set aside. Store the remaining couscous and seasoning packet for another dish.

In a medium skillet, heat 2 tablespoons of the oil over medium heat. Add the onion and cook for 3 minutes, or until the onion is softened. Meanwhile, cut ¼" slices from the tomato tops. Discard the tops. With a serrated knife or spoon, scoop out the tomato flesh, leaving ¼"-thick walls. Set aside. Finely chop the tomato flesh. Add to the onion along with the beans, parsley, Italian seasoning, pepper, and the reserved couscous and seasoning. Stir to combine. Spoon into the reserved tomato shells, mounding slightly. Spoon any extra stuffing into the base of the pan. Drizzle with the remaining 2 tablespoons of oil. Cover with aluminum foil.

Place on the grill away from direct heat. Grill, rotating the pan occasionally, for about 45 minutes, or until the tomatoes are tender and the tops are golden. Allow to stand for 20 minutes.

PORTOBELLO CAPS STUFFED WITH CHILE POLENTA AND CHEESE

Even meat lovers will respond to the toothsome texture and rich flavor of this savory mushroom main dish.

Hands-On Time: 6 minutes
Total Time: 15 minutes

Makes 4 to 6 servings

1 tube (1 pound) refrigerated green chile-cilantro polenta, cut into ½"-thick slices

8 large portobello mushroom caps, stems removed (2 ounces each; 1 pound total)

Olive oil

2 tablespoons preminced oil-packed garlic

1½ cups (6 ounces) preshredded mozzarella and provolone cheese blend

Ground black pepper

Preheat the grill or broiler. Coat a grill rack or broiler pan with cooking spray.

Place the polenta in a single layer on a microwaveable plate. Cover with plastic wrap. Microwave on high power for 3 minutes, or until heated through. Set aside.

Coat a sheet of heavy-duty aluminum foil with cooking spray. Place the mushrooms, cap side up, on the foil. Brush with olive oil to coat. Flip the mushrooms. Spread about ¼ teaspoon of the garlic over each mushroom. Pat the polenta slices into rounds that are as wide as the mushrooms. Place the polenta on the mushrooms. Sprinkle with the cheese. Drizzle with the olive oil.

Grill the mushrooms over direct heat for about 8 minutes, or until the cheese is bubbling. Season to taste with the pepper.

TERIYAKI WINGS WITH
PEPPER-BEAN-BASIL RELISH

Edamame, the fresh soy beans that are so popular for snacking on in Japan, are catching on in this country too. Look for them in the natural foods or freezer section of many supermarkets.

Hands-On Time: 10 minutes

Total Time: 22 minutes

Makes 4 to 6 servings

6 pounds premarinated teriyaki chicken wings (see note)

½ cup drained roasted red bell peppers

8 ounces (1¼ cups) frozen shelled edamame, thawed

½ cup bottled French vinaigrette dressing

¼ cup slivered fresh basil leaves

½ teaspoon ground black pepper

¼ teaspoon salt

Coat a grill rack or broiler pan with cooking spray. Preheat the grill or broiler.

Remove the wings from the marinade. Place the wings on the rack over direct heat or on the broiler pan. Cook for about 3 minutes per side, or until well browned. Move away from direct heat. Cook for about 12 minutes, or until crispy and the juices run clear.

Meanwhile, place the bell peppers in the bowl of a food processor fitted with a metal blade. Pulse about 6 times to coarsely chop. Add the edamame and dressing. Pulse about 6 times to blend. Transfer to a serving bowl. Stir in the basil, black pepper, and salt. Serve the wings with the Pepper-Bean-Basil Relish.

NOTE: If premarinated wings are not available, combine plain chicken wings with 1 cup of teriyaki baste-and-glaze sauce in an oversize zipper-lock bag (or several 1-gallon-size bags). Seal the bag(s) and massage to coat with the marinade. Refrigerate for at least 2 hours or as long as 12 hours.

WHITE CLAM PIZZAS

Five Ingredients or Less!

At your next patio party, invite
guests to shape and top their
own individual pizzas, and you'll
cut your prep time to nothing.

Hands-On Time: 10 minutes

Total Time: 25 minutes

**Makes 4 to 6 servings (8 small
pizzas)**

1 tube (10 ounces) refrigerated pizza dough

Olive oil (preferably extra-virgin)

2 tablespoons preminced oil-packed garlic

1 pouch (3 ounces) whole clams, rinsed, drained, and
patted dry, or ½ cup canned whole clams, rinsed and
drained

2 tablespoons preshredded Parmesan cheese

Preheat the grill.

Remove the dough from the package but don't unroll. Cut it
into 8 pieces. Fold the edges under and pinch to form balls. Let
them stand for 5 minutes. One at a time, roll or pat each piece
on a lightly floured surface into a 4" circle. Place each circle on
a piece of aluminum foil. Brush with the oil. Spread each round
with ¼ teaspoon of the garlic. Scatter the clams and the cheese
evenly over each round.

Place the pizzas on the grill away from direct heat. Grill, in
batches if necessary, for about 15 minutes, or until browned
and sizzling.

NORTHWEST SALMON PATTIES

These seafood patties are a wonderful main dish to pull together from the pantry. Dollop some sour cream or stone-ground mustard on the side.

Hands-On Time: 8 minutes
Total Time: 18 minutes

Makes 4 to 6 servings

1   cup Parmesan-ranch croutons

2   cans (15 ounces each) sockeye salmon, drained

1   egg

1   teaspoon hot-pepper sauce

Flour

Vegetable oil

In a food processor fitted with a metal blade, place the croutons. Pulse about 12 times, or until the croutons are coarsely chopped. Add the salmon, egg, and hot-pepper sauce. Pulse to blend well. Let stand for 3 minutes, or until the crouton pieces are softened. Turn the mixture onto a large sheet of waxed paper. Shape the salmon mixture into 8 patties. On a clean sheet of waxed paper, dust both sides with the flour.

Preheat a contact grill or a stovetop grill pan over medium-high heat. Add about 1 tablespoon of oil, or enough to generously coat the bottom of the pan. Heat until sizzling. Place the patties on the grill. Cook about 4 minutes per side, or until browned and a thermometer registers 160°F when inserted sideways into the center of a patty.

SHRIMP CALYPSO

Five Ingredients or Less!

Jerk, the preferred seasoning blend in Jamaica, is typically a combination of dried chiles, herbs, and warm spices. Serve this dish with saffron-seasoned yellow rice to soak up the spicy juices.

Hands-On Time: 10 minutes

Total Time: 10 minutes

Makes 4 to 6 servings

2   tablespoons vegetable oil

1   container (7 ounces) presliced onion and red bell pepper (2 cups)

2-2½   pounds peeled, deveined medium shrimp

1   teaspoon jerk seasoning or Cajun seasoning

¾   teaspoon salt

3   tablespoons frozen limeade concentrate

Heat the oil on a large stovetop griddle over medium-high heat. Add the onion and pepper. Cook, tossing occasionally, for 3 minutes, or until lightly browned. Scrape the onion and pepper to one side. Add the shrimp, jerk or Cajun seasoning, and salt. Cook, tossing, for 4 minutes, or until the shrimp are opaque. Add the limeade concentrate. Stir to coat.

NOTE: To prepare on a one-burner stovetop griddle, cook the onion, pepper, and shrimp in two batches, using 1 tablespoon of oil for each batch.

To cook on a portable perforated grill rack, preheat the grill. Toss the onion and pepper with ½ tablespoon of oil and the shrimp with 1½ tablespoons of oil before cooking.

GRILLED FENNEL SALMON WITH
SUN-DRIED TOMATO-ORANGE BUTTER

Bags of frozen individually wrapped boneless, skinless salmon fillets are often more economical and of better quality than the "fresh" (frequently previously frozen) salmon displayed in the seafood case. Just be sure to thaw the fillets completely according to the package instructions before grilling.

Hands-On Time: 8 minutes

Total Time: 12 minutes

Makes 4 to 6 servings

Vegetable oil

2-2$\frac{1}{2}$ pounds boneless, skinless salmon fillets

1 teaspoon crushed fennel seeds

$\frac{1}{8}$ teaspoon salt + more for seasoning

2 tablespoons butter, softened

$\frac{1}{2}$ cup drained prechopped oil-packed sun-dried tomatoes

1 tablespoon frozen orange-juice concentrate

$\frac{1}{8}$ teaspoon ground black pepper

Coat a grill rack or broiler pan with cooking spray. Preheat the grill or broiler.

Lightly drizzle oil over both sides of the salmon fillets. Evenly sprinkle the fennel seeds on both sides. Season lightly with salt. Place the fillets on the rack or pan. Grill or broil, turning once, for 8 to 10 minutes total time, or until opaque in the center.

Meanwhile, in a small bowl, combine the butter, tomatoes, juice concentrate, pepper, and the remaining $\frac{1}{8}$ teaspoon of salt. Mix to combine.

Remove the salmon to a platter. Dollop with the butter mixture.

COCONUT CATFISH WITH MELON SALSA

Frozen limeade concentrate is a wonderful ingredient to have on hand. It adds sweet tartness to many Caribbean, Mexican, and Asian dishes. Toasting the coconut takes just a few extra minutes but is well worth it because of the vibrancy it brings to the dish.

Hands-On Time: 8 minutes

Total Time: 12 minutes

Makes 4 to 6 servings

2 pounds catfish fillets

Salt

1 container (1 pound) refrigerated mixed melon cubes

¼ cup frozen limeade concentrate

½ teaspoon red-pepper flakes

⅓ cup sweetened flaked coconut

Coat a grill rack, a broiler pan, or a stovetop griddle with cooking spray. Preheat the grill, broiler, or stovetop griddle.

Coat the fish with cooking spray on both sides. Season with salt to taste. Place the fish on the grill rack, broiler pan, or griddle. Grill or broil, turning once, for 8 to 10 minutes total time, or until the fish flakes easily.

Meanwhile, in the bowl of a food processor, combine the melon, limeade concentrate, and red-pepper flakes. Pulse 12 times, or until the melon is finely chopped. Set aside.

Place the coconut in a medium heavy skillet. Cook over medium-high heat, stirring constantly with a fork, for 2 minutes, or until golden brown. Spoon the reserved salsa over the fish. Sprinkle with the coconut.

MAHI MAHI WITH MUSTARD-CAPER SAUCE

Five Ingredients or Less!

The savory mustard-caper sauce need not be reserved for mahi mahi. Try it with other "steak-type" seafood such as swordfish, shark, and halibut.

Hands-On Time: 10 minutes
Total Time: 40 minutes

Makes 4 to 6 servings

2 pounds mahi mahi steaks

½ cup bottled French vinaigrette dressing

⅓ cup dried bread crumbs

2 tablespoons Dijon mustard

2 tablespoons capers, rinsed and drained

In a large zipper-lock bag, combine the fish and dressing. Massage the bag to coat evenly. Refrigerate for 30 minutes.

Coat a grill rack or broiler pan with cooking spray. Preheat the grill or broiler.

Remove the fish from the bag, pouring the marinade into a microwaveable bowl. Cover the bowl with waxed paper. Microwave on high power for 2 minutes, or until boiling. Set aside.

Sprinkle both sides of the fish with the bread crumbs to coat. Place the fish on the rack or pan. Grill or broil, turning once, for 3 to 4 minutes per side, or until the fish is just opaque.

Meanwhile, whisk the mustard and capers into the reserved marinade. Drizzle over the fish.

LEMON-GARLIC TURKEY TENDERLOIN
WITH SALSA ROMESCO

As versatile as pesto, Spanish Romesco sauce deserves more attention from home cooks. It comes together in seconds in the food processor or blender and keeps for up to 2 weeks in the refrigerator. A dollop adds a mellow piquancy to everything from scrambled eggs to grilled shrimp.

Hands-On Time: 10 minutes

Total Time: 35 minutes

Makes 6 to 8 servings

1³⁄₄ pounds premarinated lemon-garlic turkey breast tenderloins

¹⁄₃ cup raw whole almonds

1 slice white bread or soft whole wheat bread, torn into chunks

1 cup jarred roasted red bell peppers, drained

1 teaspoon Asian chili-garlic sauce

¹⁄₄ teaspoon salt

¹⁄₄ cup olive oil (preferably extra-virgin)

Coat a grill rack or broiler pan with cooking spray. Preheat the grill or broiler. Place the tenderloins on the rack or pan. Grill or broil, turning once, for 10 minutes per side, or until browned. Move away from direct heat on the grill rack or place in a 350°F oven. Cook for 12 minutes, or until a thermometer inserted into the thickest portion registers 165°F or the juices run clear.

Meanwhile, in the bowl of a food processor fitted with a metal blade or in a blender, grind the almonds very fine. Add the bread, peppers, chili-garlic sauce, and salt. Pulse 6 times to finely chop. With the machine running, add the oil through the feed tube. Process until a coarse paste forms.

Slice the turkey. Serve the Salsa Romesco on the side.

SEASONED PEPPER TURKEY
WITH PORTUGUESE TOMATOES

The fresh herb is a major component of Portuguese Tomatoes, so select the fresh-est bunch you can find. Either parsley or cilantro works nicely.

Hands-On Time: 10 minutes
Total Time: 45 minutes

Makes 4 to 6 servings

Photo on page 142

3   pints grape tomatoes (6 cups)

¼   cup olive oil (preferably extra-virgin)

1½ tablespoons preminced oil-packed garlic

½   cup chopped fresh parsley or cilantro

½   teaspoon red-pepper flakes

¼   teaspoon salt

1¾ pounds premarinated seasoned pepper turkey tenderloins

Coat a grill rack with cooking spray. Preheat the grill.

In a 13" × 9" grillproof pan, combine the tomatoes, oil, garlic, parsley or cilantro, pepper, and salt. Toss to coat. Place on the grill over direct heat. Cook, stirring occasionally, for about 10 minutes, or until sizzling. Move the pan away from direct heat.

Place the turkey on the rack or pan. Grill, turning once, for 5 minutes per side, or until browned. Move away from direct heat on the grill rack. Cook for 10 minutes per side, or until a thermometer inserted into the thickest portion registers 165°F or the juices run clear. Let stand for 10 minutes. Slice and serve with the tomatoes.

CHINESE CHICKEN-AND-SNAP-PEAS WRAPS

In this quick-to-make variation of the classic Chinese Mu Shu Pork, flour tortillas stand in for homemade flour pancakes.

Hands-On Time: 15 minutes
Total Time: 1 hour and 20 minutes

Makes 4 to 6 servings

1½ pounds boneless, skinless chicken breasts

1 tablespoon preminced oil-packed garlic

⅔ cup hoisin sauce, divided

1 tablespoon vegetable oil

2 bags (8 ounce each) stringless sugar-snap peas

1 cup bagged shredded carrots

1 bunch scallions, all parts, cut into 3" lengths

10 (6"-wide) flour tortillas, heated

In a zipper-lock bag, combine the chicken, garlic, and ⅓ cup of the hoisin sauce. Close tightly and massage to coat the chicken evenly. Refrigerate, massaging occasionally, for 1 hour or up to 8 hours.

Heat the oil on a large stovetop griddle over medium-high heat. Add the peas, carrots, and scallions. Cook, tossing occasionally, for 5 minutes, or until lightly browned. Scrape the vegetables to one side.

Remove the chicken from the marinade. Discard the marinade. Place the chicken on the griddle. Cook for about 15 minutes, turning occasionally, or until a thermometer inserted into the thickest portion registers 160°F and the juices run clear. Let the chicken stand for 5 minutes. Cut into thin slices.

Lay the tortillas on a work surface. Spread some of the remaining hoisin sauce over each tortilla. Top with the chicken and vegetables. Roll up like soft tacos.

NOTE: To prepare on a one-burner stovetop griddle, cook the vegetables and chicken in two batches, using 1 tablespoon of oil for each batch.

BOURBON-BARBECUED PORK WITH MESQUITE SWEET-POTATO FRIES

Convenient frozen sweet-potato oven fries really spark up this barbecue plate. There's no need to thaw them before tossing on the grill.

Hands-On Time: 10 minutes
Total Time: 1 hour

Makes 4 servings

1 premarinated onion-and-garlic or oven-roasted-flavor pork roast (about 2 pounds)

1 bag (1 pound) frozen sweet-potato oven fries

¼ teaspoon mesquite seasoning

Salt (optional)

1 cup bottled barbecue sauce

2 tablespoons bourbon

Coat a grill rack and a portable perforated grill rack with cooking spray. Preheat the grill. Set the perforated grill rack on the grill away from direct heat. Place the pork on the rack. Cook for about 30 minutes. Scatter the potatoes on the rack in a single layer around the pork. Cook for about 15 minutes, tossing occasionally, or until heated. With mitts, transfer the grill rack over direct heat. Cook, watching carefully, for about 5 minutes, or until the potatoes are sizzling and browned. Remove from the grill. Sprinkle on the mesquite seasoning and salt to taste, if using. Check the pork for doneness. When a thermometer registers 175°F when inserted into the center (the pork should be well-done and very tender), remove from the grill. Let stand for 10 minutes.

Meanwhile, combine the sauce and bourbon in a microwaveable bowl. Cover with waxed paper. Microwave on high power for 2 minutes, or until hot. Remove the netting from the pork roast. Discard. Cut the pork into thin slices. Drizzle with the sauce. Serve with the potatoes on the side.

ITALIAN SAUSAGE-STUFFED ZUCCHINI

This dish is marvelous to serve to company. Preparation takes mere minutes and can be done ahead of time. Cover the zucchini with plastic wrap and refrigerate for up to 48 hours before grilling.

Hands-On Time: 12 minutes
Total Time: 57 minutes

Makes 4 to 6 servings

6 zucchini (6" long), halved lengthwise (about $3\frac{1}{2}$ pounds total)

$1\frac{1}{4}$ pounds loose-pack mild or hot Italian sausage (see note)

$\frac{3}{4}$ cup drained chopped canned pepper-onion-seasoned tomatoes

$\frac{3}{4}$ cup (3 ounces) preshredded Parmesan and Romano cheese blend, divided

Coat a grill rack or broiler pan with cooking spray. Preheat the grill or broiler.

With a melon baller or a small spoon, scoop out the pulpy seeds in the zucchini halves. Discard the seeds.

On a large sheet of waxed paper, combine the sausage, tomatoes, and $\frac{1}{2}$ cup of the cheese. Mix with hands to incorporate. Press equal amounts of the mixture on top of each zucchini half to cover evenly. Sprinkle the remaining $\frac{1}{4}$ cup of cheese over the tops. Place on the grill away from direct heat. Cook for about 45 minutes, or until the sausage is no longer pink.

NOTE: Italian sausage links may replace the loose-pack sausage. Use kitchen scissors to quickly cut the casings for removal.

PORK CHOPS ITALIANO WITH PEPPERS AND ONIONS

Five Ingredients or Less!

This standard of Italian-American backyard cookouts required advance planning and prepara- tion. The cook had to remember to place the chops in a home- made marinade a couple hours before cooking. Onion and sweet bell peppers were trimmed and sliced by hand. Cheese was shred by hand. This recipe keeps the gusto without all the fuss.

Before 2 hours and 30 minutes

After 25 minutes

Time Saved 2 hours and 5 minutes

Makes 4 to 6 servings

2 containers (7 ounces each) presliced onion and bell pepper (4 cups)

½ cup bottled Italian salad dressing

4-6 boneless premarinated Italian-seasoned pork chops (2 to 3 pounds)

2 tablespoons preshredded Romano cheese

½ teaspoon red-pepper flakes

Coat a grill rack and a portable perforated grill rack with cook- ing spray. Preheat the grill.

In a zipper-lock bag, toss the onion and bell pepper with the salad dressing. With tongs, remove the onion and bell pepper and scatter over the grill pan. Grill, stirring frequently, for about 5 minutes, or until well browned. Transfer away from direct heat.

Place the pork on the rack or pan. Grill, turning occasionally, for a total of 18 minutes, or until a thermometer inserted into the center of a chop registers 160°F and the juices run clear. Remove the pork to a platter. Scatter the onion and pepper over the pork. Sprinkle with the cheese and red-pepper flakes.

--- *We Saved Time By* ---

■ Using premarinated pork chops instead of preparing a marinade from scratch

■ Using presliced onion and bell pepper instead of peeling the onion, coring the pepper, and slicing the vegetables

■ Using bottled Italian dressing to season and oil the vegetables instead of making a dressing from scratch

■ Using preshredded cheese instead of shredding it from a block

CUBAN PORK SANDWICH

Five Ingredients or Less!

The quick meal, when eaten on the run in Miami, often features ham along with the roasted pork. This home version, although simplified, is still fabulous.

Hands-On Time: 10 minutes
Total Time: 45 minutes

Makes 4 servings

1¼ pounds premarinated honey-mustard pork fillet

Yellow mustard

4 Portuguese rolls or kaiser rolls

2 large dill pickles, thinly sliced lengthwise

4 slices (4 ounces) Swiss or Gruyère cheese

Coat a grill rack or broiler pan with cooking spray. Preheat the grill or broiler.

Place the pork on the grill rack or broiler pan. Grill or broil for about 4 minutes per side, or until browned. Move the pork to the side of the grill away from direct heat or move to a 375°F oven. Cook for about 25 minutes, or until a thermometer inserted into the center registers 155°F and the juices run clear. Let stand for 5 minutes. Do not turn off the grill. Restart the broiler.

Meanwhile, spread some mustard on both cut sides of the rolls. Cover the bottoms with the pickle slices. Cut the pork into very thin slices and layer on top of the pickles. Place a slice of cheese on top of each. If cooking on the grill, place the sandwiches away from direct heat on the grill. Grill for 5 minutes, or until the cheese is melted. If cooking in the broiler, place the sandwiches, without tops, on the broiler pan. Broil for about 4 minutes, or until the cheese is bubbling. Cover with the tops.

QUICK TIP: Grill or broil the pork fillet and allow it to cool completely. Place the pork in a zipper-lock bag and refrigerate for up to 4 days. To serve, allow the pork to stand at room temperature for 30 minutes. Cut it into thin slices. Continue with the directions for assembling and grilling or broiling the sandwiches.

CHARRED FLANK STEAK WITH PICADILLO RELISH

In many Spanish-speaking countries, picadillo is a dish of ground meat fried with vegetables and often raisins. In this variation, a whole cut of beef is grilled for added flavor, and the remaining picadillo ingredients are combined into a zesty relish.

Hands-On Time: 10 minutes

Total Time: 50 minutes

Makes 4 to 6 servings

1 beef flank steak (2 pounds)

½ cup bottled herb-garlic marinade

1 tablespoon preminced oil-packed garlic

2 tablespoons olive oil (preferably extra-virgin)

1 container (7 ounces) presliced onion and red bell pepper (2 cups)

¼ cup raisins

¼ teaspoon salt

In a large zipper-lock bag, combine the steak, marinade, and garlic. Massage the bag to coat evenly. Refrigerate, massaging occasionally, for at least 30 minutes or as long as 8 hours.

Coat a grill rack or broiler pan with cooking spray. Preheat the grill or broiler. Remove the steak from the bag, reserving the marinade. Place the steak on the rack or pan. Grill or broil, turning once, for 8 minutes per side, or until well browned. Continue cooking to desired doneness. A thermometer inserted into the center registers 145°F for medium-rare, 160°F for medium, or 165°F for well-done. Let stand for 5 minutes before cutting into thin slices across the grain.

Meanwhile, in a medium skillet, heat the oil, onion and pepper, raisins, and salt over medium-high heat. Cook, tossing, for 5 minutes, or until the onion is golden. Add the reserved marinade. Bring to a boil. Serve the relish with the steak.

BLUE CHEESEBURGERS

Five Ingredients or Less!

The flavors of beef and piquant blue cheese enjoy a long partnership—but never one so quickly realized as in these robust burgers.

Hands-On Time: 4 minutes
Total Time: 28 minutes

Makes 4 servings

$^3/_4$ cup (3 ounces) precrumbled blue cheese

4 ground beef patties (5 ounces each)

4 teaspoons Worcestershire sauce

Freshly ground black pepper

4 sesame seed hamburger buns

1 large tomato, sliced

Heat a stovetop grill pan over high heat. With hands, squeeze the cheese into 4 balls. Press slightly to flatten. Place a cheese disk on each patty. Fold the sides of the patties, flattening and spreading as necessary so that the edges meet in the middle. Press to make 4" round patties with the cheese enclosed inside. Season both sides of the patties with the Worcestershire sauce. Season with pepper.

Place the patties on the grill pan. Cook for 12 minutes per side, or until no longer pink near the center. If desired, place buns open side down on the grill pan for about 1 minute, or until toasted. Place the burgers on the bun bottoms. Top with the tomato and bun tops.

Shelf-Ready Shortcuts

BARBECUE SAUCE

Any dedicated griller has a jar of barbecue sauce in the fridge. It comes in handy for flavoring burgers, meats, chicken, and almost everything else you put on the grill. But barbecue sauce has plenty of other uses too. The flavor profile is similar to that of a spicy, smoky ketchup, and you can substitute barbecue sauce for ketchup anytime you want a richer taste than ketchup affords. Use it also to flavor braising liquids, to start up a rich salad dressing, or to make a smoky-tasting stir-fry sauce.

TURKISH BEEF WITH PEPPERS, ONION, AND SESAME

Five Ingredients or Less!

A portable perforated grill rack saves time in preparing a meal with the flavors of a Turkish kebab but without the time-consuming task of threading the ingredients on skewers. Serve warmed pita bread on the side.

Hands-On Time: 8 minutes
Total Time: 15 minutes

Makes 4 to 6 servings

2	containers (7 ounces each) presliced onion and bell pepper (4 cups)
2	tablespoons olive oil (preferably extra-virgin)
2	teaspoons dried thyme
2	teaspoons sesame seeds
½	teaspoon salt
½	teaspoon black pepper
2-2½	pounds premarinated shish-kebab beef sirloin cubes, about 2½" thick (see note)

Coat a grill rack and a portable perforated grill rack with cooking spray. Preheat the grill. In a zipper-lock bag, combine the onion and bell pepper, oil, thyme, sesame seeds, salt, and black pepper. Toss to coat. Remove the mixture from the bag and place it on the portable grill rack set over direct heat. Cook, stirring occasionally, for 5 minutes, or until well browned. Move away from direct heat.

Place the beef on the grill over direct heat. Cook, turning as needed, for about 6 minutes total, or until a thermometer registers 145°F for medium-rare, 160°F for medium, or 165°F for well-done when inserted into the center. Serve with the onion and peppers.

NOTE: Premarinated beef sirloin cubes are available in the specialty meat case of some supermarkets. If unavailable, combine beef sirloin cubes and 1 cup steak-house marinade in a zipper-lock bag. Massage to coat the beef evenly. Refrigerate for at least 1 hour.

GREEK SHRIMP WITH TOMATOES AND FETA *page 180*

CHAPTER 9

SKILLET DINNERS

These one-dish dinners are a snap to prepare because they rely on many ingredients you probably have in your cupboard. Plus, with only one pan to worry about, cleanup is a breeze.

Tex-a-Cajun Jambalaya

Chicken Braised with Corn and Chipotles

Rigatoni Carbonara with Peas

Broccoli and Bell-Pepper Toss with Tortellini

Turkey Scaloppine and Broccoli in Creamy Pan Gravy

Greek Shrimp with Tomatoes and Feta

Mediterranean Tilapia and Spinach in Spicy Tomato Sauce

Turkey Couscous with Onions, Carrots, and Peppers

Thai Catfish Curry with Green Beans and Rice

Turkey and Kale in Chinese Black-Bean Sauce

Warm Teriyaki Beef, Pineapple, and Broccoli Salad

Tuscan Pork and Chickpeas with Spinach

Curried Peppercorn Pork with Cauliflower and Potatoes

Bistro Steaks with Mushrooms and Onions

TEX-A-CAJUN JAMBALAYA

The border country between Texas and Louisiana is home to many tasty cross-cultural dishes such as jambalaya seasoned with chili powder. Serve with cornbread or hot rice. Pass the hot sauce at the table.

Hands-On Time: 7 minutes
Total Time: 25 minutes

Makes 4 to 6 servings

2 tablespoons olive oil

1 container (7 ounces) prechopped tricolor bell pepper (1 cup)

1 cup prechopped onion

1 cup prechopped celery

1½ tablespoons preminced oil-packed garlic

1 tablespoon chili powder

½ teaspoon salt

½ pound smoked fully cooked kielbasa sausage, halved lengthwise, cut into 1" chunks

2 cans (14 ounces each) diced pepper-onion seasoned tomatoes

¾ pound medium peeled, deveined shrimp

Heat the oil in a large skillet set over medium heat. Add the pepper, onion, celery, garlic, chili powder, and salt. Stir to mix. Cook, stirring occasionally, for 5 minutes, or until the onion is golden. Add the sausage. Stir to coat with the seasonings. Add the tomatoes (with juice). Reduce the heat to medium-low. Cover and simmer, stirring occasionally, for 10 minutes, or until the flavors blend.

Stir in the shrimp. Cover and simmer for 3 minutes, or until the shrimp are opaque.

EASY, HEALTHY SAUCES FOR CHICKEN BREASTS

Chicken is the cook's blank canvas. You can flavor it however you like. But sometimes, even the most creative cooks suffer from flavor fatigue. Try these easy sauces to get out of the rut. They go especially well with grilled chicken breasts. If you sauté the chicken breasts, use the same pan to make the sauce and you'll pick up even more flavor. Each sauce makes enough for about 4 chicken breast halves. Bonus: Each sauce is low in calories.

1. **Apple and Cider Sauce:** Sauté 2 thinly sliced apples in 2 teaspoons butter for 3 minutes. Add ½ cup cider and ½ cup chicken broth. Cook for about 3 minutes, or longer until slightly reduced. Stir in ¼ cup sliced scallions and cook 1 minute longer.

2. **Provençal Sauce:** Sauté ⅓ cup chopped red onion in 1 teaspoon olive oil for 5 minutes. Add 1 teaspoon preminced oil-packed garlic and 1 can (15 ounces) diced tomatoes (with juice). Cook for 5 minutes. Stir in 2 teaspoons chopped fresh rosemary and 2 tablespoons chopped oil-cured black olives.

3. **Ginger-Scallion Sauce:** Sauté 2 teaspoons preminced ginger, 1 teaspoon preminced oil-packed garlic, and 3 chopped scallions in 1 teaspoon sesame oil for 2 minutes. Stir in ¼ cup bottled stir-fry sauce and ⅓ cup chicken broth. Cook for about 3 minutes, or until thickened slightly.

4. **Creamy Chutney Sauce:** Sauté 2 chopped shallots in 1 teaspoon canola oil for 2 minutes. Stir in ½ cup chicken broth, ¼ cup prepared chutney, and ½ teaspoon curry powder. Simmer for about 3 minutes, or until thickened. Remove from the heat and stir in 1 tablespoon reduced-fat sour cream.

5. **Spiced Pineapple Sauce:** Sauté ⅓ cup prechopped onion in 1 teaspoon canola oil for 5 minutes. Stir in 1 small can (8 ounces) crushed pineapple (with juice), 2 teaspoons all-purpose flour, ½ teaspoon ground cumin, and ¼ teaspoon ground allspice. Simmer for about 4 minutes, or until thickened. Stir in 3 tablespoons chopped fresh parsley, ¼ teaspoon salt, and ⅛ teaspoon ground black pepper.

6. **Citrus-Tarragon Sauce:** Sauté 3 sliced scallions in 1 teaspoon canola oil for 1 minute. Stir in ½ cup chicken broth, ½ cup orange juice, 2 teaspoons all-purpose flour. Simmer for 3 minutes, then stir in 1 tablespoon chopped fresh tarragon, 2 teaspoons lemon juice, and 1 segmented orange.

CHICKEN BRAISED WITH CORN AND CHIPOTLES

Five Ingredients or Less!

Thanks to the complexity of chipotle salsa, this dish has a surprising depth of flavor from a mere handful of ingredients. If you love corn, serve with microwave-warmed corn tortillas.

Hands-On Time: 4 minutes
Total Time: 14 minutes

Makes 4 to 6 servings

2   tablespoons vegetable oil, divided

1   cup prechopped onion

6   boneless, skinless chicken breast halves (about 2 pounds)

2½   cups (10 ounces) frozen corn kernels

½   cup chipotle salsa

Heat 1 tablespoon of the oil in a large skillet set over high heat. Add the onion and cook, stirring, for 2 minutes, or until golden. Remove the onion and set aside.

Return the skillet to high heat. Add the remaining 1 tablespoon of oil. Place the chicken in the pan. Sauté for 2 minutes per side, or until browned. Add the corn, salsa, and the reserved onion. Lift the chicken pieces with a spatula to mix up the corn and salsa and spread some on the pan bottom. Cover. Reduce the heat to medium-low. Cook for about 8 minutes, or until the chicken is no longer pink in the center.

Shelf-Ready Shortcuts

SALSA

Years ago, salsa surpassed ketchup as America's favorite condiment. We just can't get enough chips and salsa! But don't forget that most salsa is merely a mixture of fresh chopped tomatoes, onions, and peppers with some citrus juice or vinegar added. Whenever you need these ingredients in the same dish, save some time and open a jar of salsa instead. Salsa can be used as the base for making chili, as a mildly spicy chunky tomato sauce for pasta, or in a jambalaya or other spicy rice dish.

RIGATONI CARBONARA WITH PEAS

Using ready-cooked real bacon in this family-friendly pasta saves time in two ways. It eliminates the cooking of it and the minutes spent scrubbing the griddle.

Hands-On Time: 6 minutes
Total Time: 18 minutes

Makes 4 to 6 servings

12 ounces rigatoni

    Salt

2 cups frozen petite peas

2 tablespoons olive oil

$\frac{1}{2}$ cup (2 ounces) bagged crumbled bacon

1 tablespoon preminced oil-packed garlic

4 eggs, beaten

1 cup (4 ounces) preshredded Parmesan-and-Romano cheese blend

In a large pot, cook the pasta in salted water according to the package directions. Before draining, set aside 1 cup of the cooking water. Place the peas in a large colander. Drain the pasta over the peas. Set both aside.

Return the pot to medium-low heat. Add the oil, bacon, and garlic. Cook, stirring occasionally, for 2 minutes, or until the garlic is golden. Add the reserved pasta and peas. Toss to coat with the garlic mixture.

Add $\frac{1}{2}$ cup of the reserved cooking water to the eggs in a bowl. Increase the heat of the pot to medium. Add the eggs to the pot while stirring the pasta constantly. Cook, stirring constantly, for about 4 minutes, or just until the eggs thicken and coat the pasta. Slide the pot off the burner if the eggs start to curdle. Remove from the heat. Add the cheese. Stir to mix. Add a few tablespoons more of cooking water to thin the sauce, if needed.

BROCCOLI AND BELL-PEPPER TOSS WITH TORTELLINI

Vegetarian Dish

A welcome change from jarred red sauce, this vegetable mélange takes just minutes to sauté. No need to boil the tortellini beforehand. It simmers to tenderness in the skillet with the vegetables. Pass red-pepper flakes at the table.

Hands-On Time: 4 minutes

Total Time: 12 minutes

Makes 4 to 6 servings

1 bag (8 ounces) broccoli florets

$\frac{1}{3}$ cup jarred green olive salad, drained

$\frac{1}{4}$ cup olive oil

1 cup prechopped onion

1 container (7 ounces) prechopped tricolored bell pepper (1 cup)

1 package (1$\frac{1}{4}$ pounds) refrigerated green and white cheese tortellini

1$\frac{1}{2}$ cups vegetable broth or water

$\frac{1}{2}$ cup (2 ounces) preshredded Parmesan-Romano-Asiago cheese blend

In the bowl of a food processor fitted with a metal blade, pulse the broccoli 6 times, or until coarsely chopped. Remove to a piece of waxed paper. Set aside. Without washing the bowl, pulse the olive salad 10 times, or until finely chopped. Set aside.

In a large skillet, heat the oil over high heat. Add the onion, peppers, and the reserved broccoli. Stir to mix. Cover and cook for 3 minutes, stirring occasionally, or until the broccoli is crisp-tender. Add the tortellini and broth or water. Bring to a boil. Reduce the heat so the mixture simmers gently. Cover and cook for 5 minutes, stirring occasionally, or until the tortellini is tender. Stir in the cheese and the reserved olive salad.

TURKEY SCALOPPINE AND BROCCOLI IN CREAMY PAN GRAVY

Five Ingredients or Less!

With well-selected ingredients, a restaurant-quality meal can be on your table in far less time than it takes to get pizza delivery.

Hands-On Time: 6 minutes

Total Time: 12 minutes

Makes 4 to 6 servings

1½ pounds presliced turkey breast fillets

1 teaspoon dried tarragon

2 tablespoon vegetable oil, divided

2 bags (8 ounces each) broccoli florets, cut into walnut-size chunks

1 container (10 ounces) refrigerated Alfredo sauce

Lay the turkey slices in a single layer on a work surface. With the smooth side of a meat pounder or with a spatula, press down (do not pound) on the slices to make them ¼" thick. Sprinkle the tarragon on both sides.

In a large skillet, heat ½ tablespoon of the oil over high heat. Place half of the turkey slices in the pan. Sauté for 1 to 2 minutes per side, or until browned. Remove to a tray. Repeat with ½ tablespoon of the remaining oil and the remaining slices. Remove to the tray and set aside.

Heat the remaining 1 tablespoon of oil in the pan. Reduce the heat to medium-low. Add the broccoli and toss for 2 minutes to thoroughly coat with the oil. Cover and cook for about 4 minutes, or until crisp-tender. If the broccoli is not tender enough, add 1 tablespoon of water, cover, and cook for 1 minute longer. Stir in the Alfredo sauce plus any juices accumulated on the turkey tray. Simmer for about 2 minutes, or until hot. Serve with the reserved scaloppine.

GREEK SHRIMP WITH TOMATOES AND FETA

This popular Mediterranean island dish comes together in a snap to create a dinner that's distinctive. Be sure to serve crusty bread on the side to mop up the delectable sauce.

Hands-On Time: 6 minutes
Total Time: 16 minutes

Makes 4 to 6 servings

Photo on page 170

2 tablespoons extra-virgin olive oil

½ cup prechopped onion

1 tablespoon preminced oil-packed garlic

1 can (15 ounces) diced tomatoes

1 teaspoon dried oregano

¼ teaspoon salt

½ teaspoon ground black pepper

2 pounds peeled, deveined medium or large shrimp

1½ cups (6 ounces) precrumbled feta cheese

In a large skillet, heat the oil, onion, and garlic over medium-high heat. Cook, stirring occasionally, for 4 minutes, or until golden. Add the tomatoes (with juice), oregano, salt, and pepper. Cover and reduce the heat to medium-low. Simmer for 5 minutes. Add the shrimp. Toss to coat with the sauce. Scatter the cheese on top. Cover and simmer for 4 to 5 minutes, or until the shrimp are opaque.

QUICK TIP: Bagged frozen shrimp is a convenient pantry item for hasty tasty meals. For fast thawing, soak the shrimp in a large bowl of cold water for about 30 minutes.

MEDITERRANEAN TILAPIA AND SPINACH IN SPICY TOMATO SAUCE

Other mild white-fleshed fish, such as red snapper, turbot, or flounder, can replace the tilapia. Also, bagged torn kale leaves can stand in for the spinach. Just cook for a couple minutes longer.

Hands-On Time: 5 minutes
Total Time: 20 minutes

Makes 4 to 6 servings

$\frac{1}{4}$ cup extra-virgin olive oil

1 tablespoon preminced oil-packed garlic

1 can (14 ounces) diced Italian-seasoned tomatoes

1 cup chicken broth

$\frac{1}{2}$ teaspoon red-pepper flakes

$\frac{1}{2}$ teaspoon salt

2-2$\frac{1}{2}$ pounds tilapia fillets

1 bag (10 ounces) baby spinach leaves (10 cups)

In a large skillet, heat the oil and garlic over medium heat for 2 minutes, or until fragrant. Add the tomatoes (with juice), broth, pepper, and salt. Bring to a boil. Reduce the heat to a brisk simmer. Cook for 8 minutes, or until the mixture thickens. Place the fish in the pan. Press lightly to submerge it in the sauce. Cover and cook for about 8 minutes, or until the fish flakes easily. Remove the fish to pasta bowls. Add the spinach to the skillet. Increase the heat to high. Cook, stirring occasionally, for 2 minutes, or until the spinach is wilted. Spoon over the reserved fish.

TURKEY COUSCOUS WITH ONIONS, CARROTS, AND PEPPERS

The addition of convenient premarinated turkey tenderloin adds a modern twist to this North African standard. Look for the fiery chile paste called harissa to use as a garnish. Or use Asian chili-garlic sauce.

Hands-On Time: 12 minutes
Total Time: 20 minutes

Makes 4 to 6 servings

1 box (6 ounces) roasted garlic with olive oil couscous mix

2 tablespoons olive oil, divided

1 pound premarinated lemon-pepper breast turkey tenderloin, cut into walnut-size chunks

½ bag (1 pound) frozen pearl onions, thawed (2 cups)

1 bag (1 pound) baby carrots (1½ cups)

1 large green bell pepper, cut into large chunks

1 teaspoon ground cumin

1½ cups chicken broth

½ cup fresh cilantro leaves, chopped

Remove the seasoning packet from the couscous. Set aside.

Heat 1 tablespoon of the oil in a large nonstick skillet over medium-high heat. Cook the turkey for 5 to 7 minutes, stirring with a spatula, or until all sides are browned and juices run clear. Remove to a plate and set aside.

Return the skillet to medium heat. Add the remaining 1 tablespoon of oil and the onions, carrots, pepper, cumin, and the reserved couscous seasoning packet. Cook, stirring, for 3 minutes, or until the vegetables are thoroughly coated with the seasoning. Add the broth and increase the heat to high. Scrape the pan bottom to loosen all browned bits. When the mixture begins to boil, remove from heat. Stir in the couscous and the reserved turkey, plus any juices on the plate. Cover and let stand for 5 minutes. Fluff with a fork and stir in the cilantro before serving.

THAI CATFISH CURRY WITH GREEN BEANS AND RICE

In a traditional kitchen in Thailand, preparing a curry would be an all-day affair. First, a searing chile paste would be made by grinding fresh chiles with herbs and spices. Whole coconuts would be cracked, peeled, and grated. The grated flesh would be soaked in water and then drained and squeezed to yield the precious sweet milk. Green beans would need to be trimmed and then washed. Fresh basil would be washed and dried. Then the catfish would need to be skinned and filleted. But with a few simple changes, this recipe is homemade in half the time.

Before 3 hours

After 20 minutes

Time Saved 2 hours and 40 minutes

Makes 4 to 6 servings

1 bag (1 pound) pretrimmed green beans

1 tablespoon vegetable oil

2 teaspoons preminced oil-packed garlic

1 can (14 ounces) coconut milk

½ cup vegetable broth or water

1 tablespoon Thai red curry paste (jarred or from an envelope)

1 cup instant brown rice

2 pounds catfish fillets

½ cup fresh basil leaves (optional)

Place the beans in a large skillet with enough water to come $\frac{1}{4}$" up the sides of the pan. Cover and bring to a boil. Reduce the heat so the water simmers briskly. Cook for about 4 minutes, or until the beans are bright green. Drain the beans and return to the pan. Add the oil and garlic. Cook over medium-high heat, tossing occasionally, for 2 minutes, or until the garlic is fragrant. Remove to a plate. Set aside.

Return the pan to low heat. Add the coconut milk, broth or water, and curry paste. Stir to dissolve the paste. Stir in the rice. Top with the fish. Cover and cook over medium-low heat for about 10 minutes, or until the rice is tender and the fish flakes easily. Add the reserved beans. Tilt the pan to spoon some of the curry sauce over the beans. Remove from the heat. Let stand for 4 minutes. Serve in pasta bowls garnished with basil, if using.

We Saved Time By

- Using canned or bagged red curry paste instead of grinding fresh chiles with herbs and spices

- Using canned coconut milk instead of cracking, peeling, marinating, and squeezing fresh coconut

- Using pretrimmed bagged green beans instead of trimming and washing green beans by hand

- Using purchased catfish fillets instead of skinning and filleting whole catfish

- Using preminced oil-packed garlic instead of chopping it by hand

TURKEY AND KALE IN CHINESE BLACK-BEAN SAUCE

Five Ingredients or Less!

Instant brown rice or Thai-style rice noodles are the perfect accompaniment for this sensational Asian supper.

Hands-On Time: 7 minutes

Total Time: 10 minutes

Makes 4 to 6 servings

4 tablespoons vegetable oil, divided

1 tablespoon preminced oil-packed garlic

1 bag (1 pound) kale leaves

1 pound turkey breast tenderloin, cut into walnut-size chunks

¼ cup jarred Chinese black-bean sauce with garlic

¼ cup water

In a large skillet or wok, heat 2 tablespoons of the oil and the garlic over medium-high heat until sizzling. Add the kale. Stir to coat with the oil. Cover and cook, stirring occasionally, for 2 minutes, or until wilted. Remove to a plate and set aside.

Heat the remaining 2 tablespoons of oil in the skillet or wok set over medium-high heat. Add the turkey. Cook, stirring frequently, for 4 minutes, or until the turkey is browned. Return the reserved kale to the pan. Add the black-bean sauce and the water. Stir to coat the turkey and kale with sauce. Simmer over medium-low heat for 3 minutes, or until the turkey juices run clear.

WARM TERIYAKI BEEF, PINEAPPLE, AND BROCCOLI SALAD

Enticing flavors and textures define this cross between a salad and a stir-fry. Warmed flour tortillas go great with the dish.

Hands-On Time: 8 minutes
Total Time: 20 minutes

Makes 4 to 6 servings

1½ pounds thinly sliced sirloin tip beef steaks or other sandwich steaks

½ cup thick teriyaki-with-pineapple-juice marinade

½ cup bottled low-fat sesame-ginger salad dressing, such as Newman's Own

1 bag (1 pound) shredded broccoli slaw

1 can (20 ounces) pineapple chunks in juice, drained

2 tablespoons vegetable oil, divided

In a shallow bowl, combine the beef and marinade. Toss to coat. Let marinate for 15 minutes.

Meanwhile, in a large cold skillet, combine the salad dressing, slaw, and pineapple. Cook, tossing, over high heat for about 2 minutes, or until steaming. Transfer to a serving platter. Set aside.

Return the skillet to high heat. Add 1 tablespoon of the oil. Add half of the meat mixture. Stir-fry for 2 minutes, or until browned. Remove to the platter of reserved salad and arrange the beef on top. Repeat with the remaining 1 tablespoon of oil and meat. Add to the platter and serve while warm.

TUSCAN PORK AND CHICKPEAS WITH SPINACH

Have plenty of robust Italian bread on hand to mop up the pan juices. Pass red-pepper flakes at the table.

Hands-On Time: 13 minutes

Total Time: 18 minutes

Makes 4 to 6 servings

¼ cup olive oil

½ cup prechopped onion

1¼ pounds premarinated lemon-garlic pork fillet, cut into ½"-thick slices

1 can (15 ounces) chickpeas, rinsed and drained

1 can (15 ounces) Italian-seasoned tomato sauce

½ teaspoon salt

1½ bags (10 ounces each; 15 ounces total) baby spinach leaves (15 cups)

2 tablespoons lemon juice

Heat the oil in a large skillet over medium-high heat. Add the onion. Cook, stirring occasionally, for about 2 minutes, or until fragrant. Scrape the onion to the side. Add the pork. Cook for about 4 minutes, turning once, until browned on both sides. Add the chickpeas, tomato sauce, and salt. Stir. Adjust the heat so the sauce is at a moderate simmer. Cover and cook for 5 minutes.

Add the spinach, a large handful at a time, covering the pan between each addition. Cook for about 3 minutes total, or until all the spinach wilts. Remove the pork to plates. Add the lemon juice to the pan. Stir to combine. Spoon over the pork.

CURRIED PEPPERCORN PORK
WITH CAULIFLOWER AND POTATOES

When you shop smart, you'll have all the ingredients for this warmly spiced meal at your fingertips. Tantalizing Asian chili-garlic sauce, passed at the table, is the ideal condiment.

Hands-On Time: 10 minutes

Total Time: 20 minutes

Makes 4 to 6 servings

2 bags (8 ounces each) cauliflower florets, cut into walnut-size chunks

5 tablespoons vegetable oil, divided

$\frac{1}{2}$ cup water, divided

$1\frac{1}{4}$ pounds premarinated peppercorn pork tenderloin, cut into walnut-size chunks

2 tablespoons preminced oil-packed garlic

1 tablespoon curry powder

$\frac{1}{2}$ teaspoon salt

2 cups (8 ounces) frozen potato wedges, unthawed

$\frac{1}{4}$ cup chopped fresh parsley or cilantro (optional)

In a large skillet, combine the cauliflower, 3 tablespoons of the oil, and $\frac{1}{4}$ cup of the water. Cover and bring to a boil. Reduce the heat so the mixture simmers briskly for 5 minutes. Remove the cover. Cook, tossing frequently, for 5 minutes, or until the cauliflower is lightly browned. Remove to a plate. Set aside.

Add the remaining 2 tablespoons of oil to the pan. Place over medium-high heat. Add the pork. Cook for 4 minutes total, turning once, or until browned on both sides. Reduce the heat to medium-low. Add the garlic, curry powder, salt, and the reserved cauliflower. Cook, stirring, for 1 minute, or until the garlic is fragrant. Add the remaining $1/4$ cup of water. Scrape the bottom of the pan to loosen any browned bits. Add the potatoes. Cover and cook for 5 minutes, or until the potatoes are heated through and the pork is no longer pink in the center. Sprinkle with the parsley or cilantro, if using.

QUICK TIP: *Taking a few minutes in the evening or morning before cooking to cut the cauliflower and peppercorn pork into small chunks will make the preparation even faster. Pack into zipper-lock bags and refrigerate.*

Double-Duty Gadgets
FONDUE

Back in the 1970s, Americans found fondue. They made the Swiss classic cheese fondue, chocolate fondue, and plenty of fondues in between. This popular party dish has seen a resurgence in American kitchens lately. But not everyone has a specially made fondue pot or fondue set. The good news: You can make and enjoy fondue without a fondue set. Typically, the dip for fondue is made in a pot on the stovetop, then kept warm in the middle of the table so diners can dunk their favorite ingredients in it. All you really need are a heavy-bottomed pot and some skewers or forks. What about keeping the fondue dip melted and warm? You could just reheat it on the stove if necessary. Or, better yet, put the pot on a warming tray. Don't have a warming tray? Use a heating pad instead. Voila! Instant fondue warmers.

BISTRO STEAKS WITH MUSHROOMS AND ONIONS

Five Ingredients or Less!

Like the renowned French braised entree, these pan steaks team nicely with potatoes. Pop some frozen potato wedges or frozen French fries into the oven until sizzling and golden. Sprinkle with grated Parmesan and freshly ground black pepper.

Hands-On Time: 10 minutes
Total Time: 1 hour and 35 minutes

Makes 4 to 6 servings

2-2½ pounds boneless beef bottom round steaks or other braising steaks, cut into equal portion sizes

1 cup steak-house marinade and sauce

2 tablespoons vegetable oil plus more for deglazing

1 package (8 ounces) presliced fresh mushrooms (4 cups)

1 cup (4 ounces) prechopped onion

½ teaspoon salt

½ teaspoon ground black pepper

In a large zipper-lock bag, combine the steaks and sauce. Massage the contents to coat evenly. Seal and refrigerate for 1 hour or as long as 8 hours.

Remove the steaks from the marinade. Set aside. Measure 1 cup of marinade and set aside.

In a large skillet, heat 1 tablespoon of the oil over medium-high heat. Add the mushrooms, onion, salt, and pepper. Stir. Cover and cook, stirring occasionally, for 5 minutes, or until the mushrooms are browned. Remove to a plate and set aside.

Return the skillet to medium-high heat and add the remaining tablespoon of oil. Fry the reserved steaks, in two batches to avoid crowding the skillet, for about 2 minutes per side, or until browned on both sides. Add the reserved sauce and mushroom mixture. Lift the steaks with a spatula to coat with the sauce. Reduce the heat to medium-low. Cover and simmer for about 10 minutes, or until no longer pink in the center. Let stand for 10 minutes.

CHICKEN-AND-SMOKED-SAUSAGE PAELLA *page 204*

MAKE-AHEAD MEALS

DOWN-EAST SEAFOOD CHOWDER

Don't let the ingredient list deter you from trying this seashore special. Because everything is precut and/or pretrimmed, the preparation is like a day at the beach.

Hands-On Time: 10 minutes

Total Time: 17 minutes

Makes 4 to 6 servings

2 tablespoons butter

1 cup prechopped tricolor bell pepper

1 cup prechopped onion

1 cup prechopped celery

1½ teaspoons Worcestershire sauce

½ teaspoon dried thyme

½ teaspoon salt

½ teaspoon ground black pepper

3 tablespoons flour

2 cups vegetable or fish broth

2 cups whole milk

1 pound fresh or frozen white-fleshed fish fillets, such as cod, turbot, or haddock

1 bag (8 ounces) frozen salad shrimp, thawed

1 can (10 ounces) whole clams, rinsed and drained

In a large pot, combine the butter, bell pepper, onion, celery, Worcestershire, thyme, salt, and black pepper. Cover and cook over medium-high heat for 5 minutes, or until golden. Add the flour. Stir to coat all the ingredients thoroughly. Add the broth and milk. Cook, stirring constantly, for 4 minutes, or until slightly thickened. Add the fish. Reduce the heat to medium-low. Simmer for 5 minutes. Add the shrimp and clams. Simmer for about 2 minutes, or until the fish flakes easily.

MAKE AHEAD FOR THE REFRIGERATOR: *After simmering the broth and milk, allow to cool completely. Pour into an airtight container, cover, and refrigerate for up to 3 days. To serve, reheat the chowder base in a large pot. Add the fish, shrimp, and clams. Cook according to the recipe directions.*

HEARTY CHEDDAR-VEGETABLE STEW

Pressure Cooker Dish

Vegetarian Dish

Imagine a smooth, rich cheese fondue with the dipping vegetables already mixed in and you'll have a mental taste of this pleasing meatless meal. The stew is appetizing served over a baked potato or steamed brown rice.

Hands-On Time: 8 minutes

Total Time: 10 minutes

Makes 4 to 6 servings

2 tablespoons butter

3 bags (8 ounces each) broccoli florets, cut into walnut-size pieces

12 ounces (3 cups) frozen pearl onions, thawed

1 teaspoon poultry seasoning

1 teaspoon paprika

¼ cup water

3 tablespoons flour

2 cups whole milk

2 cups (8 ounces) finely preshredded sharp Cheddar cheese

Heat the butter in a large pot set over high heat. Add the broccoli, onions, poultry seasoning, and paprika. Cook, stirring, until the vegetables are well coated with the seasonings. Add the water. Cover and reduce the heat to medium. Cook, stirring occasionally, for 4 minutes, or until the broccoli is bright green and partially cooked. Add the flour. Stir to mix well. Add the milk. Cook, stirring frequently, over medium heat for 4 minutes, or until thickened. Add the cheese, stirring constantly, until melted.

MAKE AHEAD FOR THE REFRIGERATOR: Prepare the Hearty Cheddar-Vegetable Stew to the point where the milk is thickened. Pack into an airtight container. Refrigerate for up to 3 days. To serve, place the stew base into a large pot. Cover and reheat over medium-high heat, until bubbling. Add the cheese. Cook, stirring constantly, until the cheese is melted.

SOUTHWESTERN MEATBALL SOUP

Albóndigas is the Spanish name for this piquant potage. Pass the green chile salsa at the table for people who can take more heat.

Hands-On Time: 8 minutes
Total Time: 18 minutes

Makes 4 to 6 servings

2 tablespoons olive oil

2 zucchini or yellow squash (1 pound total), shredded in the food processor (4 cups)

1½ cups prechopped onion

1 teaspoon chili powder

6 cups beef broth

12 ounces precooked cocktail-size meatballs (3 cups)

¾ cup instant brown rice

2 teaspoons refrigerated or jarred hot green chile salsa

½ cup chopped fresh cilantro

Heat the oil in a large pot set over medium-high heat. Add the zucchini or squash, onion, and chili powder. Cook, stirring occasionally, for 5 minutes, or until the zucchini loses its moisture and shrinks. Add the broth, meatballs, rice, and salsa. Bring almost to a boil. Cover partially and reduce the heat to medium-low. Simmer for 10 minutes, or until the rice is tender. Stir in the cilantro.

MAKE AHEAD FOR THE REFRIGERATOR: Prepare the soup but don't add the rice and cilantro. Allow to cool completely. Transfer to an airtight container. Refrigerate for up to 5 days. To serve, reheat the soup in a large pot. Add the rice and simmer for 10 minutes. Stir in the cilantro.

CHUNKY MESQUITE-PORK-AND-BEANS CHILI

Like all stews, the taste of this dish gets better with time. If mesquite-barbecue pork fillet is unavailable, use plain pork loin and replace the chili powder with mesquite seasoning.

Hands-On Time: 8 minutes
Total Time: 45 minutes

Makes 4 to 6 servings

¼ cup olive oil

1½ cups prechopped onion

1½ cups prechopped tricolor bell pepper

1½ tablespoons preminced oil-packed garlic

1½ tablespoons chili powder

½ teaspoon salt

1¼ pounds premarinated mesquite-barbecue pork fillet, cut into 4 chunks

1 can (40 ounces) red kidney beans, rinsed and drained

1 can (28 ounces) crushed tomatoes

1 can (14 ounces) chicken broth

In a pressure cooker pot, heat the oil over medium heat. Add the onion, pepper, garlic, chili powder, and salt. Cook, stirring occasionally, for 3 minutes, or until softened. Add the pork and beans. Stir to coat well with the seasonings. Add the tomatoes and broth. Cover the pot and lock the lid. Bring to high pressure over high heat. Reduce the heat to maintain high pressure. Cook for 10 minutes. Allow the pressure to release naturally. Remove the lid. Let stand for 30 minutes, or until the chili thickens and is cool enough to eat.

NOTE: To prepare by conventional stovetop method in a large pot, follow the recipe to the point where the tomatoes and broth are added. Cover and bring almost to a boil. Reduce the heat so the mixture simmers gently. Cook for about 1½ hours, or until the pork is fork-tender.

MAKE AHEAD FOR THE REFRIGERATOR OR FREEZER: Cool the Chunky Mesquite-Pork-and-Beans Chili completely. Pack into an airtight container. Refrigerate for up to 1 week or freeze for up to 3 months. If frozen, thaw in the refrigerator for 24 hours before reheating. To reheat, place the chili with ½ cup of water in a large pot. Cover and reheat over medium-low heat for about 15 minutes, or until heated through.

CHICKEN OKRA GUMBO

The delicate pod vegetable okra acts as a natural thickener in this hearty Louisiana soup. Pass the hot sauce at the table for extra pizzazz.

Hands-On Time: 8 minutes
Total Time: 45 minutes

Makes 4 to 6 servings

2 tablespoons olive oil

½ bag (16 ounces) frozen cut okra, thawed (2 cups)

1 cup prechopped onion

2 tablespoons preminced oil-packed garlic

1 teaspoon herbes de Provence

1 teaspoon ground black pepper

2-2¼ pounds chicken drumsticks (6 drumsticks)

2 cans (14 ounces each) chicken broth

1 can (14 ounces) diced pepper-onion-seasoned tomatoes

½ cup instant brown rice

Heat the oil in a large pot set over medium-high heat. Add the okra, onion, garlic, herbes, and black pepper. Cover and cook, stirring occasionally, for 5 minutes, or until golden. Add the chicken. Stir to coat with the seasonings. Add the broth and the tomatoes (with juice). Cover and reduce the heat to medium-low. Cook, stirring occasionally, for 30 minutes. Add the rice. Cook for about 10 minutes, or until the rice is tender and the chicken is falling off the bone. Remove the chicken. Let stand to cool slightly. Remove and discard the chicken skin and bones. Return the chicken to the pot.

MAKE AHEAD FOR THE REFRIGERATOR: Prepare the gumbo without adding the rice. Let stand to cool completely. Transfer to an airtight container. Refrigerate for up to 3 days. To serve, transfer the gumbo to a large pot. Add the rice. Bring almost to a boil. Reduce the heat and simmer for 10 minutes, or until the rice is tender.

CREOLE RED-BEANS AND RICE

This homey dish, which practically cooks itself, is a Monday supper tradition in the city of New Orleans. The flavor actually improves if prepared a few days in advance of serving. Pass extra hot-pepper sauce at the table.

Hands-On Time: 10 minutes
Total Time: 30 minutes

Makes 4 to 6 servings

2 tablespoons olive oil

1 container (7 ounces) prechopped tricolor bell pepper (1 cup)

1 cup prechopped onion

1 cup prechopped celery

1 tablespoon preminced oil-packed garlic

2 teaspoons herbes de Provence

½ teaspoon salt

1 can (40 ounces) red kidney beans, rinsed and drained

½ pound ham steak, cut into 1" chunks

½ pound smoked fully cooked kielbasa sausage, halved lengthwise, cut into 1" chunks

2 cans (14 ounces each) chicken broth

2 teaspoons hot-pepper sauce

1 cup instant brown rice

Heat the oil in a large pot over high heat. Add the pepper, onion, celery, garlic, herbes, and salt. Stir to mix. Cook, stirring occasionally, for 5 minutes, or until the onion is golden. Add the beans, ham, sausage, broth, and hot-pepper sauce. Reduce the heat to medium-low. Cover and simmer, stirring occasionally, for 10 minutes. Stir in the rice. Cover and simmer for 10 minutes, or until the rice is tender. Remove from the heat. Let stand for 5 minutes.

MAKE AHEAD FOR THE REFRIGERATOR OR FREEZER: Refrigerate in an airtight container for up to 1 week or freeze for up to 3 months. If frozen, thaw in the refrigerator for 24 hours before reheating. To reheat, place in a large pot with ½ cup water. Cover and reheat over medium-low heat for about 15 minutes, or until heated through.

CHICKEN-AND-SMOKED-SAUSAGE PAELLA

Depending upon the region of Spain in which it is prepared, this popular rice casserole can contain shellfish, pork, rabbit, or simply vegetables. This chicken and sausage version is inexpensive and quick to make for an out-of-the-ordinary weeknight supper.

Hands-On Time: 10 minutes

Total Time: 1 hour and 20 minutes

Makes 6 to 8 servings

Photo on page 194

3 tablespoons olive oil (preferably extra-virgin)

1 cup prechopped onion

1 tablespoon preminced oil-packed garlic

1 can (15 ounces) diced pepper-onion-seasoned tomatoes

1 can (14 ounces) chicken broth

1 cup drained roasted red bell peppers

1 cup (7 ounces) saffron yellow rice

½ cup frozen petite peas

½ teaspoon ground black pepper

¼ teaspoon salt

2 pounds boneless, skinless chicken thighs

½ pound smoked fully cooked kielbasa sausage, halved lengthwise, cut into 1" chunks

Preheat the oven to 350°F.

In a large glass bowl, combine the oil, onion, and garlic. Cover with plastic wrap, leaving a small corner vent. Microwave on high power for 3 minutes, or until the onion is softened. Carefully transfer the onion mixture to a 13" × 9" baking dish, along with the tomatoes (with juice), broth, roasted peppers, rice, peas, black pepper, and salt. Stir to combine. Add the chicken and sausage, pressing to embed them into the rice mixture. Cover tightly with aluminum foil. Bake for 1 hour, or until the chicken is no longer pink and the juices run clear. Let stand, covered, for 10 minutes.

QUICK TIP: Leftover Chicken-and-Smoked-Sausage Paella makes a wonderful fast supper. Spoon extra servings into an airtight container. Refrigerate for up to 4 days. To reheat, place 1 serving on a microwaveable plate. Cover with waxed paper. Microwave on medium-high power for 3 minutes, or until hot.

MAKE AHEAD FOR THE REFRIGERATOR: After cooking the onion and garlic, let them cool completely. Then transfer them to the baking dish and assemble the rest of the ingredients, cover with aluminum foil, and refrigerate for up to 2 days before baking according to the recipe directions.

— Double-Duty Gadgets —
SCISSORS

If you don't already have a pair of kitchen scissors, simply designate a pair of scissors in your house as the kitchen scissors and store them in the gadget drawer. Scissors do double, triple, and even quadruple duty in the modern kitchen. That's because almost everything is packaged in plastic these days, especially time-saving convenience foods like premarinated meats, presliced cheeses, and refrigerated stuffed pasta—the very ingredients used throughout this book. Use your scissors to open these packages quickly. You can also use them to save time cutting up chives, scallions, and herbs and slicing precut baby carrots into coins.

NEW ORLEANS BARBECUED SHRIMP

Who knows why these richly sauced shrimp are called "barbecued" when they're not? Just enjoy every drop of this delicious concoction. For a truly decadent meal, serve Cajun Potato Salad (page 102) with the shrimp.

Hands-On Time: 4 minutes

Total Time: 10 minutes

Makes 4 to 6 servings

3 tablespoons butter, divided

1 tablespoon vegetable oil

1 tablespoon preminced oil-packed garlic

2 teaspoons Cajun seasoning

½ cup chicken broth or flat beer

2 tablespoons Worcestershire sauce

2-2½ pounds peeled, deveined medium shrimp

½ cup chopped fresh parsley

In a large skillet, heat 2 tablespoons of the butter and the oil and garlic over medium-low heat for 2 minutes, or until the garlic is fragrant. Add the seasoning, broth or beer, and Worcestershire sauce. Increase the heat to medium-high. Simmer, swirling the pot frequently, for 4 minutes, or until reduced by one-third.

Add the shrimp. Cook, stirring for 2 minutes, or until the shrimp are opaque. Add the parsley and the remaining 1 tablespoon of butter. Stir until the butter melts.

MAKE AHEAD FOR THE REFRIGERATOR OR FREEZER: Prepare the sauce portion of the recipe. Cool completely. Refrigerate in an airtight container for up to 2 weeks or freeze for up to 3 months. To serve, reheat the sauce in a large skillet. Add the shrimp and cook according to the recipe directions.

FRENCH VEGETABLE GRATIN WITH GOAT CHEESE

Vegetarian Dish

With the availability of presliced fresh vegetables, preparing sophisticated meatless main dishes has never been more convenient. Choose an oven-proof high-sided skillet—old-fashioned cast iron works beautifully—to brown the peppers, mushrooms, and onions, and you won't have to dirty a baking dish.

Hands-On Time: 10 minutes

Total Time: 30 minutes

Makes 4 to 6 servings

2 tablespoons olive oil

2 containers (7 ounces each) prechopped tricolor bell pepper

1 package (8 ounces) presliced brown mushrooms

$1^1/_2$ cups prechopped onion

$1^1/_2$ teaspoons herbes de Provence

$^1/_2$ teaspoon salt

2 tablespoons cornmeal

2 logs (4 ounces each) goat cheese

1 cup part-skim ricotta cheese

2 eggs

$^1/_2$ teaspoon ground black pepper

Preheat the oven to 350°F.

Heat the oil in a 10" ovenproof skillet over medium-high heat. Add the bell pepper, mushrooms, onion, herbes, and salt. Toss. Cover and cook over medium-high heat for about 3 minutes, or until the vegetables give off liquid. Remove the cover. Cook, tossing occasionally, for about 6 minutes, or until the vegetables are browned. Reduce the heat if the onions are browning too quickly. Stir in the cornmeal.

Meanwhile, place the goat cheese in a mixing bowl. Mash with a fork. Mix in the ricotta cheese, eggs, and black pepper. Beat until smooth. Dollop over the vegetables, spreading to cover. Bake for about 20 minutes, or until the topping is set.

MAKE AHEAD FOR THE REFRIGERATOR: Assemble the dish and cover tightly with plastic wrap. Refrigerate for up to 3 days before baking according to the recipe directions.

GREEN AND WHITE LASAGNA

Vegetarian Dish

Classic creamy northern Italian vegetable-pesto lasagna can take the better part of a day to prepare. Pasta is kneaded and hand-rolled, cheeses are grated by hand, the white sauce demands constant stirring while it simmers, the basil pesto is made from scratch, the spinach requires several washings, and the peas must be shelled. Only then is the whole dish assembled and baked. This up-to-date adaptation comes together pronto but tastes as satisfying as the day-long version.

Before 3 hours

After 1 hour and 15 minutes

Time Saved 1 hour and 45 minutes

Makes 6 to 8 servings

1½ bags (10 ounces each; 15 ounces total) baby spinach leaves

1 carton (15 ounces) part-skim ricotta cheese

3 eggs, beaten

1¾ cups whole milk

1 container (7 ounces) refrigerated basil pesto

2 teaspoons ground black pepper

1 box (8 ounces) oven-ready lasagna noodles

1½ cups (6 ounces) frozen petite peas

1 container (5 ounces) shredded Parmesan-Romano cheese blend, divided

Preheat the oven to 375°F. Coat a 13" × 9" glass or ceramic baking dish with cooking spray.

In the microwave oven, cook the spinach in the bags according to the package directions. Drain the spinach and pat dry with paper towels.

In a mixing bowl, combine the ricotta cheese, eggs, milk, pesto, and pepper. With a fork, beat until smooth. Pour 1 cup of the pesto mixture into the prepared baking dish. Place 3 lasagna noodles in the dish. Drizzle with 1 cup of the pesto mixture. Scatter one-third of the spinach, one-third of the peas, and one-quarter of the Parmesan-Romano cheese over the top. Repeat layering the noodles, pesto mixture, spinach, peas, and Parmesan-Romano cheese two times. Top with the 3 remaining noodles and drizzle with the remaining pesto mixture. Sprinkle with the remaining Parmesan-Romano cheese.

Cover with aluminum foil. Bake for 45 minutes, or until the noodles are tender when pierced with a knife. Let stand for 10 minutes.

QUICK TIP: Bake the Green and White Lasagna on the weekend and refrigerate it for speedy homemade meals during the workweek. To reheat, place one serving on a microwaveable dish. Cover loosely with waxed paper. Cook in the microwave oven on medium-high power for 3 minutes.

MAKE AHEAD FOR THE REFRIGERATOR: After draining the spinach, cool it completely. Assemble the lasagna in a refrigerator-to-ovenproof baking dish. Cover tightly with aluminum foil. Refrigerate for up to 24 hours. Bake according to the recipe directions.

We Saved Time By

- Using prewashed spinach instead of washing and trimming the leaves

- Cooking the spinach in the bag instead of using a skillet and then washing it

- Using preshredded cheese instead of shredding it from a block

- Using ricotta cheese instead of cooking a white sauce in a pan and then washing the pan

- Using refrigerated prepared basil pesto instead of preparing pesto from scratch

- Using oven-ready lasagna noodles instead of making fresh noodles and boiling them in a large pot, then washing the pot

- Using frozen petite peas instead of shelling fresh peas

CURRIED CHICKEN, BROCCOLI, AND PENNE PASTA BAKE

Here's an interesting twist on an Italian favorite. Curry powder lends a wonderful color to the pasta, while precooked chicken makes prep time a breeze.

Hands-On Time: 15 minutes
Total Time: 1 hour and 5 minutes

Makes 4 to 6 servings

½ box (1 pound) uncooked mini penne pasta (2 cups)

2 bags (8 ounces each) broccoli florets

1 cup prechopped onion

2 tablespoons olive oil

1 teaspoon curry powder

1 teaspoon dried thyme

½ teaspoon ground black pepper

½ bag (20 ounces) cooked chicken breast strips (2 cups)

1 carton (16 ounces) creamy small-curd cottage cheese (2 cups)

½ cup preshredded Parmesan cheese

Cook the pasta according to the package directions but for half of the normal cooking time. Add the broccoli during the last 2 minutes of cooking. Reserve 1 cup of the cooking water. Drain and rinse with cold water. Set aside.

Meanwhile, preheat the oven to 375°F. Coat a 13" × 9" glass or ceramic baking dish with cooking spray.

Combine the onion, oil, curry powder, thyme, and pepper in a small glass dish or measuring cup, preferably one with a handle. Cover with plastic wrap, leaving a small corner vent. Microwave on high power, stirring once, for 5 minutes, or until sizzling. Using a rubber spatula, carefully scrape the spice mixture into the prepared baking dish. Add the chicken, cottage cheese, Parmesan cheese, and the reserved cooking water. Mix completely. Cover with aluminum foil. Bake for 30 minutes. Remove the foil. Bake for about 20 minutes longer, or until golden and bubbling.

MAKE AHEAD FOR THE REFRIGERATOR: Allow the broccoli, pasta, cooking water, and onion mixture to cool completely before assembling the dish. Cover tightly with plastic wrap. Refrigerate for up to 3 days. To serve, remove the plastic and bake according to the recipe directions.

TURKEY PAPRIKÁS

Pressure Cooker Dish

This rosy-hued, velvety-sauced stew is a treat served over buttered noodles with an accompaniment of sautéed spinach.

Hands-On Time: 10 minutes
Total Time: 35 minutes

Makes 4 to 6 servings

2 tablespoons vegetable oil

12 ounces turnips, peeled, cut into sticks the size of baby carrots

1 bag (1 pound) baby carrots (1½ cups)

½ bag (1 pound) frozen pearl onions (2 cups)

1 tablespoon preminced oil-packed garlic

1½ teaspoons paprika

½ teaspoon dried rosemary

½ teaspoon salt

1 can (14 ounces) chicken broth

3 pounds turkey drumsticks (4 drumsticks)

½ cup sour cream

2 tablespoons flour

Heat the oil over medium-high heat in the pressure cooker pot. Add the turnips, carrots, onions, garlic, paprika, rosemary, and salt. Cook, stirring occasionally, for 4 minutes, or until slightly softened. Add the broth and turkey. Cover the pot and lock the lid. Bring to high pressure over high heat. Reduce the heat to maintain high pressure. Cook for 10 minutes.

Allow the pressure to release naturally. Remove the lid. Transfer the turkey to a platter. Let stand for 15 minutes, or until cool enough to handle. Remove the skin and discard. Remove the turkey meat from the bones. Discard the bones.

In a bowl, whisk together the sour cream and flour. Whisk in about 1 cup of the sauce from the pot. Over medium heat, pour the sour cream mixture into the pot, whisking constantly.

Simmer for 5 minutes, whisking constantly, or until slightly thickened. Return the turkey to the pot to coat with sauce before serving.

NOTE: *To prepare Turkey Paprikás by conventional stovetop method in a large pot, follow the recipe. Cover and bring almost to a boil. Reduce the heat so the mixture simmers gently. Cook for about 1½ hours, or until the turkey is fork tender. Continue according to the recipe directions.*

MAKE AHEAD FOR THE REFRIGERATOR OR FREEZER: *Cool the Turkey Paprikás completely. Do not add the sour cream mixture. Pack into an airtight container. Refrigerate for up to 1 week or freeze for up to 3 months. If frozen, thaw in the refrigerator for 24 hours before reheating. To reheat, place the paprikás in a large pot. Cover and reheat over medium-low heat for about 15 minutes, or until heated through. Add the sour cream mixture according to the recipe directions.*

CREAMY BLUE-CHEESE CHICKEN

Cleaned and trimmed bagged sugar-snap peas add color and crunch to this meal. Serve them on the side, either raw or stir-fried for 1 minute in a hot skillet filmed with oil, seasoned with salt to taste and a splash of lemon juice.

Hands-On Time: 10 minutes
Total Time: 1 hour

Makes 4 to 6 servings

1 bag (1 pound) baby carrots ($1\frac{1}{2}$ cups)

1 container (10 ounces) refrigerated Alfredo sauce, divided

1 cup whole milk

1 cup uncooked orzo

$2-2\frac{1}{2}$ pounds boneless, skinless chicken thighs

1 bunch scallions, white and light green parts, sliced ($\frac{1}{3}$ cup)

1 teaspoon ground black pepper

$\frac{1}{2}$ teaspoon poultry seasoning

$\frac{1}{4}$ cup dried bread crumbs

$\frac{3}{4}$ cup (3 ounces) precrumbled blue cheese

Preheat the oven to 375°F. Coat a 13" × 9" glass or ceramic baking dish with cooking spray.

Place the carrots in an 8" × 8" microwaveable baking dish. Add enough water to come $\frac{1}{4}$" up the sides of the dish. Cover with plastic wrap, leaving a small corner vent. Microwave on high power for 4 minutes, or until partially cooked. Drain and set aside.

Meanwhile, in a bowl, whisk the Alfredo sauce and the milk until smooth. Pour half into the prepared 13" × 9" dish. Sprinkle the orzo evenly over the sauce. Top with the chicken, scallions, pepper, poultry seasoning, and the reserved carrots. Pour the remaining sauce evenly over the top. Sprinkle on the bread crumbs and the cheese. Cover with aluminum foil. Bake for 40 minutes. Remove the foil. Bake for 10 minutes longer, or until the chicken is no longer pink and the juices run clear.

MAKE AHEAD FOR THE REFRIGERATOR: Assemble the ingredients in the baking dish, cover with aluminum foil, and refrigerate for up to 2 days before baking.

CHICKEN BREASTS GLAZED WITH ORANGE AND MINT

Prepare a couscous mix with toasted pine nuts as a side dish. Toss some prewashed greens with your favorite dressing, and dinner is served.

Hands-On Time: 5 minutes

Total Time: 30 minutes

Makes 4 to 6 servings

¼ cup olive oil (preferably extra-virgin)

2 tablespoons frozen orange-juice concentrate

¼ cup coarsely chopped fresh mint

1 tablespoon preminced oil-packed garlic

½ teaspoon salt

½ teaspoon ground black pepper

2-2½ pounds boneless, skinless chicken breast halves

½ cup (2 ounces) preshredded Parmesan cheese

Preheat the oven to 375°F. Coat a 13" × 9" baking dish with cooking spray.

Combine the oil, orange-juice concentrate, mint, garlic, salt, and pepper in the dish. Mix until blended. Add the chicken, turning the pieces to coat well with the sauce. Sprinkle on the cheese.

Bake for about 20 minutes, or until the chicken is no longer pink and the juices run clear. Increase the oven temperature to broil and place the chicken 9" from the heat source for about 3 minutes, or until browned.

MAKE AHEAD FOR THE REFRIGERATOR: Assemble the dish, cover tightly with plastic wrap, and refrigerate for up to 24 hours. Remove the plastic wrap before baking according to the recipe directions.

CHICKEN POT PIE WITH BISCUITS

Old-fashioned chicken pot pie made on the farm was an excellent recipe for using older hens that were too tough to roast. The chicken was first poached for an hour or so with water and aromatics to cook and tenderize. After cooling, the chicken was removed from the bones. Some of the flavorful chicken broth would be seasoned, thickened, and simmered into gravy. Then came the peeling and dicing of the carrots and onions. For the crowning touch, flaky biscuits were mixed, rolled, and cut by hand. Only then would the pot pie be ready for the oven. We've brought Chicken Pot Pie from the farm to the fast lane with all the savory goodness intact.

Before 4 hours

After 1 hour

Time Saved 3 hours

Makes 6 to 8 servings

1 bag (1 pound) baby carrots, halved crosswise (1$\frac{1}{2}$ cups)

1 rotisserie chicken or 1 pound boneless roasted chicken

2 cans (10 ounces each) sage and black-pepper chicken gravy

$\frac{1}{3}$ cup sour cream

2 tablespoons flour

1 teaspoon poultry seasoning

1 teaspoon hot-pepper sauce

2 cups (8 ounces) frozen pearl onions

1 cup (4 ounces) frozen petite peas

1 tube (16 ounces) large-size refrigerated biscuits (8 biscuits)

Preheat the oven to 375°F. Coat a 13" × 9" glass or ceramic baking dish with cooking spray.

Place the carrots in an 8" × 8" microwaveable baking dish. Add enough water to come $\frac{1}{4}$" up the sides of the dish. Cover with plastic wrap, leaving a small corner vent. Microwave on high power, stirring once, for 3 to 4 minutes, or until partially cooked. Remove and drain.

Meanwhile, if using rotisserie chicken, remove the skin and bones. Discard them. Tear or cut the chicken into big chunks. If using boneless roasted chicken, tear or cut the chicken into chunks.

In the prepared baking dish, whisk the gravy, sour cream, flour, poultry seasoning, and hot-pepper sauce until smooth. Add the chicken, onions, peas, and reserved carrots. Stir to coat with the gravy. Place the biscuits on top. Cover with aluminum foil. Bake for 40 minutes, or until the sauce is bubbling. Remove the foil. Bake for 5 minutes longer, or until the biscuits are browned.

MAKE AHEAD FOR THE REFRIGERATOR OR FREEZER: Cool the carrots completely after draining. Assemble the pot pie in a freezer-to-ovenproof baking dish. Cover with plastic wrap and then with aluminum foil. To bake from the refrigerator, remove the plastic wrap and discard. Re-cover with the foil. Bake for about 50 minutes, removing the foil for the last 10 minutes. To bake from the freezer, remove the plastic wrap and discard. Re-cover with the foil. Bake for about 2 hours and 15 minutes, removing the foil for the last 15 minutes.

--- *We Saved Time By* ---

- Using prewashed baby carrots instead of washing and cutting regular carrots

- Using preroasted chicken instead of roasting the chicken

- Using seasoned canned gravy instead of making broth and gravy from scratch

- Using refrigerated biscuits instead of mixing the dough, rolling, and cutting the biscuits by hand

- Using frozen peeled baby onions instead of peeling the onions by hand

- Using frozen petite peas instead of shelling fresh peas by hand

HEARTLAND PORK, POTATO, AND APPLE BAKE

This dinner is as versatile as it is easy. Golden Delicious is a good choice for the apples, or use Granny Smith for more tartness. As for the potatoes, other seasoning mixes of frozen oven-roast potatoes will work fine.

Hands-On Time: 5 minutes

Total Time: 1 hour

Makes 4 to 6 servings

1¼ pounds premarinated peppercorn pork tenderloin

1 pound (4 cups) frozen French onion oven-roast potatoes

1 cup chunky unsweetened applesauce

2 apples, cored, cut into walnut-size chunks

2 tablespoons stone-ground mustard

Preheat the oven to 375°F. Coat a 17" × 11" baking pan or other large shallow baking pan with cooking spray.

Place the pork, potatoes, applesauce, and apples in the pan. Toss to coat with the applesauce. Clear a diagonal strip in the center of the pan. Place the pork in the cleared space.

Bake for about 45 minutes, or until a thermometer inserted into the center of the pork reaches 155°F and the juices run clear. Remove the pork to a cutting board. Let stand for 10 minutes. Cut the pork into thin slices. Stir the mustard into the potato-apple mixture.

QUICK TIP: Cool the Heartland Pork, Potato, and Apple Bake completely. Store in an airtight container. Refrigerate. To reheat, place one serving on a microwaveable plate. Cover with waxed paper. Microwave on medium power for 2 minutes, then on high power for 1 minute. Let stand for 1 minute.

MAKE AHEAD FOR THE REFRIGERATOR: Assemble the Heartland Pork, Potato, and Apple Bake. Cover tightly with plastic wrap. Refrigerate for up to 3 days. Remove the plastic wrap before baking according to the recipe directions.

BRAISED PROVENÇAL LAMB SHANKS

Pressure Cooker Dish

Here's an amazing way to get incredible "all-day-in-the-kitchen" flavor in less than an hour. Pair with the French Vegetable Gratin with Goat Cheese (page 207) for a perfect spring buffet.

Hands-On Time: 10 minutes
Total Time: 40 minutes

Makes 4 to 6 servings

2	tablespoons olive oil (preferably extra-virgin)
1	bag (12 ounces) precut carrot and celery sticks
1	cup prechopped onion
2	tablespoons preminced oil-packed garlic
1	cup dry red wine
3½–4	pounds lamb shanks (6 shanks)
1	can (14 ounces) diced tomatoes with Burgundy wine and olive oil
1	teaspoon herbes de Provence
½	teaspoon salt
½	teaspoon ground black pepper

Heat the oil over medium-high heat in the pressure cooker pot. Add the carrot and celery, onion, and garlic. Cook, stirring occasionally, for 5 minutes, or until golden. Add the wine. Allow to come to a boil. Add the lamb, tomatoes (with juice), herbes, salt, and pepper. Stir to combine. Cover the pot and lock the lid. Bring to high pressure over high heat. Reduce the heat to maintain high pressure. Cook for 20 minutes.

Allow the pressure to release naturally. Remove the lid. Transfer the meat to a platter. Let stand for 15 minutes, or until the meat is cool enough to handle. Remove the meat from the bones. Discard the bones and any fat or gristle. Return the meat to the pot.

NOTE: To prepare by conventional stovetop method in a large pot, follow the recipe to the point where the lamb, tomatoes, and seasonings are added. Cover and bring almost to a boil. Reduce the heat so the mixture simmers gently. Cook for about 2 hours, or until the lamb is fork-tender.

MAKE AHEAD FOR THE REFRIGERATOR OR FREEZER: Cool the Braised Provençal Lamb Shanks completely. Remove the meat from the bones, discarding the bones. Return the meat to the sauce. Transfer to a large bowl. Refrigerate, uncovered, overnight. Remove the layer of hardened fat from the surface. Discard the fat. Pack the stew into an airtight container. Refrigerate for up to 1 week or freeze for up to 3 months. If frozen, thaw in the refrigerator for 24 hours before reheating. To reheat, place the stew in a large pot. Cover and reheat over medium-low heat for about 15 minutes, or until heated through.

BASQUE SHEPHERD'S PIE

A heavy-duty, high-sided oven-proof skillet is a real time-saving investment. When you sauté and bake in the same pan, it cuts dishwashing in half.

Hands-On Time: 10 minutes
Total Time: 40 minutes

Makes 4 to 6 servings

3/4 bag (12 ounces) pretrimmed greens beans, halved

1 1/2 pounds ground lamb

1 cup prechopped onion

1 can (14 ounces) diced tomatoes with Burgundy wine and olive oil

1 1/2 teaspoons herbes de Provence

3/4 teaspoon salt

3/4 teaspoon ground black pepper

1 pound (4 cups) refrigerated or frozen mashed potatoes, thawed

1/2 cup (4 ounces) preshredded Parmesan-Romano cheese blend

Preheat the oven to 400°F. Place the beans in a large non-reactive ovenproof skillet. Add enough water to come 1/4" up the sides. Cover and cook over high heat for 3 minutes, or until the beans are crisp-tender. Drain and set aside.

Return the skillet to the stovetop over high heat. Add the lamb and onion. Break the lamb into small clumps with a spatula. Cook, stirring occasionally, for about 5 minutes, or until no pink remains. Tip the skillet so that the oil pools on one side. Spoon out excess oil and discard. Add the tomatoes (with juice), herbes, salt, pepper, and reserved beans. Stir to mix.

In a bowl, combine the potatoes and the cheese. Stir to mix thoroughly. Spread over the meat mixture. Bake for about 30 minutes, or until golden and bubbling.

MAKE AHEAD FOR THE REFRIGERATOR OR FREEZER: **To refrigerate before baking, cool the meat mixture completely before spreading on the potato mixture. Cover tightly with plastic wrap. Refrigerate for up to 3 days. Remove the plastic wrap before baking according to the recipe directions.**

To freeze before baking, cool the skillet mixture completely. Transfer to a platter.

Wash and dry the skillet. Line the skillet with heavy-duty aluminum foil. Coat with cooking spray. Pour the meat mixture into the pan. Spread on the potato mixture. Freeze, uncovered, for 24 hours. Remove the frozen foil bundle. Wrap tightly in heavy-duty aluminum foil. Freeze for up to 3 months. To bake, remove the outer foil wrapping. Insert the frozen foil bundle into the original pan. Cover with aluminum foil. Bake for about 1 hour, removing the foil for the last 15 minutes.

CHILAQUILES WITH BEEF AND PINK BEANS

The Mexican equivalent of lasagna, this easy layered oven dish deserves to be better known in American kitchens. To dry the tortillas slightly, leave them out on a paper towel–lined tray overnight.

Hands-On Time: 10 minutes

Total Time: 1 hour and 10 minutes

Makes 6 to 8 servings

2 tablespoons vegetable oil

1 cup prechopped onion

1 pound ground beef

2 cans (14 ounces each) diced zesty chili-style tomatoes

1 can (14 ounces) pink beans, rinsed and drained

¾ cup frozen corn kernels

1 teaspoon ground black pepper

10 (5"-wide) corn tortillas, slightly dried, halved

3 cups (12 ounces) preshredded Mexican four-cheese blend, divided

Heat the oil in a medium skillet over medium heat. Add the onion and cook, stirring occasionally, for 3 minutes, or until softened. Crumble in the beef. Cook over high heat, stirring occasionally, for 4 minutes, or until the meat is no longer pink. Stir in the tomatoes (with juice), beans, corn, and pepper. Set aside.

Preheat the oven to 375°F. Coat a 13" × 9" glass or ceramic baking dish with cooking spray.

Spread 2 cups of the skillet mixture over the bottom of the dish. Cover with one-third of the tortillas, tearing some into small pieces to fit in an even layer. Cover with 2 cups of the skillet mixture and 1 cup of the cheese. Repeat with another layer of tortillas, sauce, and cheese. Top with the remaining tortillas, remaining 2 cups of the skillet mixture, and the remaining 1 cup of cheese. Cover with aluminum foil. Bake for 35 minutes. Remove the foil. Bake for 15 minutes longer, or until browned and bubbling. Let stand for 10 minutes.

QUICK TIP: The Chilaquiles taste even better a few days after baking. To reheat, place one serving on a microwaveable dish. Cover loosely with waxed paper. Cook in the microwave oven on medium-high power for 3 minutes.

MAKE AHEAD FOR THE REFRIGERATOR: After cooking, allow the skillet mixture to cool completely. Assemble the ingredients in the baking dish, cover with aluminum foil, and refrigerate for up to 2 days before baking according to recipe directions.

EASY MAKE-AHEAD MARINADES FOR CHICKEN

Chicken breasts take extremely well to marinating, and the flavor possibilities are endless. Use the marinades below to take your next make-ahead chicken meal to new heights of taste. After removing the chicken from the marinade, grill it, broil it, or pan-fry it until the chicken juices run clear (about 160°F). Discard the marinade.

1. **Moroccan Chicken:** In a food processor, combine ½ cup fresh parsley leaves, ½ cup fresh cilantro leaves, 1 teaspoon preminced oil-packed garlic, 3 tablespoons vegetable oil, 1 tablespoon lemon juice, ½ teaspoon ground cumin, ½ teaspoon paprika, ½ teaspoon salt, and ¼ teaspoon ground black pepper. Process until smooth and pour into a zipper-lock bag. Add 4 to 6 boneless, skinless chicken breast halves to coat, then seal the bag. Marinate in the refrigerator for 2 to 6 hours before cooking.

2. **Mexican Chicken:** In a zipper-lock bag, combine ¼ cup vegetable oil, 2 tablespoons lime juice, 1 teaspoon preminced oil-packed garlic, 2 teaspoons chili powder, and 1 teaspoon ground cumin. Add 4 to 6 boneless, skinless chicken breast halves to coat, then seal the bag. Marinate in the refrigerator for 1 to 2 hours before cooking.

3. **Tarragon Chicken:** In a zipper-lock bag, combine ½ cup dry white wine, ¼ cup lemon juice, ¼ cup olive oil, ½ teaspoon preminced oil-packed garlic, 2 teaspoons dried tarragon, ½ teaspoon salt, and ¼ teaspoon ground black pepper. Add 4 to 6 boneless, skinless chicken breast halves to coat, then seal the bag. Marinate in the refrigerator for 1 to 2 hours before cooking.

4. **Mediterranean Chicken:** In a zipper-lock bag, combine ¼ cup olive oil, ¼ cup lemon juice, ¼ cup shredded fresh basil, ¼ cup chopped fresh parsley, ½ teaspoon dried oregano, ½ teaspoon salt, ¼ teaspoon ground black pepper, and ⅛ teaspoon ground red pepper. Add 4 to 6 boneless, skinless chicken breast halves to coat, then seal the bag. Marinate in the refrigerator for 1 to 4 hours before cooking.

5. **Curried Chicken:** In a food processor or blender, combine ¾ cup plain yogurt, ½ cup prechopped onion, 2 tablespoons lemon juice, 1 teaspoon preminced oil-packed garlic, 1 tablespoon curry powder, and ¼ teaspoon ground red pepper. Process until smooth. Scrape into a zipper-lock bag and add 4 to 6 boneless, skinless chicken breast halves to coat, then seal the bag. Marinate in the refrigerator for 1 to 2 hours before cooking.

6. **Italian Chicken:** In a zipper-lock bag, combine ½ cup olive oil, 2 tablespoons lemon juice, 1½ tablespoons white wine vinegar, 3 crumbled bay leaves, 1½ teaspoons preminced oil-packed garlic, 1½ teaspoons salt, 1½ teaspoons dried oregano, 1 teaspoon dried basil, 1 teaspoon dried thyme, and ½ teaspoon ground black pepper. Add 4 to 6 boneless, skinless chicken breast halves to coat, then seal the bag. Marinate in the refrigerator for 24 hours before cooking. (Due to the long marinating time, the chicken may begin to turn white on the surface before cooking, which is okay.)

CHAPTER 11

DOUBLE-DUTY DINNERS

Why start from scratch every night of the week? Instead, give yourself a head start with these clever recipes that help you transform leftovers from one meal into a fabulous new creation the next night.

Minestrone Grande/Tuscan Vegetable-and-Ham Gratin

Pan-Seared Salmon with Scallions and Tarragon/Creamed Salmon on Crisp Potato Cakes

Greek-Style Lemon-Garlic Chicken/Chicken Cacciatora on Polenta

Breaded Dijon Chicken Breasts/Provençal Chicken-and-Vegetable Main Dish Salad

Roasted Chicken and Turnips in Peanut Sauce/Thai Chicken Noodle Salad

Honey-Glazed Ham with Carrots, Onions, and New Potatoes/Pennsylvania Dutch Stovetop Pot Pie with Noodles

Chicken and Wild Mushroom Puff-Pastry Roulade/Risotto with Chicken, Wild Mushrooms, Feta, and Spinach

Peppercorn Pork with Grilled Tomatoes, Zucchini, and Basil/Shredded-Pork Burritos

Roasted Italian-Sausage and Vegetables/Bean-and-Sausage Farfalle

Leg of Lamb Roasted with Herbs and Red Wine/Gyros with Creamy Cucumber-Dill Sauce in Pita

Balsamic Rosemary-Grilled Beef/Fajitas

The Easiest Meat Loaf/Rigatoni with Chunky Meat Sauce

MINESTRONE GRANDE

In English, the Italian word minestrone translates as "big soup." This minestrone, with the addition of hunks of smoky ham, is a big, big soup that's grand enough for a meal.

Hands-On Time: 12 minutes
Total Time: 1 hour and 12 minutes

Makes 4 to 6 servings

2 tablespoons olive oil

2 cups prechopped onion

2 cups prechopped celery

2 cups baby carrots, halved

2 tablespoons preminced oil-packed garlic

1 teaspoon dried Italian seasoning

½ teaspoon salt

½ teaspoon red-pepper flakes

2 cans (15 ounces each) cannellini beans, rinsed and drained

1 pound thick boneless ham steak, cut into ½" cubes

1 can (15 ounces) diced Italian-seasoned tomatoes

10 cups chicken broth

½ bag (½ pound) prechopped kale (4 cups)

3 cups cooked orzo

In a large pot set over high heat, combine the oil, onion, celery, carrots, garlic, Italian seasoning, salt, and red-pepper flakes. Cover and cook, stirring occasionally, for 5 minutes. Add the beans, ham, tomatoes (with juice), and broth. Bring almost to a boil. Reduce the heat to low. Cover partially and simmer for 45 minutes, or until the carrots are softened. Add the kale. Cover partially and simmer for 15 minutes, or until the kale is tender.

Ladle 7 cups into a shallow container. Let stand to cool completely. Transfer to an airtight container. Refrigerate for up to 3 days. Use this minestrone to make Tuscan Vegetable-and-Ham Gratin (opposite).

Meanwhile, stir the orzo into the minestrone in the pot.

MINESTRONE GRANDE *opposite*

TUSCAN VEGETABLE-AND-HAM GRATIN

Five Ingredients or Less!

Called "la ribollita" in Tuscany, this dish is the country cook's creative use of leftover soup. Serve with a mixed greens salad, followed by a winter fruit salad of diced apples, pears, kiwifruit, and oranges tossed with some lemon juice and sugar.

Hands-On Time: 5 minutes

Total Time: 1 hour and 5 minutes

Makes 4 to 6 servings

7   cups Minestrone Grande (opposite)

$^1/_4$ cup tomato paste

$^3/_4$ loaf (1 pound) sesame semolina bread, cut into $^1/_2$"-thick slices, toasted

$1^1/_2$ cups (6 ounces) preshredded mozzarella and provolone cheese blend

Preheat the oven to 350° F. Coat a 13" × 9" glass or ceramic baking dish with cooking spray.

Ladle the minestrone into the dish. Stir in the tomato paste to thoroughly dissolve. Cover with a layer of the bread and the cheese. With a fork, submerge the bread and cheese. Pierce the bread so it can soak up the soup. Let stand for 5 minutes.

Bake for 45 minutes, or until browned and the bread puffs up like a soufflé. Let stand for 10 minutes.

PAN-SEARED SALMON WITH SCALLIONS AND TARRAGON

Want an elegant meal on the table fast? This skillet salmon and some herbed rice can be ready in about 20 minutes.

Hands-On Time: 10 minutes
Total Time: 12 minutes

Makes 4 to 6 servings

3-3½ pounds skinless salmon fillet, divided

Flour

4 tablespoons butter, divided

2 tablespoons olive oil, divided

1 teaspoon dried tarragon leaves, divided

½ teaspoon salt, divided

¼ teaspoon pepper, divided

3 bunches scallions, white and green parts, cut into 1" lengths, divided

½ cup dry white wine, divided

Lay the salmon on a work surface. Sprinkle flour over both sides to coat. Shake off any excess.

Place 2 tablespoons of the butter and 1 tablespoon of the oil in each of 2 large skillets set over medium-high heat. When the foam subsides, add half of the salmon to each pan. Sprinkle evenly with the tarragon, salt, and pepper. Cook for 2 minutes per side, or until seared. Add half of the scallions to each pan in the space between the fillets. Add ¼ cup of the wine to each pan. Bring to a boil. Cover. Reduce the heat to medium-low. Cook for about 3 minutes, or until the salmon is opaque.

Set aside about one-third of the salmon and scallions (about 1 pound). Let stand to cool completely. Place the reserved salmon and scallions in a zipper-lock bag. Refrigerate for up to 2 days. Use the salmon to make Creamed Salmon on Crisp Potato Cakes (opposite).

CREAMED SALMON ON CRISP POTATO CAKES

Thinking outside the box—or the container in this case—pays delicious dividends. Instead of using prepared Alfredo sauce only for pasta, try it in this luscious seafood main course.

Hands-On Time: 10 minutes
Total Time: 10 minutes

Makes 4 to 6 servings

1 container (10 ounces) refrigerated Alfredo sauce

1 pound Pan-Seared Salmon with Scallions and Tarragon (opposite)

3 cups (12 ounces) frozen potato wedges, thawed

1 egg yolk

½ teaspoon hot-pepper sauce

Flour

Vegetable oil

In a saucepan, heat the Alfredo sauce. Add the salmon and scallions. Break the salmon into smaller pieces with a spoon. Simmer over low heat for 5 minutes, or until heated through.

Meanwhile, in the bowl of a food processor fitted with a metal blade, process the potatoes for about 1 minute, or until finely ground. Add the egg yolk and hot-pepper sauce. Process just to mix. Shape the mixture into twelve ¼"-thick patties. Dust both sides lightly with flour.

Heat ¼" oil in a large nonstick skillet over medium-high heat. Fry the patties for 2 minutes per side, or until browned and crisp. Serve with the creamed salmon.

GREEK-STYLE LEMON-GARLIC CHICKEN

As the lemon slices roast, the natural sugars caramelize. They make a tantalizing accompaniment to the herbed chicken. Be sure to scrub the lemon well before roasting so you can eat the slices peel and all. Accompany with mashed potatoes. For a more elaborate meal, precede the chicken with Spring Greens, Chickpeas, and Tomatoes with Feta Dressing (page 107).

Hands-On Time: 10 minutes
Total Time: 55 minutes

Makes 4 to 6 servings

7 pounds split bone-in chicken breasts (10 breast halves)

½ cup olive oil (preferably extra-virgin)

1 lemon, thinly sliced

8 cloves garlic, halved

8 bay leaves

1 teaspoon dried oregano

1 teaspoon ground black pepper

½ teaspoon salt

Preheat the oven to 400°F.

Place the chicken on a 17" × 11" baking pan or other large shallow baking pan. Add the oil, lemon, garlic, bay leaves, oregano, pepper, and salt. Toss to coat all the chicken pieces with oil and seasoning. Overlap the chicken breasts slightly if necessary. Tuck the garlic and bay leaves underneath the chicken. Place the lemon slices over the chicken.

Bake for about 45 minutes, or until a thermometer inserted into the thickest portion registers 160°F and the juices run clear. Set aside 3 breast halves. Let stand to cool completely. Place in a zipper-lock bag and refrigerate for up to 3 days. Use these chicken breasts to make Chicken Cacciatora on Polenta (opposite).

Meanwhile, place the remaining chicken on a platter. Remove and discard the bay leaves. Place the garlic in a microwaveable bowl. Smash with a fork. Tip the baking pan. Skim off any fat and discard. Scrape with a spatula to remove all the browned bits. Pour the pan juices with the lemon slices into the dish with the garlic. Microwave on high power for 2 minutes, or until bubbling. Pour over the reserved chicken.

CHICKEN CACCIATORA ON POLENTA

This rustic Italian chicken stew is also wonderful served with country-style bread or spooned over cooked pasta.

Hands-On Time: 5 minutes
Total Time: 15 minutes

Makes 4 to 6 servings

Photo on page 236

¼ cup extra-virgin olive oil

1 container (7 ounces) presliced onion and red bell pepper (2 cups)

1½ cups (3 ounces) presliced mushrooms

3 Greek-Style Lemon-Garlic Chicken breasts (opposite), boned, skinned, and cut or torn into chunks

2 cans (15 ounces each) diced basil-garlic-oregano-seasoned tomatoes

½ teaspoon salt

½ teaspoon ground black pepper

1 tube (1 pound) refrigerated basil-garlic polenta, cut into ½"-thick slices

Heat the oil in a large skillet set over medium heat. Add the onion and bell pepper and mushrooms. Stir to combine. Cover and cook for 4 minutes, or until the mushrooms are browned.

Add the chicken and the tomatoes (with juice) to the skillet. Add the salt and black pepper. Bring the mixture to a brisk simmer, then reduce the heat so the mixture simmers gently for 10 minutes.

Meanwhile, place the polenta in a single layer on a microwaveable plate. Cover with waxed paper. Microwave on high power for 2 minutes, or until heated. Spoon the stew over the polenta.

CHICKEN CACCIATORA ON POLENTA *page 235*

POLENTA AROUND THE WORLD

Most produce sections stock prepared polenta in the refrigerated case. Slice the polenta cross-wise into rounds, then bake, grill, or sauté the rounds until browned on both sides. Top with any of the following international toppings.

1. **Italian:** olive oil, canned tomatoes, basil, and preshredded Parmesan cheese

2. **Greek:** pitted olives, precrumbled feta cheese, lemon juice, oregano, and ground lamb

3. **Indonesian:** peanut butter and teriyaki sauce

4. **Thai:** canned coconut milk, jarred curry paste, and cilantro

5. **French:** canned white beans, canned tuna, and rosemary

6. **Southern American:** prepared mushroom gravy and chicken breasts

BREADED DIJON CHICKEN BREASTS

The chicken goes nicely with Cajun Potato Salad (page 102) and Southern Greens with Bacon (page 296).

Hands-On Time: 10 minutes
Total Time: 35 minutes

Makes 4 to 6 servings

Olive oil

3 cups dried bread crumbs

2 teaspoons herbes de Provence

2 teaspoons paprika

4-4½ pounds boneless, skinless chicken breast halves

½ cup Dijon mustard

Arrange two shelves in the center of the oven. Preheat the oven to 400°F. Drizzle oil generously onto two 17" × 11" baking pans or other large shallow baking pans.

On a large sheet of waxed paper, combine the bread crumbs, herbes, and paprika. On another large sheet of waxed paper, lay the chicken in a single layer. Coat both sides evenly with the mustard. One at a time, dip both sides of the chicken into the bread crumb mixture. Shake off any excess. Place in a single layer on the prepared pans. Drizzle with oil.

Bake for 15 minutes. Rotate the pans. Bake for about 10 minutes longer, or until a thermometer inserted into the thickest portion registers 160°F and the juices run clear.

Set aside 4 chicken breast halves. Let stand to cool completely. Place in a zipper-lock bag and refrigerate for up to 3 days. Use these chicken breasts to make Provençal Chicken-and-Vegetable Main Dish Salad (page 240).

BREADED DIJON CHICKEN BREASTS *opposite* and **SOUTHERN GREENS WITH BACON** *page 296*

PROVENÇAL CHICKEN-AND-VEGETABLE
MAIN DISH SALAD

The French call this type of salad "composed" to differentiate it from a tossed salad. The appeal of the dish is obvious. From already-cooked ingredients and staple condiments, you can create a colorful masterpiece.

Hands-On Time: 6 minutes
Total Time: 12 minutes

Makes 4 to 6 servings

½ bag (8 ounces) pretrimmed green beans (2 cups)

1 bag (5 ounces) spring salad mix

4 Breaded Dijon Chicken Breasts (page 238), thinly sliced

½ cup drained presliced roasted red bell peppers

3 pre-hard-cooked eggs, sliced

1 bunch scallions, white and light green parts, sliced (⅓ cup)

¾ cup French vinaigrette salad dressing

Place the beans in an 8" × 8" microwaveable baking dish. Add enough water to come ¼" up the sides of the dish. Cover with plastic wrap, leaving a small corner vent. Microwave on high power for 6 minutes, or until the beans are crisp-cooked. Drain and rinse with cold water to stop the cooking. Pat dry. Let stand to cool.

Meanwhile, arrange the spring mix on a large serving platter. Top with the chicken, peppers, eggs, scallions, and the reserved beans. Drizzle the dressing over the salad.

ROASTED CHICKEN AND TURNIPS IN PEANUT SAUCE

Five Ingredients or Less!

The slightly bitter bite of the turnips marries well with the sweet distinctive peanut sauce.

Hands-On Time: 5 minutes
Total Time: 50 minutes

Makes 4 to 6 servings

1½ pounds turnips, peeled and cut into walnut-size chunks

4½ pounds skinless chicken thighs

½ teaspoon salt

1 tablespoon vegetable oil

1 cup bottled Thai peanut sauce

Preheat the oven to 375°F.

Place the turnips in a 8" × 8" microwaveable baking dish. Add enough water to come ¼" up the sides of the dish. Cover with plastic wrap, leaving a small corner vent. Microwave on high power for 5 minutes, or until partially cooked. Drain and set aside.

Coat a 17" × 11" baking pan or other large shallow baking pan with cooking spray. Place the chicken in the pan, overlapping slightly if necessary. Scatter the turnips in the pan. Sprinkle with the salt. Drizzle with oil.

Bake for 45 to 50 minutes, or until it is sizzling, the chicken is no longer pink, and the juices run clear. Drizzle the sauce over the chicken and turnips. Stir to coat well. Turn on the broiler and place the chicken approximately 6" from the heat source for about 4 minutes, or until browned. Set aside 4 thighs. Let stand to cool completely. Place in a zipper-lock bag and refrigerate for up to 3 days. Use these chicken thighs to make Thai Chicken-Noodle Salad (page 244).

THAI CHICKEN-NOODLE SALAD

If flat rice noodles are not available, replace them with dried fettuccine boiled just until al dente. Pass Asian chili-garlic sauce at the table.

Hands-On Time: 5 minutes
Total Time: 25 minutes

Makes 4 to 6 servings

12 ounces Thai-style flat rice noodles

3 tablespoons vegetable oil, divided

1 bag (8 ounces) stringless sugar snap-peas or Chinese pea pods (2 cups)

1 cup (3 ounces) bagged shredded carrots

2 tablespoons preminced oil-packed garlic, divided

4 thighs from Roasted Chicken and Turnips in Peanut Sauce (page 243), deboned and cut into thin slices

1 bunch scallions, white and light green parts, sliced (⅓ cup)

½ cup sesame-ginger salad dressing

Fill a large pot with hot tap water. Add the noodles and stir. Let stand, stirring occasionally, for 20 minutes, or until softened but still firm. Drain.

In a large skillet or wok, heat 1 tablespoon of the oil over medium-high heat. Add the peas, carrots, and 1 tablespoon of the garlic. Cook, tossing, for 1 minute, or until sizzling. Remove to a plate. Set aside. Add the remaining 2 tablespoons of oil and 1 tablespoon of garlic to the pan. Add the noodles. Cook, tossing, for 2 minutes, or until sizzling. Remove from the heat. Add the chicken, scallions, reserved peas and carrots, and dressing. Toss.

HONEY-GLAZED HAM WITH CARROTS, ONIONS, AND NEW POTATOES

Nothing beats the homemade comfort of this slow-roasted dish. Assemble the ingredients on a Sunday afternoon and let your oven do the rest of the work.

Hands-On Time: 6 minutes

Total Time: 1 hour and 16 minutes

Makes 4 to 6 servings

1½ bags (1½ pounds total) baby carrots

1½ bags (1½ pounds total) frozen pearl onions

1½ pounds prewashed new red potatoes

2 tablespoons vegetable oil

Salt

1 fully cooked boneless ham shank (3¾-4 pounds)

¼ cup honey

¼ cup stone-ground mustard

½ teaspoon ground cloves

Preheat the oven to 375°F. Coat two 17" × 11" baking pans or other large shallow baking pans with cooking spray.

Place the carrots, onions, and potatoes in the pans. Drizzle 1 tablespoon of oil into each pan. Toss the vegetables to coat. Sprinkle lightly with salt. Bake for 35 minutes, rotating the pans if needed.

Place the ham on a cutting board. With a large knife, cut into 2 pieces, one a bit larger than the other.

With a spatula, scrape the vegetables to the outer edge of the pans. Place 1 piece of ham in the center of each pan. Bake for 30 minutes.

Meanwhile, in a small bowl, combine the honey, mustard, and cloves. Whisk to blend well. Drizzle over the ham and vegetables. Bake for about 5 minutes, or until a thermometer registers 140°F when inserted into the center of the ham and the vegetables are browned. Cut the larger piece of ham into thin slices. Serve with the roasted vegetables.

NOTE: Allow the pan with the smaller piece of ham and vegetables to cool completely. Package the ham and vegetables in an airtight plastic container for up to 3 days. Use the ham and vegetables to make Pennsylvania Dutch Stovetop Pot Pie with Noodles (below).

PENNSYLVANIA DUTCH STOVETOP POT PIE WITH NOODLES

Packaged dried egg noodles make quick work of this folksy dish, typically made with hand-made square flour-and-egg dumplings.

Hands-On Time: 15 minutes
Total Time: 25 minutes

Makes 4 to 6 servings

Photo on page 228

12 ounces wide egg noodles

Honey-Glazed Ham with Carrots, Onions, and New Potatoes (opposite)

8 cups chicken broth

½ cup chopped parsley

1 teaspoon ground black pepper

Prepared horseradish

Cook the noodles according to the package directions but 2 minutes less than directed. Meanwhile, cut the ham into 1" chunks.

Drain the noodles. Return them to the pot. Add the broth, ham, vegetables, parsley, and pepper. Cook over medium-high heat for about 5 minutes, or until heated. Serve in wide soup bowls. Pass the horseradish at the table.

CHICKEN AND WILD MUSHROOM
PUFF-PASTRY ROULADE

Porcini, wild Italian dried mush-rooms, are sold in cellophane packets in the produce section of most supermarkets. The deep, rich flavor that porcini contribute to this dish is well worth the few minutes needed to reconstitute them.

Hands-On Time: 20 minutes

Total Time: 45 minutes

Makes 4 to 6 servings

1/2 cup (1/2 ounce) dried porcini mushrooms

1/2 cup hot water

2 tablespoons butter

1 cup prechopped onion

2 packages (10 ounces each) presliced brown mushrooms

2 teaspoons dried rosemary

1/2 teaspoon salt

1 teaspoon ground black pepper, divided

1 bag (20 ounces) cooked chicken breast strips (4 cups)

1 carton (15 ounces) part-skim ricotta cheese

1 cup (4 ounces) preshredded Parmesan-Romano-Asiago cheese blend

1 box (17 ounces) frozen puff-pastry sheets, thawed

Preheat the oven to 400°F. Coat a baking sheet with cooking spray.

In a measuring cup, combine the porcini and water. Set aside for 5 minutes, or until softened.

Meanwhile, melt the butter in a large skillet over high heat. Add the onion, brown mushrooms, rosemary, salt, and 1/2 teaspoon of the pepper. Stir to combine. Cover and cook for about 4 minutes, or until the mushrooms give off liquid. Remove the cover and cook, stirring for about 8 minutes.

Meanwhile, holding a fine sieve over the skillet, drain the porcini so the mushroom liquid goes into the skillet. Rinse the porcini. Chop and add to the skillet. Cook until all of the mushrooms are browned. Stir in the chicken.

Remove from the heat. Measure 3 cups of the chicken-mushroom mixture onto a plate. Let stand to cool completely. Pack into a zipper-lock bag. Refrigerate for up to 3 days. Use this chicken-mushroom mixture to make Risotto with Chicken, Wild Mushrooms, Feta, and Spinach (page 250).

To the skillet, add the ricotta cheese, Parmesan-Romano-Asiago cheese blend, and the remaining $\frac{1}{2}$ teaspoon of pepper. Stir and set aside.

Lay the pastry sheets on a work surface with two of the short sides touching. Overlap those two sides about $\frac{1}{4}$". Press down to seal. Spoon the chicken-mushroom mixture over the sheet, leaving a 1" border on all sides. Starting at a short end, roll the pastry into a log without pressing down. With a large spatula, carefully transfer to the baking sheet, seam side down. Press the edges together to seal. Coat with cooking spray. Bake for 25 minutes, or until browned and sizzling. Let stand for 10 minutes. Cut with a serrated knife into 1" thick slices.

RISOTTO WITH CHICKEN, WILD MUSHROOMS, FETA, AND SPINACH

Pressure Cooker Dish

While the risotto cooks, combine a salad of bagged baby spinach leaves and a handful of preshredded carrots in a large bowl. Drizzle with bottled Italian salad dressing and toss just before serving.

Hands-On Time: 4 minutes

Total Time: 12 minutes

Makes 4 to 6 servings

2	tablespoons butter
$\frac{1}{2}$	cup prechopped celery
$1\frac{1}{2}$	cups Arborio rice
4	cups chicken broth, divided
3	cups Chicken and Wild Mushrooms (page 248)
$\frac{3}{4}$	cup (3 ounces) precrumbled herbed feta cheese
$\frac{1}{4}$	teaspoon salt

Combine the butter and celery in the pressure cooker pot. Cook over medium-low heat, stirring occasionally, for 2 minutes, or until softened. Add the rice and stir to coat thoroughly with the celery mixture. Add $3\frac{1}{2}$ cups of the broth. Stir to combine. Cover the pot and lock the lid. Bring to high pressure over high heat. Reduce the heat to maintain high pressure. Cook for 5 minutes.

Using the quick-release method, reduce the pressure. Uncover the pot. Add the Chicken and wild mushrooms and $\frac{1}{4}$ cup of the remaining broth. Cook, stirring, over low heat for about 2 minutes, or just until the chicken is heated. Test a grain of rice. If it is still hard in the center, add up to $\frac{1}{4}$ cup of the remaining broth. Cook, stirring, over medium heat, for 1 minute, or until the broth is absorbed. Remove from the heat. Stir in the cheese and salt.

PEPPERCORN PORK WITH GRILLED TOMATOES, ZUCCHINI, AND BASIL

Any time you want to dress up this dish for company, replace the zucchini with baby squash and the regular cherry tomatoes with yellow ones.

Hands-On Time: 5 minutes

Total Time: 1 hour and 5 minutes (plus 10 minutes standing time)

Makes 4 to 6 servings

2 cartons (1 pint each) cherry or grape tomatoes

2 zucchini (12 ounces total), cut into walnut-size chunks

2 tablespoons extra-virgin olive oil

½ teaspoon salt

½ teaspoon ground black pepper

3 pounds premarinated peppercorn pork tenderloin or premarinated peppercorn pork roast

½ cup slivered fresh basil leaves

Preheat the oven to 375°F. Coat a 17" × 11" baking pan or other large shallow baking pan with cooking spray.

Place the tomatoes, zucchini, oil, salt, and pepper in the pan. Stir to coat the tomatoes and zucchini. Pushing the tomatoes and zucchini aside, place the pork in the pan, and arrange to avoid touching edges of the pan or other foods.

Roast for 45 minutes to 1 hour (the tenderloin will be cooked sooner than the roast), or until a thermometer inserted into the center registers 155°F and the juices run clear. Let stand 10 minutes. Cut off approximately one-third of the total amount of pork (about 1 pound). Let stand to cool completely. Cut the remaining pork into thin slices. Serve with the tomatoes and zucchini, sprinkled with the basil.

Place the reserved pork in a zipper-lock bag. Refrigerate for up to 3 days. Use to prepare the Shredded-Pork Burritos (opposite).

SHREDDED-PORK BURRITOS

With this Mexican-style main dish, you'll have the satisfaction of home-cooked flavor faster than the fastest fast food.

Hands-On Time: 8 minutes

Total Time: 12 minutes

Makes 4 to 6 servings

1 can (16 ounces) refried beans

1 pound Peppercorn Pork (opposite), very thinly sliced

8 large (10"-wide) burrito-style flour tortillas, heated

2 cups preshredded romaine lettuce or mixed greens

1 cup (4 ounces) finely preshredded sharp Cheddar cheese

½ cup sour cream

Hot or mild refrigerated or jarred tomato salsa

In a nonstick skillet, cook the beans over medium heat for 2 minutes, or until heated. Add the pork. Cook, stirring, for 2 minutes, or just until the pork is heated.

Lay the tortillas on a work surface. Spoon on the bean-pork mixture. Top with the lettuce or greens, cheese, and sour cream. Season with salsa to taste. One at a time, fold opposite sides of each tortilla to meet in the middle. Fold the opposite sides together to make a bundle. Serve seam side down.

Double-Duty Gadgets

ZIPPER-LOCK BAGS

Plastic storage bags are pretty standard in most kitchens these days. They do a great job of sealing up sandwiches, refrigerating leftovers, and packing foods for the freezer. But why stop there? The bags have plenty of other uses. There's no better tool for marinating meats, because the bag keeps the marinade against the food at all times, and when you're done, simply throw away the bag with nothing else to clean. You can also use zipper-lock bags to save time crushing chips or cookies or coating foods with flour or batter.

ROASTED ITALIAN-SAUSAGE AND VEGETABLES

*With main course and vegeta-
bles roasted in one pan, all
that's needed is an interesting
grain side dish. Prepared refrigerated basil-garlic polenta or
roasted garlic–olive oil couscous mix are both good
choices.*

Hands-On Time: 15 minutes

Total Time: 1 hour and 10 minutes

Makes 4 to 6 servings

1¼ pounds fennel bulbs, quartered

1½ pounds peeled red onions, quartered

1½ pounds mild Italian sausage links, cut into 3" pieces

1 pound portobello mushroom caps, quartered

6 tablespoons extra-virgin olive oil

1 teaspoon salt, divided

3 tablespoons frozen lemon-juice concentrate

Ground black pepper

Preheat the oven to 400°F. Coat two 17" × 11" baking pans or
other large shallow baking pans with cooking spray.

If any leaves are attached to the fennel, remove about ½ cup
and set aside.

Cut the fennel and onions crosswise into 1" chunks. Place half
of the sausage, mushrooms, fennel, onions, oil, and salt in each
pan. Toss to coat with oil.

Roast for about 50 minutes, stirring occasionally and rotating the
pans if necessary, or until the vegetables are well browned. Remove
both pans. Transfer about one-quarter of the sausage mixture
from 1 pan to the other pan. Drizzle the lemon-juice concentrate
over the pan with the greater amount of ingredients. Toss. Roast
for about 5 minutes, or until the glaze is sizzling.

Meanwhile, chop the reserved fennel leaves. Sprinkle over the
glazed sausage mixture. Season to taste with pepper.

Meanwhile, set the pan with the smaller amount of the sausage
mixture aside. Allow to cool completely. Pack into a large
zipper-lock bag. Refrigerate for up to 3 days. Use the sausage
mixture to make Bean-and-Sausage Farfalle (opposite).

BEAN-AND-SAUSAGE FARFALLE

A crisp tossed salad with bagged prewashed mixed greens and creamy Italian dressing can be made in the time it takes to cook the pasta.

Hands-On Time: 8 minutes
Total Time: 18 minutes

Makes 4 to 6 servings

12   ounces dried farfalle (bow-tie pasta)

     Roasted Italian-Sausage and Vegetables (opposite)

1   cup cannellini beans, rinsed and drained

1   can (15 ounces) Italian-seasoned diced tomatoes

½   cup preshredded Parmesan-Romano-Asiago cheese blend plus additional for garnish

½   teaspoon red-pepper flakes

Cook the pasta according to the package directions. Before draining, reserve ½ cup of the cooking water. Drain the pasta. Set aside.

Meanwhile, cut the sausage into small chunks.

Return the pot to medium-high heat. Add the beans and Roasted Italian-Sausage and Vegetables. Toss for about 2 minutes, or until sizzling. Add the tomatoes (with juice). Cook for 2 minutes, or until bubbling. Add the pasta. Toss to mix well. Add a few tablespoons of the reserved cooking water, if needed, to loosen the sauce. Remove from the heat. Add ½ cup of the cheese and the pepper flakes. Toss to mix. Pass additional cheese at the table.

LEG OF LAMB ROASTED WITH HERBS
AND RED WINE

This main course is elegant enough for company, and it yields the benefit of a quick-and-easy weeknight meal. Serve Risotto with Cheese and Peas (page 301) and a big tossed salad dressed in vinaigrette with the roast.

Hands-On Time: 15 minutes

Total Time: 1 hour and 55 minutes

Makes 4 to 6 servings

3½-4 pounds boneless leg of lamb

1 tablespoon preminced oil-packed garlic

2 tablespoons extra-virgin olive oil

1 teaspoon Italian seasoning

½ teaspoon salt

½ teaspoon ground black pepper

½ cup dry red wine

1 cup water or beef broth, heated

Preheat the oven to 375°F. Coat a small roasting pan with cooking spray.

If the lamb is enclosed in string mesh, remove it and discard. Set the lamb in the pan. Rub the garlic, oil, Italian seasoning, salt, and pepper over the lamb, including the cavity where the leg bone was removed. Add the wine to the pan.

Roast for about 1 hour and 30 minutes, adding small amounts of the water or broth to the pan if juices are evaporated, or until a thermometer inserted into the center registers 145°F for medium rare, 160°F for medium, or 170°F for well-done.

Set the lamb on a cutting board with a well. Let stand for 10 minutes. Meanwhile, deglaze the pan with what remains of the water or broth. Scrape to remove browned bits. Slice about two-thirds of the lamb very thinly. Serve drizzled with the pan juices.

Set aside the uncut lamb (1-1¼ pounds). Let stand to cool completely. Place in a zipper-lock plastic bag and refrigerate for up to 3 days. Use this lamb to make Gyros with Creamy Cucumber-Dill Sauce in Pita (opposite).

GYROS WITH CREAMY CUCUMBER-DILL SAUCE IN PITA

Chunky Broccoli-Spinach Soup (page 89) makes a wonderful companion to these speedy sandwiches.

Hands-On Time: 8 minutes
Total Time: 8 minutes

Makes 4 servings

$^1/_3$ English cucumber (15 ounces)

1 bunch scallions, white and light green parts

$^1/_2$ cup (4 ounces) plain yogurt or sour cream

$^1/_4$ teaspoon dried dillweed

$^1/_4$ teaspoon salt

$^1/_4$ teaspoon ground black pepper

1 teaspoon lemon juice

4 pitas (6" wide), halved and toasted

1-1$^1/_4$ pounds Leg of Lamb Roasted with Herbs and Red Wine (opposite), thinly sliced

In a food processor fitted with the slicing blade, slice the cucumber and then the scallions. Remove the cucumber and scallions to a sheet of waxed paper. Insert the steel blade into the food processor. Return the cucumber and scallions to the work bowl. Add the yogurt or sour cream, dillweed, salt, pepper, and lemon juice. Pulse 12 times just to combine. Open the pita halves and spread the interior with some of the yogurt sauce. Tuck the lamb slices into the pitas. Spoon the remaining sauce over the lamb.

BALSAMIC ROSEMARY-GRILLED BEEF

Five Ingredients or Less!

It's hard to believe that a dish that's so easy can taste so fabulous. Round out the meal with Couscous with Chickpeas, Pine Nuts, and Peppadew (page 304) and Sicilian Cauliflower-Olive Salad (page 106).

Hands-On Time: 30 minutes

Total Time: 2 hours and 30 minutes

Makes 4 to 6 servings

2 beef flank steaks (1½–1¾ pounds each; 3–3½ pounds total)

1 cup bottled balsamic salad dressing

1 tablespoon preminced oil-packed garlic

2 tablespoons minced fresh rosemary or crumbled dried rosemary

In a large zipper-lock bag, combine the steaks, dressing, garlic, and rosemary. Massage to coat the steaks evenly. Refrigerate for 2 hours or as long as 12 hours.

Coat a grill rack or broiler pan with cooking spray. Preheat the grill or broiler. Remove the beef from the marinade. Set aside the marinade. Place the beef on the rack or pan. Cook, turning once, for 8 minutes per side, or until a thermometer inserted into the thickest portion registers 145°F for medium-rare, 160°F for medium, or 165°F for well-done. Let stand for 5 minutes.

Meanwhile, pour the marinade into a microwaveable cup. Cover with waxed paper. Microwave on high power for 3 minutes, or until boiling. Cut one steak into very thin slices across the grain. Serve, drizzled with the marinade.

Let the second steak stand to cool completely. Place in a zipper-lock bag and refrigerate for up to 3 days. Use this steak to make Fajitas (opposite).

FAJITAS

For a casual party, grill several beef flank steaks in advance and set out extra toppings such as fresh cilantro and shredded Monterey Jack or Cheddar cheese.

Hands-On Time: 10 minutes
Total Time: 10 minutes

Makes 4 to 6 servings

2   tablespoons olive oil

2   containers (7 ounces each) presliced onion and bell pepper (4 cups)

1½ teaspoons ground cumin

¼   teaspoon salt

1   Balsamic Rosemary-Grilled Beef steak (opposite), thinly sliced

10 (7"-wide) flour tortillas, warmed

¾   cup sour cream

¾   cup refrigerated or jarred mild or hot tomato salsa

½   container (8 ounces) prepared guacamole (1 cup)

Heat the oil in a large skillet set over medium-high heat. Add the onion and bell pepper, cumin, and salt. Cover and cook, tossing, for about 5 minutes, or until browned. Add the beef. Toss for 1 minute just to heat. Serve buffet-style, allowing diners to fill and roll tortillas with the beef-pepper-onion mixture, sour cream, salsa, and guacamole.

THE EASIEST MEAT LOAF

With the aid of plastic wrap and a little sleight of hand, you use only a single pan to mix and bake two meat loaves.

Hands-On Time: 10 minutes
Total Time: 1 hour

Makes 4 to 6 servings

$\frac{1}{2}$ cup whole milk

1 egg, beaten

1 teaspoon dried thyme

$1\frac{1}{2}$ teaspoons salt

$1\frac{1}{2}$ teaspoons ground black pepper

2 pounds ground round beef

1 pound ground pork

$1\frac{1}{2}$ cups coarsely crumbled day-old Italian bread

1 cup chopped fresh parsley

2 tablespoons preminced oil-packed garlic

2 teaspoons vegetable oil

1 jar (12 ounces) prepared beef gravy (optional)

Preheat the oven to 350°F. Coat a 17" × 11" baking pan or other large shallow baking pan with cooking spray. Line the pan with plastic wrap.

In a measuring cup, beat the milk, egg, thyme, salt, and pepper with a fork. Set aside. Place the beef, pork, bread crumbs, parsley, and garlic in the center of the prepared pan. With hands, combine the meat mixture until well mixed. Gradually drizzle in the milk mixture while mixing with the other hand until all of the liquid is absorbed. Shape the mixture into two loaves, about 9" × 5", parallel with the shorter side of the pan. Cut the plastic sheet in half between the loaves. Either pull the plastic sheets out from under the loaves or flip each loaf upside down to remove the plastic. Position the loaves at least 5" apart. Drizzle 1 teaspoon of the oil over each of the loaves.

Bake for about 50 minutes, or until a thermometer inserted horizontally into the center registers 160°F and the meat is no longer pink. Let stand 15 minutes before slicing. Cut off three-quarters of 1 meat loaf (1 pound). Transfer to a plate. Allow to cool completely. Place in a zipper-lock bag and refrigerate for up to 3 days. Use this meat loaf to make Rigatoni with Chunky Meat Sauce (page 263). Serve meat loaf with prepared gravy, if desired.

THE EASIEST MEAT LOAF *opposite* and **SICILIAN BROCCOLI** *page 294*

RIGATONI WITH CHUNKY MEAT SAUCE

If you told them, people wouldn't believe how simple this southern Italian–style pasta dish is. So don't let them in on the secret.

Hands-On Time: 4 minutes
Total Time: 10 minutes

Makes 4 to 6 servings

2   tablespoons extra-virgin olive oil

1   cup prechopped onion

1   pound The Easiest Meat Loaf (page 260), cut into walnut-size chunks

2   cans (14 ounces each) diced Italian-seasoned tomatoes

½   teaspoon salt

1   teaspoon ground black pepper

12   ounces dried rigatoni pasta

¼   cup pregrated Pecorino Romano cheese + additional for the table

In a large skillet, heat the oil over high heat. Add the onion. Cook, stirring occasionally, for 3 minutes, or until well browned. Add the meat loaf, tomatoes (with juice), salt, and pepper. Stir to combine. Reduce the heat to medium-low. Cover and simmer for about 4 minutes, or until the tomatoes are softened.

Meanwhile, cook the pasta according to the package directions. Before draining, reserve ½ cup of the cooking water. Drain and place the pasta in the skillet. Add ¼ cup of the cheese and toss to coat. Add a bit of the reserved cooking water, if needed, to moisten the sauce. Serve with additional cheese at the table.

PORK POSOLE *page 278*

CHAPTER 12

Slow Cooker Favorites

These tantalizing dishes are designed to make your life easier. Just a few minutes of hands-on time in the morning and you can come home to a dinner that tastes like you were in the kitchen all day.

Mediterranean Lentil Stew

Braised Vegetables with Polenta Dumplings

Brazilian Feijoado

Un-Stuffed Cabbage

Asian Chicken-Noodle Soup

Chinese Sweet-and-Sour Chicken

Coq au Vin

Turkey with Boston Bacon Beans

Turkey-Sausage Cassoulet

Pork Posole

Moroccan Lamb Tagine

Alsatian Smoked Pork Chops and Sauerkraut

Chuck Wagon Barbecued-Beef Sandwiches

New England Pot Roast

Beef Short Ribs with Sweet-and-Sour Red Cabbage

MEDITERRANEAN LENTIL STEW

Vegetarian Dish

This legume stew tastes as robust as any prepared with meat. A crispy mixed green salad with creamy Parmesan dressing is a fast and tasty side dish.

Hands-On Time: 5 minutes

Total Time (low heat): 7 hours and 5 minutes

Makes 4 to 6 servings

4 cups vegetable broth

1 pound dry lentils, rinsed and drained

³/₄ cup prechopped onion

³/₄ cup bagged baby carrots, quartered

³/₄ cup prechopped celery

¹/₄ cup olive oil (preferably extra-virgin)

1¹/₂ tablespoons preminced oil-packed garlic

1¹/₂ teaspoons Italian seasoning

¹/₂ teaspoon ground black pepper

¹/₄ teaspoon salt

Balsamic vinegar

Pregrated Romano cheese

Coat the inside of a 3¹/₂-quart slow cooker pot with cooking spray.

Add the broth, lentils, onion, carrots, celery, oil, garlic, Italian seasoning, pepper, and salt to the pot. Stir to combine. Cover and cook on the low-heat setting for 7 to 8 hours.

Drizzle each serving with vinegar and sprinkle with cheese to taste.

NOTE: Mediterranean Lentil Stew can be cooked on the high-heat setting for 3¹/₂ to 4 hours.

BRAISED VEGETABLES WITH POLENTA DUMPLINGS

Vegetarian Dish

This is one of those lazy meals to make on a weekend after-noon when you're at home. The slow cooker does most of the work. All you have to do is stir-fry the broccoli just before serv-ing so it keeps its bright color and crisp texture.

Hands-On Time: 12 minutes
Total Time (low heat): 5 hours and 12 minutes

Makes 4 to 6 servings

1 can (15 ounces) Italian-seasoned tomato sauce

$^1/_2$ cup dry red wine

3 tablespoons flour

$1^1/_2$ teaspoons dried rosemary

$^3/_4$ teaspoon salt

$^3/_4$ teaspoon ground black pepper

2 large sweet potatoes ($1^1/_4$ pounds), cut into large chunks

1 bag (1 pound) frozen pearl onions

1 package (10 ounces) small brown mushrooms

2 tablespoons olive oil

2 bags (8 ounces each) broccoli florets, cut into walnut-size chunks

1 tube (1 pound) refrigerated basil-garlic polenta, cut into 1" chunks

Coat the inside of a $3^1/_2$-quart slow cooker pot with cooking spray.

Combine the tomato sauce, wine, flour, rosemary, salt, and pepper in the pot. Whisk until smooth. Add the sweet potatoes, onions, and mushrooms. Stir to coat evenly with the sauce. Cover and cook on the low-heat setting for 5 to 6 hours.

In a large skillet, heat the oil over medium-high heat. Add the broccoli. Toss. Cover and cook, tossing occasionally, for 2 to 3 minutes, or until the broccoli is crisp-tender. Add the slow cooker mixture. Stir to combine. Place the polenta pieces over the skillet mixture. Cover and simmer over medium heat for about 8 minutes, or until the polenta is heated through.

NOTE: To use the high-heat setting, cook for $2^1/_2$ to 3 hours.

BRAZILIAN FEIJOADO

Serve over cooked rice. In Brazil, sliced oranges are the traditional accompaniment, but a simple side salad garnished with orange wedges can be just as nice.

Hands-On Time: 5 minutes
Total Time (low heat): 7 hours and 5 minutes

Makes 4 to 6 servings

1 cup beef broth

1 teaspoon dried thyme

$^1/_2$ teaspoon salt

3 cans (16 ounces each) black beans, rinsed and drained

$1^1/_4$ pounds premarinated oven-roasted-flavor pork chops

$1^1/_4$ pounds fully cooked smoked kielbasa sausage, cut into 2" pieces

1 cup prechopped onion

2 tablespoons preminced oil-packed garlic

2 bay leaves

Hot-pepper sauce

Coat the inside of a 5- to 6-quart slow cooker pot with cooking spray.

In the pot, combine the broth, thyme, and salt. Stir to blend well. Add the beans, pork, sausage, onion, garlic, and bay leaves. Stir to coat all the ingredients with broth. Cover and cook on the low-heat setting for 7 to 8 hours. Remove and discard the bay leaves. With the back of a large spoon, mash some of the beans to thicken the sauce. Serve with hot-pepper sauce at the table.

NOTE: Brazilian Feijoado can be cooked on the high-heat setting for $3^1/_2$ to 4 hours.

UN-STUFFED CABBAGE

Meat-and-rice-stuffed cabbage leaves can make a wonderful homey meal, but it requires time and patience to stuff and wrap each leaf separately. This dish retains all those robust ingredients but takes a mere 5 minutes of hands-on time to prepare.

Hands-On Time: 5 minutes
Total Time (low heat): 5 hours and 5 minutes

Makes 4 to 6 servings

1 can (14 ounces) diced pepper-onion-seasoned tomatoes

2 tablespoons tomato paste

1 tablespoon preminced oil-packed garlic

1 teaspoon salt

$1\frac{1}{2}$ teaspoons ground black pepper

2 bags (10 ounces each) preshredded green cabbage

$1\frac{1}{4}$ pounds garlic turkey-sausage patties or links, broken into walnut-size chunks

1 cup prechopped onion

$\frac{1}{2}$ cup instant brown rice

1 cup chopped fresh parsley

Coat the inside of a 5- to 6-quart slow cooker pot with cooking spray.

Combine the tomatoes, tomato paste, garlic, salt, and pepper in the pot. Stir to mix. Add the cabbage, sausage, onion, and rice. Stir to mix. Cover and cook on the low-heat setting for 5 to 6 hours. Add the parsley.

NOTE: Mild Italian turkey sausage can replace the garlic turkey sausage. Un-Stuffed Cabbage can be cooked on the high-heat setting for $2\frac{1}{2}$ to 3 hours.

ASIAN CHICKEN-NOODLE SOUP

In Vietnam, pho is a steaming rice-noodle soup typically prepared with beef. This variation calls for chicken in a warming main dish that's familiar, yet exotic.

Hands-On Time: 10 minutes
Total Time (low heat): 5 hours and 10 minutes

Makes 4 to 6 servings

1 broiler-fryer chicken (3³/₄ pounds)

2 cans (14 ounces each) chicken broth

1 quart water

1 bag (12 ounces) carrot and celery sticks, cut into 1" pieces

2 slices (¹/₄"-thick) fresh ginger

¹/₄ teaspoon ground cinnamon

¹/₂ teaspoon cracked fennel seeds or 1 star anise

¹/₄ cup fish sauce or soy sauce

6 ounces Thai-style flat rice noodles

1 bunch scallions, all parts, sliced (¹/₂ cup)

1 cup torn fresh basil leaves

Asian chili-garlic sauce

Place the chicken, breast side up, in the pot of a 5- to 6-quart slow cooker. Add the broth, water, carrot and celery, ginger, cinnamon, fennel seeds or star anise, and fish sauce or soy sauce. Cover and cook on the low-heat setting for 5 to 6 hours.

Thirty minutes before serving, fill a large pot with hot tap water. Add the noodles and stir. Let stand, stirring occasionally, for 30 minutes, or until softened.

With a wide skimmer or two slotted spoons, remove the chicken to a casserole dish. With two forks, remove the skin and discard. Remove the ginger and discard. Remove the chicken from the bones (it will fall off very easily) and return to the slow cooker. Discard the bones. Add the noodles to the pot. Garnish with the scallions and basil. Pass the chili-garlic sauce at the table.

NOTE: *Asian Chicken-Noodle Soup can be cooked on the high-heat setting for 2½ to 3 hours.*

QUICK TIP: *There's no need to use a cutting board and knife to cut the carrots and celery. Holding several vegetable sticks at a time in one hand over the pot, simply use kitchen scissors to snip 1" pieces.*

Double-Duty Gadgets

CHEESECLOTH

Recipes often call for cheesecloth when you need to strain liquids or for making a spice bundle (bouquet garni) that will be dropped into hot liquids to infuse them with flavor. If you don't have cheesecloth, don't despair. You don't always need it. For straining liquids, use nylon mesh, such as clean nylon stockings, which make a perfectly acceptable substitute for cheesecloth. You can also use a clean coffee filter for small straining jobs. And a coffee filter works well for wrapping spices or herbs to make a bouquet garni.

CHINESE SWEET-AND-SOUR CHICKEN

Take just a few extra minutes to prepare steamed instant brown rice and stir-fried broccoli florets or spinach. You'll be glad you did!

Hands-On Time: 6 minutes
Total Time (low heat): 5 hours and 11 minutes

Makes 4 to 6 servings

1 can (20 ounces) pineapple chunks in juice

¼ cup brown sugar

¼ cup rice vinegar or white wine vinegar

3 tablespoons soy sauce

2 tablespoons cornstarch

1 tablespoon preminced oil-packed garlic

1 tablespoon jarred grated fresh ginger

2 pounds boneless, skinless chicken thighs

1 container (7 ounces) prechopped tricolor bell pepper (1 cup)

1 container (7 ounces) prechopped onion (1 cup)

½ cup baby carrots

Coat the inside of a 5- to 6-quart slow cooker pot with cooking spray.

Drain the pineapple and set it aside, reserving 1 cup of juice. In the pot, combine the sugar, vinegar, soy sauce, cornstarch, garlic, ginger, and the reserved juice. Whisk until smooth. Add the chicken, pepper, onion, and carrots. Stir to coat with sauce. Cover and cook on the low-heat setting for 5 to 6 hours. Stir in the reserved pineapple. Cook for 5 minutes, or until the pineapple is heated.

NOTE: Chinese Sweet-and-Sour Chicken can also be cooked on the high-heat setting for 2½ to 3 hours.

COQ AU VIN

Over the centuries, French cooks have perfected the art of slow-braising chicken simmered in red wine and aromatics. You can master the dish in just a few hours with a slow cooker.

Hands-On Time: 10 minutes

Total Time (low heat): 5 hours and 10 minutes

Makes 4 to 6 servings

1 cup dry red wine

½ cup tomato paste

3 tablespoons flour

1½ teaspoons herbes des Provence

1½ teaspoons salt

1½ teaspoons ground black pepper

2½-3 pounds boneless, skinless chicken thighs

½ bag (1 pound) frozen pearl onions (2 cups)

8 ounces small cremini mushrooms (2 cups)

6 precooked bacon slices, coarsely chopped

1 tablespoon preminced oil-packed garlic

Coat the inside of a 5- to 6-quart slow cooker pot with cooking spray. In the pot, combine the wine, tomato paste, flour, herbes, salt, and pepper. Whisk until smooth. Add the chicken, onions, mushrooms, bacon, and garlic. Stir to coat the chicken with the sauce. Cover and cook on the low-heat setting for 5 to 6 hours.

NOTE: Coq au Vin can be cooked on the high-heat setting for 2½ to 3 hours.

TURKEY WITH BOSTON BACON BEANS

Old-fashioned Boston baked bean recipes often call for fatty salt pork. This modern version uses healthier turkey and a small amount of bacon for traditional flavor.

Hands-On Time: 10 minutes

Total Time (low heat): 7 hours and 10 minutes

Makes 4 to 6 servings

1½ cups prechopped onion

4 slices (4 ounces) uncooked bacon, cut into 2" strips

1 tablespoon vegetable oil

¾ cup ketchup

¼ cup maple syrup

1 tablespoon Worcestershire sauce

1 tablespoon Dijon mustard

1 teaspoon ground black pepper

3 cans (16 ounces) navy beans, rinsed and drained

1 cup loose-packed chopped fresh parsley

2¾-3 pounds bone-in turkey thighs (2 thighs)

Coat the inside of a 5- to 6-quart slow cooker pot with cooking spray.

In an 8" × 8" microwaveable baking dish, combine the onion, bacon, and oil. Stir. Cover with plastic wrap, leaving a small corner vent. Microwave on high power, stirring once, for 5 minutes, or until golden. Set aside.

Meanwhile, combine the ketchup, maple syrup, Worcestershire sauce, mustard, and pepper in the pot. Stir to mix. Add the beans, parsley, and reserved onion mixture. Stir to mix. Insert the turkey so it is partially covered with the bean mixture. Cover and cook on the low-heat setting for 7 to 8 hours. Remove the turkey. Take off the skin and remove the bones from the turkey. Discard the skin and bones. Break the turkey into big chunks and return them to the pot.

NOTE: Turkey with Boston Bacon Beans can be cooked on the high-heat setting for 3½ to 4 hours.

TURKEY-SAUSAGE CASSOULET

The genuine bean-and-mixed-meat casserole of southwestern France is truly a labor of love. With this no-work version, the love stays in, but the labor evaporates.

Hands-On Time: 10 minutes

Total Time (low heat): 7 hours and 10 minutes

Makes 4 to 6 servings

1 cup prechopped onion

³/₄ cup bagged baby carrots, halved

¹/₄ cup olive oil (preferably extra-virgin)

2 tablespoons preminced oil-packed garlic

1¹/₄ pounds Italian turkey sausage, cut into 2" lengths

1 can (15 ounces) tomato sauce

2 teaspoons herbes de Provence

1 teaspoon ground black pepper

2 cans (15 ounces each) great Northern beans, rinsed and drained

¹/₂ cup (2 ounces) bagged precooked crumbled bacon

In an 8" × 8" microwaveable baking dish, combine the onion, carrots, oil, and garlic. Cover with plastic wrap, leaving a small corner vent. Microwave on high power for 4 minutes, or until sizzling. Set aside.

Coat the inside of a 3¹/₂-quart slow cooker pot with cooking spray. Add the sausage, tomato sauce, herbes, pepper, and the reserved onion mixture. Stir to combine. Cover and cook on the low-heat setting for 7 to 8 hours. Add the beans to the pot in the last hour of cooking. Stir gently to combine.

Place the bacon on a microwaveable plate. Microwave on high power for 1 minute, or until sizzling. Sprinkle on each serving.

NOTE: To use the high-heat setting, cook for 3¹/₂ to 4 hours.

PORK POSOLE

A Mexican and Southwestern specialty, this main dish is a cross between a soup and a stew. Hominy, the same type of dried hulled corn that's ground into grits, is the star ingredient. Typically, it is topped with a variety of flavorful uncooked garnishes. Choose from among the recommended ones in the recipe.

Hands-On Time: 10 minutes

Total Time (low heat): 7 hours and 10 minutes

Makes 4 to 6 servings

Photo on page 264

2 containers (7 ounces each) prechopped onion (2 cups)

2 tablespoons olive oil

2 tablespoons preminced oil-packed garlic

2 teaspoons chili powder

1¼ pounds premarinated Italian-seasoned pork tenderloin, cut into 3 chunks

2 cans (15 ounces each) hominy, drained

1 can (15 ounces) chicken broth

1 cup crumbled tortilla chips (optional)

1 cup chopped lettuce (optional)

½ cup (2 ounces) shredded Cheddar cheese (optional)

½ cup chopped cilantro (optional)

½ cup radishes (optional)

1 cup refrigerated or jarred green or red salsa (optional)

In a 12" × 8" microwaveable baking dish, combine the onion, oil, garlic, and chili powder. Cover with plastic wrap, leaving a small corner vent. Microwave on high power, stirring once, for 4 minutes, or until sizzling. Set aside.

Coat the inside of a 3½-quart slow cooker pot with cooking spray. Place the pork, hominy, broth, and reserved onion mixture into the pot. Stir to combine. Cover and cook on the low-heat setting for 7 to 8 hours. Serve in pasta dishes or big soup bowls. If desired, offer chips, lettuce, cheese, cilantro, radishes, and salsa for garnishing.

NOTE: Pork Posole can be cooked on the high-heat setting for 3½ to 4 hours.

MOROCCAN LAMB TAGINE

Warm spices and tart fruits give this North African stew complexity. Serve with quick couscous or toasted pita bread.

Hands-On Time: 5 minutes
Total Time (low heat): 7 hours and 5 minutes

Makes 4 to 6 servings

1   cup pomegranate-cherry juice

2   tablespoons flour

1   teaspoon apple pie spice

1   teaspoon salt

1   teaspoon ground black pepper

3   pounds lamb shoulder steaks or lamb stew meat

2   Granny Smith apples (1 pound total), cut into eighths

1   cup prechopped onion

½   cup raisins

2   tablespoons preminced oil-packed garlic

½   cup chopped fresh cilantro (optional)

Coat the inside of a 5- to 6-quart slow cooker pot with cooking spray. Combine the juice, flour, pie spice, salt, and pepper. Whisk until smooth. Add the lamb, apples, onion, raisins, and garlic. Cover and cook on the low-heat setting for 7 to 8 hours. Stir in the cilantro, if using.

NOTE: Moroccan Lamb Tagine can be cooked on the high-heat setting for 3½ to 4 hours.

ALSATIAN SMOKED PORK CHOPS AND SAUERKRAUT

Whether you're returning from the ski slopes or just a winter commute, this mountain dish is sure to restore you. Select a Riesling or other fruity-style German wine to round out your meal. Or, for an alcohol-free alternative, serve with apple juice.

Hands-On Time: 5 minutes
Total Time (low heat): 8 hours and 5 minutes

Makes 4 to 6 servings

2 pounds smoked pork chops

1 bag (2 pounds) refrigerated sauerkraut, rinsed and drained

$^3/_4$ pound prescrubbed small red potatoes

1 cup fruity white wine

$^1/_2$ cup bagged baby carrots

$^1/_2$ cup prechopped onion

1 teaspoon ground black pepper

1 teaspoon dried thyme

Coat the inside of a $3^1/_2$-quart slow cooker pot with cooking spray. Cut the pork, if necessary, into pieces that fit into the pot. Place the pork, sauerkraut, potatoes, wine, carrots, onion, pepper, and thyme into the pot. Cover and cook on the low-heat setting for 8 to 9 hours.

NOTE: Alsatian Smoked Pork Chops and Sauerkraut can be cooked on the high-heat setting for 4 to $4^1/_2$ hours.

CHUCK WAGON BARBECUED-BEEF SANDWICHES

Campfire cooks can't afford to waste any ingredients. This ingenious recipe makes use of leftover brewed coffee to produce a distinctive barbecue.

Hands-On Time: 8 minutes

Total Time (low heat): 8 hours and 8 minutes

Makes 6 to 8 servings

$3/4$ cup brewed coffee

$1/4$ cup tomato paste

$1/4$ cup brown sugar

2 tablespoons apple cider vinegar

1 tablespoon cornstarch

1 tablespoon chili powder

1 teaspoon salt

$1/2$ teaspoon ground black pepper

1 container (7 ounces) presliced onion and bell pepper (2 cups)

$1/2$ cup raisins

2 beef eye round roasts (about $3^3/4$ pounds total)

12 hamburger buns

Coat the inside of a 5- to 6-quart slow cooker pot with cooking spray. Combine the coffee, tomato paste, sugar, vinegar, cornstarch, chili power, salt, and pepper. Whisk until smooth. Add the onion and bell pepper and raisins. Add the beef, turning the pieces to coat with the sauce. Cover and cook on the low-heat setting for 8 to 9 hours.

Remove the beef to a cutting board. Transfer the sauce to a food processor fitted with a meat blade. Process until smooth. Or, with an immersion blender, puree the sauce until smooth. If using the food processor, return the sauce to the pot. Slice the beef (it will be very tender and will almost fall apart) and return it to the pot. Spoon the barbecue onto the buns.

NOTE: Chuck Wagon Barbecued-Beef can be cooked on the high-heat setting for 4 to $4^1/2$ hours.

NEW ENGLAND POT ROAST

Your family and friends may suspect that Grandma is visiting when you serve this hearty meal that prepares itself. Grandma never had it so good.

Hands-On Time: 5 minutes
Total Time (low heat): 8 hours and 5 minutes

Makes 6 to 8 servings

$\frac{1}{2}$ cup flour

1 can (14 ounces) beef broth

3 tablespoons tomato paste

1 teaspoon dried thyme

1 teaspoon salt

1 teaspoon ground black pepper

$2\frac{1}{2}$ pounds boneless beef chuck roast or top sirloin roast

1 bag (12 ounces) precut carrot and celery sticks

1 cup prechopped onion

1 pound small prescrubbed new potatoes

Prepared horseradish

Coat the inside of a 5- to 6-quart slow cooker pot with cooking spray. Place the flour in the pot. Add the broth gradually, whisking constantly, until smooth. Add the tomato paste, thyme, salt, and pepper. Whisk to combine. Place the beef, carrot and celery, onion, and potatoes into the pot. Spoon some of the sauce over the beef. Cover and cook on the low-heat setting for 8 to 9 hours, or until the beef is fork tender. Serve with the horseradish.

NOTE: New England Pot Roast can also be cooked on the high-heat setting for 4 to 4$\frac{1}{2}$ hours.

BEEF SHORT RIBS WITH
SWEET-AND-SOUR RED CABBAGE

The Onion-Rye Beer Bread (page 311) is a fine flavor complement to this classic dish.

Hands-On Time: 5 minutes
Total Time (low heat): 7 hours and 5 minutes

Makes 4 to 6 servings

3 tablespoons flour

2 tablespoons brown sugar

$\frac{1}{2}$ cup dry red wine

2 tablespoons red wine vinegar

1 cup canned diced tomatoes

$\frac{1}{2}$ teaspoon salt

$\frac{1}{2}$ teaspoon ground black pepper

$\frac{1}{4}$ teaspoon ground cloves

2 bags (10 ounces each) preshredded red cabbage (7 cups)

$1\frac{1}{2}$ cups prechopped onion

2 bay leaves

$2\frac{1}{2}$-3 pounds beef short ribs

Prepared horseradish

Coat the inside of a 5- to 6-quart slow cooker pot with cooking spray. Add the flour and sugar. Whisk to combine. Add the wine and vinegar. Whisk until smooth. Add the tomatoes (with juice), salt, pepper, and cloves. Stir to mix well. Add the cabbage, onion, and bay leaves. Stir to coat well with the seasoning mixture. Insert the ribs so they are partially covered with the cabbage mixture. Cover and cook on the low-heat setting for 7 to 8 hours. Remove and discard the bay leaves. Serve with the horseradish.

NOTE: Beef Short Ribs with Sweet-and-Sour Red Cabbage can be cooked on the high-heat setting for $3\frac{1}{2}$ to 4 hours.

FLAVORED BUTTER

Nothing could be simpler than flavored butter. You soften a stick of butter in a bowl, stir in some flavorings, then shape the butter into a log in a piece of plastic wrap. Refrigerate the plastic-wrapped butter, and when it is cold, you have a time-saving flavor enhancer right there in the butter bin. Slice off a pat to top a sautéed chicken breast, melt onto grilled steak, slather onto corn on the cob, or enliven steamed broccoli. Here are six flavor combinations to try and some serving suggestions. Each recipe makes about ½ cup.

1. **Caraway Butter:** Combine 1 stick softened butter, 2 teaspoons lightly crushed caraway seeds, ¼ teaspoon salt, and ¼ teaspoon ground black pepper. Use on wedges of steamed cabbage and fresh ham.

2. **Chipotle Butter:** Combine 1 stick softened butter, 1 tablespoon finely chopped canned chipotle chile peppers packed in adobo sauce, and ¼ teaspoon salt. Serve over roasted, boiled, or baked potatoes or over fish fillets or chicken breasts.

3. **Ginger Butter:** Combine 1 stick softened butter, 1½ tablespoons pregrated ginger, 2 teaspoons lime juice, ¼ teaspoon salt, and ¼ teaspoon ground black pepper. Wonderful over broiled fish fillets, chicken, pork, and simple noodles. As an Asian variation, omit the salt and add 2 to 3 teaspoons soy sauce and ½ teaspoon toasted sesame oil.

4. **Tomato Butter:** Combine 1 stick softened butter, ¼ cup tomato paste, ½ teaspoon dried oregano, ½ teaspoon dried basil, ¼ teaspoon salt, and ¼ teaspoon ground black pepper. Great over broiled tomatoes and grilled steak, chicken, or vegetables.

5. **Watercress Butter:** Combine 1 stick softened butter, ¼ cup chopped watercress leaves, 1 to 2 teaspoons lemon juice, ¼ teaspoon salt, and ¼ teaspoon ground black pepper. A delight over steak, seafood, pork chops, or chicken. Also try it over baked potatoes.

6. **Paprika Butter:** Combine 1 stick softened butter, 1 tablespoon paprika, 1 teaspoon orange juice, and ¼ teaspoon salt. Perfect with seafood, pork, or potatoes.

MESQUITE-BARBECUED CORN ON THE COB *page 290*

CHAPTER 13

SIDES WORTH SAVORING

Here are more than a dozen delicious ways to make your main dish shine a little brighter. You might even find these easy accompaniments so tasty that your family will want to build a meal around them instead!

Teriyaki-Glazed Carrots

Creamed Pearl Onions

Mesquite-Barbecued Corn on the Cob

Fluffy Garlic Mashed Potatoes

Dilled Cauliflower and Peas

Sicilian Broccoli

Broccoli with Oyster Sauce

Southern Greens with Bacon

Creamy Garlic Spinach

Charred Radicchio with Balsamic and Bacon

Sherried Squash

Risotto with Cheese and Peas

Curried Basmati Rice with Broccoli

Mixed Grain–Almond Pilaf

Couscous with Chickpeas, Pine Nuts, and Peppadew

Marinated Black-Eyed Peas

Brown Rice with White and Black Beans

Italian Hazelnut Couscous with Tuna

Spinach-Artichoke Bread

Cheese-Herb-Pepper Bread

Onion-Rye Beer Bread

TERIYAKI-GLAZED CARROTS

Five Ingredients or Less!

This exotic-tasting vegetable dish harmonizes with pork chops, chicken breasts, or grilled fish.

Hands-On Time: 2 minutes
Total Time: 12 minutes

Makes 4 to 6 servings

1 bag (1 pound) baby carrots

2 tablespoons teriyaki baste-and-glaze sauce

2 tablespoons water

1 tablespoon vegetable oil

1 bunch scallions, white and light green parts, sliced ($\frac{1}{3}$ cup)

In a large saucepan, combine the carrots, teriyaki sauce, water, and oil. Stir to mix. Cover and bring to a boil. Reduce the heat. Simmer for about 8 minutes, or until the carrots are tender when pierced with a knife. Remove the lid and increase the heat to high. Cook, stirring, for about 1 minute, or until the carrots are glazed. Add the scallions and toss.

CREAMED PEARL ONIONS

Five Ingredients or Less!

This classic American vegetable dish is a tradition at many a holiday table, served alongside the stuffed roasted turkey or glazed ham. Unfortunately, the tedious chore of blanching and peeling enough tiny onions to serve a large gathering can take the better part of an hour. This rapid rendition takes only 10 minutes of unattended cooking time. So invite as many guests as you like. The recipe can be easily doubled or tripled.

Before 1 hour and 10 minutes

After 10 minutes

Time Saved 1 hour

Makes 4 to 6 servings

1   bag (1 pound) frozen pearl onions, thawed

1   cup refrigerated Alfredo sauce

$\frac{1}{4}$ teaspoon ground black pepper

$\frac{1}{8}$ teaspoon dried thyme

In a saucepan, combine the onions, sauce, pepper, and thyme. Stir to mix. Cook, stirring occasionally, over medium heat for about 10 minutes, or until heated through.

--- *We Saved Time By* ---

- ■ Using frozen pearl onions instead of peeling and cooking the onions from scratch

- ■ Using refrigerated Alfredo sauce instead of preparing a white sauce from scratch on the stovetop

MESQUITE-BARBECUED CORN ON THE COB

Five Ingredients or Less!

Here's an easy way to dress up a summertime favorite. The spicy seasonings are the perfect complement to fresh sweet corn.

Hands-On Time: 5 minutes
Total Time: 30 minutes

Makes 4 to 6 servings

Photo on page 286

4   ears corn, halved

2   tablespoons butter, softened

3   scallions, white and light green parts, sliced

1   teaspoon mesquite seasoning

Preheat the grill or broiler.

Place the corn in a single layer in an extra heavy duty foil cooking bag. Add the butter, scallions, and mesquite seasoning. Close the bag. Fold tightly several times to seal. Place the bag in a broiler pan. Grill or broil for 25 minutes, or until sizzling hot, occasionally rotating and shaking the bag to distribute the seasonings.

Double-Duty Gadgets
SWIVEL-BLADE VEGETABLE PEELER

A traditional, straight swivel-bladed vegetable peeler has many uses beyond peeling vegetables and fruits. There is no better tool for extracting capers from those tall and annoyingly skinny jars in which they are often packed. Slip in the straight peeler, capturing a row of capers, and the salty packing liquid drains between the blades, staying in the jar where it belongs. You can also use a peeler to make beautiful chocolate shavings and Parmesan shavings. Just run the peeler along the narrow edge of the chocolate bar or block of Parmesan as if you are peeling it.

FLUFFY GARLIC MASHED POTATOES

Here's a garlic-lover's dream—light and fluffy mashed potatoes laced with garlic, butter, and scallions. Be prepared to make a double batch—these will disappear quickly.

Hands-On Time: 7 minutes
Total Time: 27 minutes

Makes 4 servings

4 medium russet or Yukon gold potatoes, cut into eighths

2 tablespoons preminced oil-packed garlic

½ cup buttermilk

1 tablespoon butter

½ teaspoon salt

¼ teaspoon freshly ground black pepper

1 tablespoon snipped fresh chives, dill, or scallion greens

Place a steamer basket in a large saucepan with ½" of water. Place the potatoes and garlic in the steamer. Bring to a boil over high heat. Reduce the heat to medium, cover, and cook for 20 minutes, or until the potatoes are very tender.

Place the potatoes and garlic in a bowl, and mash with a potato masher. Add the buttermilk, butter, salt, pepper, and chives. Mash until well blended.

DILLED CAULIFLOWER AND PEAS

Five Ingredients or Less!

The dill adds a refreshing note to this easy steamed vegetable dish, a wonderful complement for salmon, chicken, or pork chops.

Hands-On Time: 2 minutes
Total Time: 8 minutes

Makes 4 to 6 servings

2   bags (8 ounces each) cauliflower florets, cut into walnut-size chunks

1   bunch scallions, white and light green parts, sliced (⅓ cup)

½   cup water

2   tablespoons butter

½   teaspoon dried dillweed

1   cup frozen petite peas

In a large skillet, combine the cauliflower, scallions, water, butter, and dillweed. Toss to mix. Cover and cook over medium heat, stirring occasionally, for about 6 minutes, or until the cauliflower is tender. Stir in the peas. Cook, tossing, for 2 minutes, or until the peas are heated.

CAULIFLOWER

Cauliflower is among the healthiest vegetables, along with other cruciferous vegetables such as broccoli. Precut cauliflower makes it easy to enjoy any time. Try the following sauces to dress up about 4 cups of steamed or roasted cauliflower florets, roughly the equivalent of 1½ pounds of cauliflower or 1 small head. You could also use these sauces on the same amount of broccoli.

1. **Herbed Butter Sauce:** Cook 1 tablespoon minced onion, 1 teaspoon dried tarragon (or basil, chervil, or dill), ½ cup white wine, and 2 tablespoons white wine vinegar in a small skillet over high heat until reduced to ¼ cup total volume. Reduce the heat to low and swirl in ½ stick (¼ cup) butter and 1 teaspoon finely chopped fresh parsley.

2. **Garlic Sauce:** In a small bowl, combine ½ teaspoon preminced oil-packed garlic, 2 tablespoons mayonnaise, and 1 teaspoon Dijon mustard. Whisk in 2 tablespoons white wine vinegar and ⅓ cup olive oil in a slow stream.

3. **Mustard Sauce:** Sauté 1 tablespoon finely chopped onion in ½ teaspoon butter until soft. Remove from the heat and stir in ⅓ cup sour cream and 1 tablespoon brown mustard.

4. **Yogurt and Herb Sauce:** Sauté 2 tablespoons chopped leeks and ¼ teaspoon minced garlic in 1 tablespoon olive oil until the leek is softened. Add 3 tablespoons chopped fresh herbs and ½ cup broth (vegetable, chicken, or fish). Cook over medium-high heat for about 10 minutes, or until the liquid is reduced to ¼ cup. Remove from the heat and stir in ½ cup plain yogurt.

5. **Creamy Anchovy Sauce:** Mix 2 tablespoons mayonnaise, 1 tablespoon anchovy paste, 1 tablespoon extra-virgin olive oil, 2 teaspoons lemon juice, and ¼ teaspoon preminced oil-packed garlic.

6. **Cheddar Cheese Sauce:** Melt 2 teaspoons butter in a saucepan over medium heat. Add 1 tablespoon all-purpose flour and stir for 1 minute. Gradually add ¼ cup warm milk, whisking constantly to break up any lumps. Add another ¼ cup warm milk, whisking until smooth. Cook for about 2 minutes, or until thick and smooth. Stir in 6 tablespoons shredded sharp Cheddar cheese, ¼ teaspoon Dijon mustard, ¼ teaspoon salt, ¼ teaspoon paprika, a pinch of ground black pepper, and a pinch of grated nutmeg (optional).

SICILIAN BROCCOLI

When the vegetable is this zesty, there's no need for a fussy protein main course. A simple pan-grilled chicken breast with a splash of lemon is the perfect companion. Pass red-pepper flakes at the table.

Hands-On Time: 5 minutes

Total Time: 10 minutes

Makes 4 to 6 servings

Photo on page 261

2 tablespoons olive oil (preferably extra-virgin)

2 bags (8 ounces each) broccoli florets, cut into walnut-size pieces

1 tablespoon preminced oil-packed garlic

1 can (15 ounces) diced Italian-seasoned tomatoes

2 tablespoons raisins

¼ teaspoon salt

In a large skillet, warm the oil over medium-high heat. Add the broccoli and garlic. Stir to coat with the oil. Cover and cook for 2 minutes, or until the broccoli is bright green. Add the tomatoes (with juice), raisins, and salt. Reduce the heat to medium-low. Cook, stirring occasionally, for about 5 minutes, or until the broccoli is crisp-tender.

Double-Duty Gadgets

STEAMER

Steaming quickly and gently softens vegetables and retains more nutrients and flavor than most other cooking methods. If you don't have one of those collapsible steamer baskets, here are three options.

1. Line the bottom of a pot with balls of crumpled aluminum foil. Put a small metal colander, strainer, or wire rack (such as one from a toaster oven) over the foil balls to create a makeshift steaming basket. Add water to the bottom of the pot, bring it to a simmer, and put the food in your basket. Cover tightly and steam away.

2. Use a heatproof plate and a metal trivet or clean empty tuna can (with both ends removed) in a similar way to the above method. Put the trivet or empty tuna can in the bottom of the pot and set the plate on top to use as a steaming rack.

3. Use your microwave oven, which is ideal for steaming. Put the food to be steamed in a microwave-safe container, add a little water, cover with plastic wrap, and cook on high power until the food is just cooked through.

BROCCOLI WITH OYSTER SAUCE

Serve this quick broccoli stir-fry alongside any Asian dish. Toasted sesame seeds make a nice garnish.

Hands-On Time: 6 minutes

Total Time: 6 minutes

Makes 4 servings

2 teaspoons cornstarch

1/3 cup chicken broth, cold or at room temperature

1/4 cup oyster sauce

2 tablespoons bottled teriyaki sauce

1 teaspoon toasted sesame oil

2 tablespoons vegetable oil

3 cups fresh broccoli florets

2 tablespoons water

2 scallions, sliced

1 tablespoon preminced oil-packed ginger

1/2 teaspoon preminced oil-packed garlic

In a small bowl, dissolve the cornstarch in the broth. Stir in the oyster sauce, teriyaki sauce, and sesame oil. Set aside.

Heat 1 tablespoon of the vegetable oil in a wok or large, deep skillet over medium-high heat. When hot, add the broccoli and water (it should sizzle). Cover and cook for 1 minute, shaking the pan occasionally. Uncover and add the remaining 1 table-spoon of oil and the scallions, ginger, and garlic. Stir-fry for 10 to 15 seconds, or until fragrant, then spread the vegetables to the sides of the pan. Stir the reserved sauce to recombine, then pour into the center of the pan. Stir for about 30 seconds, or until the sauce boils and thickens, then stir in the vegetables until coated.

SOUTHERN GREENS WITH BACON

Either tastes have changed or "pot" greens have become more tender. Simmering greens for hours is a cooking technique of the past. Welcome to the delicious, nutritious side dish of the New South.

Before 3 hours

After 10 minutes

Time Saved 2 hours and 50 minutes

Makes 4 to 6 servings

Photo on page 239

3 tablespoons vegetable oil

1 cup prechopped onion

1 bag (1 pound) collard greens or kale

$\frac{1}{2}$ cup chicken broth or water

$\frac{1}{2}$ teaspoon salt

$\frac{3}{4}$ teaspoon ground black pepper

$\frac{1}{4}$ cup (1 ounce) bagged precooked crumbled bacon

1 tablespoon cider vinegar or white wine vinegar

Heat the oil in a large pot over medium heat. Add the onion. Stir to combine. Cook, stirring occasionally, for 2 minutes, or until softened. In two batches, add the collard or kale. Stir to coat with the onion mixture. Add the broth or water, salt, and pepper. Cover and cook over medium-low heat for 4 minutes, or until wilted. Add the bacon and vinegar. Toss to combine.

We Saved Time By

- Using prechopped onion instead of peeling and chopping the onion by hand

- Using pretrimmed, prewashed, pretorn cooking greens instead of doing multiple washings (to remove all sand), then trimming and cutting by hand

- Using precooked bacon pieces instead of cooking chunk bacon or ham hocks from scratch

- Cooking the greens contemporary-style—just until brightly colored and crisp-tender—to preserve texture and nutrients instead of cooking them for hours

---

CREAMY GARLIC SPINACH

Five Ingredients or Less!

Here's a quick, updated creamed spinach for people who like sautéed spinach with a little pizzazz. To make this more sophisticated, use herbed goat cheese in place of the cream cheese.

Hands-On Time: 6 minutes
Total Time: 6 minutes

Makes 4 servings

2 tablespoons butter

2 tablespoons prechopped onion

½ teaspoon preminced oil-packed garlic

2 bags (20 ounces) baby spinach leaves

2 ounces herbed cream cheese

Melt the butter in a large skillet over medium heat. Add the onion and garlic and cook for about 4 minutes, or until soft. Add the spinach and cook for about 2 minutes, or just until wilted. Stir in the cream cheese until melted.

CHARRED RADICCHIO WITH BALSAMIC AND BACON

Five Ingredients or Less!

Fans of this bittersweet Italian chicory love it with rosemary roasted chicken or pork.

Hands-On Time: 2 minutes

Total Time: 6 minutes

Makes 4 to 6 servings

2 heads radicchio (about 12 ounces), cored and sliced into 1"-wide cross-sections

Olive oil

¼ cup (1 ounce) bagged precooked crumbled bacon

2 tablespoons balsamic vinegar

Salt

Ground black pepper

Preheat the broiler. Line a broiler pan with aluminum foil. Coat with cooking spray.

Place the radicchio in a single layer on the pan. Drizzle with oil. Broil 6" from the heat source for 3 minutes, or until the top of the leaves are browning. Flip the radicchio. Drizzle with oil. Scatter the bacon over the top. Broil 6" from the heat source for 2 minutes, or until browned and sizzling. Sprinkle with the vinegar. Season to taste with salt and pepper.

SHERRIED SQUASH

This comforting casserole makes a great accompaniment to just about any roasted pork or chicken dish. Using precut squash dramatically reduces the hands-on time required.

Hands-On Time: 5 minutes
Total Time: 42 minutes

Makes 8 servings

1 package (20 ounces) precut butternut squash

1 tablespoon water

½ cup milk

2 tablespoons all-purpose flour

1 egg

2 teaspoons cream sherry or apple juice

⅓ cup packed brown sugar

½ teaspoon salt

¼ teaspoon ground white or black pepper

⅛ teaspoon ground cinnamon

Preheat the oven to 325°F.

Arrange the squash in an 8" × 8" microwave-safe baking dish. Add the water and cover with plastic wrap, leaving a small corner vent. Microwave on high power for 7 minutes, or until the squash is very tender.

In a large bowl with a mixer at medium speed, beat the squash, milk, flour, egg, sherry or apple juice, brown sugar, salt, pepper, and cinnamon.

Spray a baking dish with cooking spray and fill with the squash mixture. Bake for 30 minutes, or until a wooden toothpick inserted into the center comes out clean.

RISOTTO WITH CHEESE AND PEAS

Pressure Cooker Dish

Velvety Italian risotto isn't difficult to prepare, but many home cooks resist making it because it needs constant attention. The traditional cooking method requires that the broth be added to the simmering rice ½ cupful at a time so the rice can soften by absorbing the liquid gradually. This lightning-speed version could fool even an Italian nonna.

Before 35 minutes

After 10 minutes

Time Saved 25 minutes

Makes 6 to 8 servings

2	tablespoons butter
½	cup prechopped onion
1½	cups Arborio rice
4	cups vegetable broth, divided
¾	cup frozen petite peas
¾	cup preshredded Parmesan-Romano cheese blend
¼	teaspoon salt

Combine the butter and the onion in the pressure cooker pot. Cook over medium-low heat, stirring occasionally, for 2 minutes, or until softened. Add the rice and stir to coat thoroughly with the onion mixture. Add 3½ cups of the broth. Stir to combine. Cover the pot and lock the lid. Bring to high pressure over high heat. Reduce the heat to maintain high pressure. Cook for 6 minutes.

Using the quick-release method, reduce the pressure. Uncover the pot. Test a grain of rice. If it is still hard in the center, add a remaining ¼ cup of broth and cook, stirring, over medium heat until the broth is absorbed. Continue stirring in broth, if needed. Remove from the heat. Stir in the peas, cheese, and salt.

--- *We Saved Time By* ---

- Using frozen petite peas instead of shelling and washing fresh peas

- Using preshredded cheese instead of grating a block of cheese by hand

- Using a pressure cooker instead of stirring the rice in a conventional pot during the entire cooking time

CURRIED BASMATI RICE WITH BROCCOLI

Basmati rice cooks just as quickly as white rice but has a more complex, nutty aroma. It's a popular rice in India and is sold near the other rice in many American grocery stores.

Hands-On Time: 5 minutes
Total Time: 20 minutes

Makes 4 servings

1³⁄₄ cups water

¹⁄₂ teaspoon salt

1 cup basmati rice, rinsed thoroughly

10 ounces fresh broccoli florets (about 1¹⁄₂ cups)

1 tablespoon butter

¹⁄₂ cup pine nuts

¹⁄₂ teaspoon curry powder

1¹⁄₂ tablespoons lemon juice

Bring the water to a boil in a medium saucepan. Add the salt and stir in the rice. Cover tightly and simmer over low heat for 12 minutes. Add the broccoli and simmer for 3 minutes, or until all the water has been absorbed by the rice and the broccoli is crisp-tender. Remove from the heat and let rest for 5 minutes.

Melt the butter in a another medium saucepan over medium heat. Add the pine nuts and cook, stirring occasionally, for about 3 minutes, or until golden and fragrant. Stir in the curry powder and lemon juice. Add the rice mixture and toss to combine.

MIXED GRAIN-ALMOND PILAF

Before the advent of par-cooked whole grains, a pilaf could take nearly an hour to prepare. By combining a multi-rice mix with quick-cooking barley, this grain medley is ready in half the time.

Hands-On Time: 5 minutes
Total Time: 30 minutes

Makes 4 to 6 servings

1 box (6 ounces) long-grain and wild-rice mix

2 tablespoons butter

¼ cup sliced almonds

¼ cup prechopped onion, minced

¼ cup bagged preshredded carrot

½ teaspoon ground black pepper

3 cups vegetable broth

½ cup quick-cooking barley

Remove the seasoning packet from the long-grain and wild-rice mix. Measure 2 tablespoons and discard the remainder. Set aside.

In a medium saucepan, combine the butter and the almonds over medium heat. Cook, stirring with a fork, for 2 minutes, or until the almonds are golden. Use the fork to transfer the almonds to a plate, leaving the butter in the pan. Add the rice, onion, carrot, and pepper. Cook, stirring, for 2 minutes, or until the rice is glazed with butter. Add the broth and the reserved seasoning. Bring almost to a boil. Reduce the heat to medium-low. Cover and simmer for 15 minutes. Stir in the barley. Cover and cook for 10 minutes, or until all the broth is absorbed. Sprinkle the reserved almonds over each serving.

COUSCOUS WITH CHICKPEAS, PINE NUTS, AND PEPPADEW

Peppadew, a sweet-hot bright red chile from South Africa, adds interest to this good grain side dish.

Hands-On Time: 3 minutes
Total Time: 7 minutes

Makes 4 to 6 servings

1 box (6 ounces) couscous mix with toasted pine nuts

2 tablespoons olive oil

1 teaspoon preminced oil-packed garlic

1 cup canned chickpeas, rinsed and drained

1½ cups vegetable broth

¼ cup drained jarred Peppadew or pimientos, chopped

Remove the seasoning packet from the couscous. Set aside.

In a large saucepan, heat the oil and garlic over high heat for 30 seconds, or until sizzling. Add the chickpeas and the contents of the reserved seasoning packet. Cook, tossing, for 2 minutes, or until the chickpeas are thoroughly coated with the seasonings. Add the broth and couscous. Bring to a boil. Stir. Reduce the heat to medium-low. Cover and simmer for 4 minutes, or until all the broth is absorbed. Stir in the Peppadew or pimientos.

MARINATED BLACK-EYED PEAS

Black-eyed peas are enjoyed all over the southern United States. The flavors here are more Southwest than Southeast, but you could serve this dish with any Southern meal. Make the peas ahead of time since they need at least a couple hours in the refrigerator to marinate.

Hands-On Time: 5 minutes
Total Time: 2 hours and 5 minutes

Makes 6 servings

⅓ cup olive oil

¼ cup lemon or lime juice

¼ cup chopped fresh cilantro

½ teaspoon preminced oil-packed garlic

1 teaspoon ground cumin

1 teaspoon dried oregano

½ teaspoon salt

¼ teaspoon sugar

2 cans (15 ounces each) black-eyed peas, rinsed and drained

1 small tomato, finely chopped (optional)

In a large bowl, whisk together the oil, lemon or lime juice, cilantro, garlic, cumin, oregano, salt, and sugar. Stir in the peas. Cover and marinate in the refrigerator for at least 2 hours or up to 2 days. Top each serving with 1 tablespoon of the tomato, if using.

BROWN RICE WITH WHITE AND BLACK BEANS

This Southwest side dish is full of bold flavor and heart-healthy fiber. Serve it with any Mexican dish to help fill out the meal.

Hands-On Time: 5 minutes
Total Time: 45 minutes

Makes 6 servings

1 tablespoon olive oil

1 cup prechopped onion

1 can (4 ounces) diced green chile peppers, drained

½ teaspoon preminced oil-packed garlic

3 tablespoons chili powder

1 tablespoon ground cumin

1 teaspoon dried oregano

2 teaspoons ground coriander (optional)

2 cups brown rice

5 cups vegetable or chicken broth

½ can (15-ounce can) black beans (about 1 cup), rinsed and drained

½ can (15-ounce can) small white beans (about 1 cup), rinsed and drained

1 tablespoon chopped fresh cilantro

Heat the oil in a medium saucepan over medium heat. Add the onion, peppers, and garlic and cook for about 5 minutes, or until tender. Add the chili powder, cumin, oregano, and coriander, if using, and cook for 1 minute longer. Stir in the rice. Add the broth, cover, and simmer for 35 to 45 minutes, or until the liquid is absorbed and the rice is tender. Gently stir in the black beans and white beans and cook 1 minute longer. Stir in the cilantro.

ITALIAN HAZELNUT COUSCOUS WITH TUNA

Five Ingredients or Less!

Unlike most pasta, instant couscous is ready in 5 minutes simply by pouring boiling water
over it. Here it's mixed with
pantry ingredients for a simple
side dish to accompany any
Italian- or Mediterranean-style
meal. Look for hazelnuts in the
nut aisle of your grocery store.

Hands-On Time: 2 minutes

Total Time: 10 minutes

Makes 4 servings

1   box (10 ounces) instant couscous

1   can (6 ounces) olive oil-packed tuna

½   cup chopped hazelnuts

1   teaspoon preminced oil-packed garlic

2   tablespoons chopped fresh dill

¼   teaspoon salt

⅛   teaspoon ground black pepper

Prepare the couscous according to the package directions.
Fluff with a fork and toss with the tuna (with oil), hazelnuts,
garlic, dill, salt, and pepper.

Shelf-Ready Shortcuts

SALAD DRESSING

Most home cooks keep a few different salad dressings in the refrigerator. Generally, these dressings come in two basic styles: thinner vinaigrettes and thicker creamy dressings. Both types have
myriad uses beyond their traditional role atop salad greens. You can use almost any vinaigrette
as an instant marinade. Marinate chicken in Caesar salad dressing, portobello mushrooms in
balsamic vinaigrette, or beef in garlic vinaigrette. Creamy dressings can double as vegetable or
chip dips, as quick sauces (when thinned out with a little milk or buttermilk) to serve alongside a
simple meal, or as final flavor boosters for creamy soups and sauces. Blue cheese dressing is
particularly good when added to Italian soups and creamy pasta sauces. One caveat: When
using salad dressing in a long-cooking mixture such as a soup or sauce, add the dressing at the
end of the cooking time and heat it only briefly to prevent the dressing from separating.

SPINACH-ARTICHOKE BREAD

Flavored breads are simple to make at home. Thaw some bread dough, then fill with your favorite flavors! To jazz this up even more, sprinkle a layer of pregrated Parmesan cheese onto the bread dough before adding the filling.

Hands-On Time: 20 minutes

Total Time: 2 hours and 5 minutes (plus 15 minutes cooling time)

Makes 1 loaf (4 servings)

1 tablespoon olive oil

1½ cups prechopped onion

½ teaspoon preminced oil-packed garlic

½ package (10-ounce package) frozen chopped spinach, thawed and drained

½ teaspoon salt

⅛ teaspoon ground black pepper

Pinch nutmeg

½ jar (6-ounce jar) marinated artichoke hearts, drained and chopped

½ pound frozen white bread dough, thawed

Heat the oil in a medium skillet over medium heat. Add the onion and garlic and cook, stirring occasionally, for about 5 minutes, or until soft. Add the spinach and cook for about 3 minutes, or until almost dry. Season with the salt, pepper, and nutmeg. Remove from the heat and stir in the artichoke hearts.

On a lightly floured work surface, pat the dough into a 6" × 8" rectangle. Spoon the spinach mixture over the dough and roll it up like a jelly roll, starting at a wide side. Pinch the ends closed and place, seam side down, on a greased baking sheet. Cover it with a damp towel and let it rise in a warm spot for about 1 hour, or until almost doubled in size.

Preheat the oven to 400°F. Slash the top of the loaf in a few places with a sharp knife. Brush the surface with ice cold water and bake for about 40 minutes, or until crisp and golden. Cool on a rack for 15 minutes before slicing and serving.

ONION-RYE BEER BREAD (top) *page 311*; SPINACH-ARTICHOKE BREAD (center) *opposite page*; and CHEESE-HERB-PEPPER BREAD (bottom) *page 310*

CHEESE-HERB-PEPPER BREAD

Five Ingredients or Less!
Bread Machine Dish

Gorgeously browned with a high dome, the aroma of this bread will drive your family crazy as it bakes. If you set the delay button, you can have the hot loaf ready with your slow cooker New England Pot Roast (page 283) when you arrive home for supper. Who needs a private chef?

Hands-On Time: 5 minutes

Total Time: 3 hours and 35 minutes

Makes 1 loaf (1½ pounds)

Photo on page 309

1 cup room-temperature water

2 tablespoons olive oil (preferably extra-virgin)

1 box (14 ounces) Italian herb bread-machine mix

1 cup (4 ounces) preshredded Parmesan cheese

½ cup loosely packed chopped fresh parsley

1 teaspoon red-pepper flakes

In the canister of a 1½-pound bread machine, place the water, oil, bread mix, and yeast (from the bread mix). Select the settings for white bread, medium crust, and large loaf. Press the start button. When the add-in signal beeps, add the cheese, parsley, and pepper flakes.

When the machine beeps done, remove the bread to a rack to cool completely.

ONION-RYE BEER BREAD

Five Ingredients or Less!
Bread Machine Dish

This old-world bakery-style loaf is a natural with corned beef or pastrami sandwiches. It's also unbeatable with Beef Short Ribs with Sweet-and-Sour Red Cabbage (page 284).

Hands-On Time: 5 minutes

Total Time: 4 hours and 5 minutes

Makes 1 loaf (1½ pounds)

Photo on page 309

1   cup room-temperature flat dark beer, such as stout

2   tablespoons vegetable oil

1   box (16 ounces) caraway-rye bread-machine mix

1½   cups (3 ounces) canned French-fried onions

In the canister of a 1½-pound bread machine, place the beer, oil, bread mix, and yeast (from the bread mix). Select the settings for whole wheat bread, medium crust, and large loaf. Press the start button. When the add-in signal beeps, add the onions.

When the machine beeps done, remove the bread to a rack to cool completely.

DEEP-DISH GOLDEN DELICIOUS APPLE PIE *page 336*

CHAPTER 14

THE PERFECT FINALE—DESSERTS

Add an extra-special ending to your family meal with one of these supereasy creations. The sweetest part is that you're the only one who has to know how quick they really are.

Warm Blueberry Biscuit Shortcakes

Chocolate-Hazelnut Bar Cookies

Banana Bars with Fudge Frosting

Pistachio Cream Tarts in Flaky Pastry Shells

Orange-Glazed Pears with Chocolate Drizzles

Clementine Tart with White Chocolate-Macadamia Cookie Crust

French Mixed-Fruit Galette

Lemon-Raspberry Trifle

Austrian Walnut-White Chocolate Torte with Lemon Frosting

Chocolate-Almond Torte with Orange Sauce

Fudgy Chocolate-Peanut Butter Torte

Pecan-Cinnamon Bundt Cake

Carrot-Cranberry-Pineapple Snack Cake with Cream Cheese-Walnut Frosting

Apricot-Ginger Crumble

Cinnamon-Raisin Bread Pudding with Whiskey Sauce

Chocolate-Walnut-Cherry Tart

Deep-Dish Golden Delicious Apple Pie

Southern Sour Cream-Coconut Layer Cake

Tiramisu Cheesecake

Maple Cream-Peach Parfaits with Toffee Topping

Pumpkin Panna Cotta

Raspberry Sundaes in Fudge-Glazed Waffle Bowls

Tropical-Fruit Cream Pie

Banana-Glazed Pecan Ice-Cream Sundaes

Rainbow-Sorbet Angel Cake

WARM BLUEBERRY BISCUIT SHORTCAKES

You can savor a taste of summer anytime with these oh-so-easy berry delights.

Hands-On Time: 10 minutes

Total Time: 20 minutes (plus 10 minutes cooling time)

Makes 8 servings

1 tube (16 ounces) large-size refrigerated biscuits (8 biscuits)

2 tablespoons brown sugar

¼ teaspoon ground cinnamon

2 tablespoons frozen limeade concentrate

¼ cup granulated sugar

2 teaspoons cornstarch

1 bag (12 ounces) frozen loose-pack blueberries, thawed

1 can (7 ounces) refrigerated whipped cream

Preheat the oven to 350°F.

Place the biscuits on a baking sheet. On a small sheet of waxed paper, combine the brown sugar and cinnamon. Set half of the mixture to one side. Use the remainder to sprinkle over the biscuits. Bake for 18 minutes, or until browned. Remove to a rack.

Meanwhile, in a saucepan, combine the limeade concentrate, granulated sugar, and cornstarch. Whisk until smooth. Add the berries (with juice). Cook, stirring constantly, over medium-high heat for about 5 minutes, or until the mixture is thickened. Allow to cool for 10 minutes.

Split the reserved biscuits in half. Place the bottoms, cut side up, on individual plates or a platter. Sprinkle with the reserved cinnamon sugar. Spoon the berry mixture over the bottoms. Spritz generously with whipped cream. Cover with the biscuit tops. Spritz whipped cream on top.

CHOCOLATE-HAZELNUT BAR COOKIES

Five Ingredients or Less!

Look for Nutella next to the peanut butter in the supermarket. The Italian chocolate spread is giving the all-American goober a run for its money.

Hands-On Time: 6 minutes

Total Time: 36 minutes

Makes 32 bars

Flour for dusting hands

2 tubes (18 ounces each) refrigerated sugar cookie dough

1 jar (13 ounces) hazelnut-skim milk-cocoa spread, such as Nutella

⅓ cup corn syrup with brown sugar flavoring

1 egg yolk

Preheat the oven to 350°F. Coat a 13" × 9" baking pan with cooking spray.

With floured palms, pat one tube of the cookie dough to cover the bottom of the pan.

In a mixing bowl, combine the hazelnut-skim milk-cocoa spread, corn syrup, and egg yolk. Mix until smooth. Spoon onto the crust in small dollops. With palms or the back of a spoon, flatten the filling to cover the dough. With floured palms, press small chunks of the remaining tube of dough into flat pieces. Place over the filling. (Small gaps are fine.) Bake for 30 minutes, or until the crust is lightly browned. (Do not overbake.) Cool in the pan on a rack.

BANANA BARS WITH FUDGE FROSTING

With a moist fruity bottom layer, a lighter cake center, and chocolate fudge frosting, these dessert bars are outrageously yummy.

Hands-On Time: 10 minutes
Total Time: 50 minutes

Makes 24 bars

Flour for dusting pan

1 box (18 ounces) butter-recipe golden cake mix

10 tablespoons butter, softened

1 cup mashed ripe bananas (about 2 medium)

½ cup water

3 eggs

¼ cup sugar

2 teaspoons vanilla extract

1 bag (6 ounces) semisweet chocolate morsels

½ cup sour cream

Preheat the oven to 350°F. Coat a 13" × 9" baking pan with cooking spray. Dust with flour, shaking out the excess.

In the bowl of an electric mixer, combine the cake mix, butter, bananas, water, eggs, sugar, and vanilla. Blend for about 30 seconds, or until the dry ingredients are moistened. Beat at medium speed for 3 minutes, or until smooth and fluffy. Pour into the prepared pan. Bake for about 40 minutes, or until a tester inserted into the center comes out clean. Cool in the pan on a rack.

Place the chocolate morsels in a microwaveable bowl. Microwave on high power for 2 minutes, or until glossy. Stir until smooth. Add the sour cream. Stir until smooth and glossy. Spread over the cake.

QUICK TIP: Purchase over-ripe bananas on the sale table in the produce department to have on hand any time the urge hits for banana bars. Mash the bananas and place 1-cup measures in zipper-lock freezer bags. Freeze for up to 3 months. To use, place in the microwave oven. Microwave on the defrost setting for 2 to 3 minutes, or until softened.

PISTACHIO CREAM TARTS IN FLAKY PASTRY SHELLS

Five Ingredients or Less!

Pale green and pretty, these individual desserts are just the thing for a tea or luncheon.

Hands-On Time: 5 minutes

Total Time: 20 minutes (plus 1 hour cooling time)

Makes 6 servings

6 frozen puff-pastry shells

1 box (3 ounces) instant pistachio pudding mix

1 cup half-and-half

½ cup shelled unsalted pistachio nuts, coarsely chopped, divided

Confectioners' sugar in a shaker can

Preheat the oven to 400°F.

Place the shells on a baking sheet. Bake for about 15 minutes, or until browned and puffed. Allow to cool on a rack for at least 1 hour.

Meanwhile, measure ¼ cup of the pudding mix into a bowl. (Reserve the remainder for another recipe.) Add the half-and-half. Whisk until smooth. Set aside 2 tablespoons of the pistachios. Stir the remaining pistachios into the pudding. Cover with plastic wrap and refrigerate.

Remove the tops from the pastry shells. Set aside. Place each shell bottom on a dessert plate. Spoon the pudding mixture into the shells. Sprinkle the reserved nuts over the pudding and onto the plates. Place the reserved tops askew over the pudding. Dust the shells and plates with sugar.

NOTE: The cooled shells can be stored in an airtight metal tin for up to 12 hours before serving.

ORANGE-GLAZED PEARS
WITH CHOCOLATE DRIZZLES

When you have a bar of high-quality chocolate on hand, this dessert from the cupboard becomes something special. Use a vegetable peeler to shave the chocolate right over the pears. Offer shortbread cookies on the side.

Hands-On Time: 2 minutes
Total Time: 8 minutes

Makes 6 servings

3   tablespoons frozen orange-juice concentrate

1   tablespoon butter

3   cans (15 ounces each) pear halves in juice, drained

1   ounce bittersweet or semisweet chocolate, shaved

In a skillet large enough to hold the pears in a single layer, combine the juice concentrate and butter. Cook over medium heat for 2 minutes, or until bubbling. Arrange the pears, cut side down, in the pan. Cook for about 1 minute. Gently flip the pears. Cook for about 1 minute, or just until the pears are glazed. Sprinkle on the chocolate.

Double-Duty Gadgets

KITCHEN TIMER

Most kitchens use inexpensive plastic white timers for setting cooking times. Invariably, these timers break after a while. If you find yourself without a timer, use an alarm clock instead. Or if you wear a sport watch with a timer, use that.

CLEMENTINE TART WITH WHITE CHOCOLATE-MACADAMIA COOKIE CRUST

Five Ingredients or Less!

This sophisticated European-style dessert is truly easy enough for a child to prepare.

Hands-On Time: 8 minutes

Total Time: 28 minutes (plus 30 minutes chilling time)

Makes 8 to 10 servings

1 package (18 ounces) refrigerated white chocolate-macadamia nut cookie dough

$\frac{1}{3}$ cup sweet orange marmalade

2 containers ($3\frac{1}{2}$ ounces each) snack-pack vanilla pudding

5 clementines, peeled and sections separated

Preheat the oven to 350°F. Coat a 9" or 10" springform pan with cooking spray.

Press the cookie dough into the pan and $\frac{1}{2}$" up the sides. Bake for 20 minutes, or until well browned. Allow to cool completely on a rack.

Meanwhile, place the marmalade in a microwaveable bowl. Cover with waxed paper. Cook on high power for 90 seconds, or until bubbling. Set aside.

Remove the pan sides. Set the crust on a serving plate. Spread the pudding on the crust. Starting at the outer edge of the crust, set the clementine sections slightly overlapping in a ring. Repeat with smaller rings until the entire crust is covered (some pudding will show through). With a spoon, drizzle the marmalade over the fruit. Spread with the back of the spoon. Refrigerate, uncovered, for at least 30 minutes.

FRENCH MIXED-FRUIT GALETTE

Five Ingredients or Less!

This rustic tart is the kind that home cooks prepare in France. It requires no top crust, so it comes together very quickly. If mixed berries aren't available, replace them with halved frozen strawberries or frozen raspberries.

Hands-On Time: 5 minutes

Total Time: 1 hour and 5 minutes

Makes 8 servings

1 refrigerated piecrust (not frozen)

1 jar (12 ounces) peach preserves

3 tablespoons cornstarch

1 bag (1 pound) frozen mixed berries, thawed

   Confectioners' sugar in a shaker can

Preheat the oven to 375°F. Coat a 9" cake or pie pan with cooking spray.

Fit the crust into the pan, allowing excess crust to flop over the sides.

In a mixing bowl, combine the preserves and cornstarch. Whisk until smooth. Add the berries and stir to mix thoroughly. Pour into the prepared pan. Fold the excess crust toward the center. (There will be an uncovered center portion of filling.)

Bake for 1 hour, or until the filling bubbles in the center. Cool in the pan on a rack. Just before serving, sprinkle with the sugar.

LEMON-RASPBERRY TRIFLE

Simultaneously refreshing, creamy, fruity, and dreamy, trifle is the British name for a luscious cake and pudding mélange.

Hands-On Time: 10 minutes

Total Time: 10 minutes (plus 1 hour chilling time)

Makes 8 to 10 servings

2 boxes (3 ounces each) instant lemon pudding mix

4 cups whole milk

1 package (12 ounces) frozen loose-pack raspberries (3 cups)

½ cup seedless raspberry jam

1 package (1 pound) frozen pound cake, cut into ½"-thick slices

Whipped cream

In a mixing bowl, combine the pudding mix and milk. Whisk until smooth. Set aside. In a mixing bowl, stir the raspberries and jam to mix.

Spoon 1 cup of the pudding mixture into an 8- to 10-cup glass serving dish, preferably straight-sided. Cover with 4 cake slices, trimming to fit in an even layer. Spread on 1 cup of the raspberry mixture. Repeat with two layers each of the pudding, cake, and raspberry mixture. Spread the remaining pudding on the top. If the bowl is not straight-sided, 2 or 3 slices of cake may remain. Wrap in plastic for another use.

Refrigerate, uncovered, for 1 hour for the berries to thaw and the flavors to blend. Spoon onto dessert dishes or shallow bowls. Serve with whipped cream.

AUSTRIAN WALNUT-WHITE CHOCOLATE TORTE WITH LEMON FROSTING

This triple-layered European confection is more dense and moist than a layer cake. It's wonderful served with steaming brewed tea or coffee.

Hands-On Time: 10 minutes
Total Time: 30 minutes

Makes 8 to 10 servings

2¼ cups chopped walnuts

1½ cups white chocolate morsels

¾ cup biscuit baking mix

¾ cup + 3¾ cups confectioners' sugar

6 eggs

1 stick (½ cup) butter, softened

2-3 tablespoons lemon juice

Preheat the oven to 350°F. Coat three 8" round cake pans with cooking spray. Dust with flour to coat; shake out any excess.

In the work bowl of a food processor fitted with a metal blade, combine the walnuts, white chocolate morsels, biscuit mix, and ¾ cup of the sugar. Process for about 2 minutes, or until the nuts are finely ground. Add the eggs. Process for about 1 minute, or until smooth. Pour into the prepared pans, spreading evenly. Bake for about 20 minutes, or until the torte springs back when lightly pressed. Let stand on a rack for 10 minutes. Turn the layers onto a rack to cool completely.

Meanwhile, in the bowl of an electric mixer, combine the butter, 2 tablespoons of the lemon juice, and the remaining 3¾ cups of sugar. Blend on low speed for about 1 minute, or until moistened. Beat on high speed for 3 minutes longer, or until smooth and fluffy. Add up to 1 tablespoon more lemon juice, if needed, to make a spreadable frosting. Frost the torte between layers and on the top but not on the sides.

CHOCOLATE-ALMOND TORTE WITH ORANGE SAUCE

No one but the baker will know that this elegant European-style confection is created from a boxed brownie mix. Both the sauce and the toasted almonds can be prepared days ahead of serving. Refrigerate the sauce. Place the almonds in an airtight container.

Hands-On Time: 10 minutes

Total Time: 55 minutes

Makes 8 to 10 servings

$\frac{1}{3}$ cup water

$\frac{1}{3}$ cup vegetable oil

1 egg

1 teaspoon almond extract

1 box (20 ounces) double-chocolate brownie mix

$1\frac{1}{4}$ cups orange marmalade

2 tablespoons lemon juice

$\frac{1}{4}$ cup slivered almonds

Preheat the oven to 325°F. Coat an 8" springform pan with cooking spray.

In a mixing bowl, combine the water, oil, egg, and extract. Beat with a fork. Add the brownie mix. Stir until the dry ingredients are moistened. Pour into the prepared pan. Bake for 45 minutes, or until slightly puffed. The center may appear underbaked but cools to doneness. Cool in the pan on a rack.

Meanwhile, combine the marmalade and lemon juice. Whisk to mix.

In a small skillet, toast the almonds over medium-high heat, stirring often, for 5 minutes, or until toasted. Remove to a plate to cool.

Remove the side of the springform pan. Cut the torte into wedges. Place the wedges on dessert plates. Surround with drizzles of orange sauce and the almonds.

FUDGY CHOCOLATE–PEANUT BUTTER TORTE

Decadent, rich, and over-the-top are just a few descriptors for this outrageous dessert. This is the treat for peanut-butter chocoholics.

Hands-On Time: 10 minutes

Total Time: 1 hour and 5 minutes

Makes 12 to 14 servings

1 tube (18 ounces) refrigerated peanut-butter cookie dough

¾ cup creamy peanut butter

½ cup corn syrup with brown sugar flavoring

2 eggs, separated

⅓ cup vegetable oil

⅓ cup water

1 box (20 ounces) double-chocolate brownie mix

¼ cup dry roasted peanuts, finely chopped

Preheat the oven to 325°F. Coat a 9" or 10" springform pan with cooking spray.

Press the cookie dough into the pan.

In a mixing bowl, combine the peanut butter, corn syrup, and 1 egg. Beat with a fork until smooth. Pour into the pan. In the same bowl, combine the oil, the water, and the remaining egg. Beat with a fork. Add the brownie mix. Stir until the dry ingredients are moistened. Pour into the prepared pan. Bake for 30 minutes. Sprinkle the peanuts over the torte. Bake for 25 minutes, or until the center is puffed but still jiggles. The center may appear underbaked but cools to doneness. Cool in the pan on a rack.

PECAN-CINNAMON BUNDT CAKE

This cake offers a crisp cinnamon-sugar crust and an ultra-moist crumb. It's a good keeping cake—if there's any left to keep.

Hands-On Time: 10 minutes

Total Time: 1 hour and 10 minutes (plus 10 minutes cooling time)

Makes 12 servings

2/3 cup + 1 tablespoon butter, softened, divided

1 box (22 ounces) cinnamon-swirl cake mix with pudding

1/2 cup corn syrup with brown sugar flavoring

4 eggs, divided

1 bag (2 ounces) chopped pecans (1/2 cup)

3/4 cup whole milk

Preheat the oven to 350°F. Coat the inside of a 12-cup Bundt pan with 1 tablespoon of the butter.

Pour the cinnamon seasoning packet from the cake mix into the pan. Coat the sides with the mixture, shaking out the excess into a mixing bowl. Add the corn syrup, 1/3 cup of the butter, and 1 egg. Beat with a spoon until smooth. Stir in the pecans. Set aside.

In the bowl of an electric mixer, combine the cake mix, milk, the remaining 1/3 cup of butter, and the remaining 3 eggs. Blend for about 30 seconds, or until the dry ingredients are moistened. Beat at high speed for 3 minutes, or until smooth and fluffy. Dollop the pecan mixture over the cake batter. With a spatula, fold the pecan mixture into the batter about 6 times, so wide streaks are visible. Pour into the pan.

Bake for about 1 hour, or until a tester inserted into the center comes out clean. Cool for 10 minutes in the pan on a rack. Turn the cake onto a cooling rack to cool completely.

CARROT-CRANBERRY-PINEAPPLE SNACK CAKE WITH CREAM CHEESE–WALNUT FROSTING

For all those who believe the boxed mix just isn't carroty enough, this cake brings the flavor home in bunches. This is a fine family dessert.

Hands-On Time: 10 minutes
Total Time: 45 minutes

Makes 8 servings

1 bag (2 ounces) chopped walnuts (½ cup)

1 cup bagged preshredded carrot

1 box (18 ounces) carrot cake mix with pudding

2 jars (4 ounces each) baby-food pureed carrots

4 eggs

½ cup vegetable oil

⅓ cup whole milk

1 teaspoon pure orange or lemon extract

1 can (8 ounces) crushed pineapple in juice

¾ cup dried cranberries

2 cartons (8 ounces each) honey-nut cream cheese spread, at room temperature

⅓ cup confectioners' sugar

Preheat the oven to 350°F. Coat a 13" × 9" cake pan with cooking spray. Dust with flour to coat; shake out any excess.

In the bowl of a food processor fitted with a metal blade, chop the walnuts for about 1 minute, or until finely chopped. Transfer to a sheet of waxed paper. Remove 2 tablespoons and set aside. Add the carrot to the work bowl. Process for about 1 minute, or until finely chopped. Set aside.

In the bowl of an electric mixer, combine the cake mix, pureed carrot, eggs, oil, milk, and orange or lemon extract. Blend for about 30 seconds, or until the dry ingredients are moistened. Beat at medium speed for 3 minutes, or until smooth and fluffy. Stir in the pineapple (with juice), cranberries, reserved nuts, and reserved carrots. Pour into the cake pan. Bake for about 35 minutes, or until the cake springs back when pressed with fingertips. Cool completely in the pan on a rack

In a mixing bowl, combine the cream cheese and sugar. With a spoon, stir until smooth. Frost the cake. Sprinkle with the reserved 2 tablespoons of walnuts.

NOTE: Store the frosted cake in the refrigerator.

APRICOT-GINGER CRUMBLE

Crumbles are such homey, versatile desserts. In this recipe, you can replace the apricots with canned pineapple chunks, peaches, or pears.

Hands-On Time: 6 minutes

Total Time: 36 minutes

Makes 6 to 8 servings

2 jars (24 ounces each) apricots in light syrup or 2 cans (29 ounces each) apricots in syrup

2 tablespoons + $\frac{1}{2}$ cup flour

5 individual packets (6 ounces total) maple and brown sugar instant oats

$\frac{1}{2}$ cup (1 stick) cold butter, cut into small chunks

1 bag (2 ounces) chopped walnuts ($\frac{1}{2}$ cup)

$\frac{1}{3}$ cup chopped candied ginger

Preheat the oven to 400°F. Coat a 12" × 8" glass or ceramic baking dish with cooking spray.

Drain the apricots, reserving 1 cup of the syrup. Discard the remaining syrup. Place 2 tablespoons of the flour into a mixing bowl. Add the syrup, whisking constantly until smooth. Add the apricots. Stir to mix. Transfer to the baking dish. In the same mixing bowl, combine the oats, butter, and the remaining $\frac{1}{2}$ cup of flour. With a fork or a pastry blender, cut the butter until coarse crumbs form. Stir in the walnuts and ginger. Scatter the mixture over the fruit. Bake for about 30 minutes, or until browned and bubbling. Serve warm or cold.

CINNAMON-RAISIN BREAD PUDDING
WITH WHISKEY SAUCE

A taste of old New Orleans cooking is yours in a jiffy when you start with packaged cinnamon-raisin bread.

Hands-On Time: 12 minutes

Total Time: 42 minutes (plus 10 minutes standing time)

Makes 8 servings

6 eggs

3 cups half-and-half

½ cup brown sugar

2 teaspoons vanilla extract

1 loaf (1 pound) cinnamon-raisin bread, toasted (12 slices)

1 jar (12 ounces) caramel sauce

¼ cup whiskey

Preheat the oven to 325°F. Coat a 13" × 9" ceramic or glass baking dish with cooking spray.

Break the eggs into the baking dish. Tipping the dish slightly, beat the eggs with a fork. Add the half-and-half, sugar, and vanilla. Stir to mix. Place a solid layer of toast into the dish, tearing slices to fit. Press with a fork to saturate. Cover with a layer of the remaining toast. Press with a fork. Let stand for 5 minutes, pressing frequently, until the toast is thoroughly saturated. Bake for about 30 minutes, or until the top puffs up and the custard is set. Let stand for 10 minutes.

Meanwhile, in a microwaveable bowl, combine the caramel sauce and whiskey. Stir until smooth. Cover with waxed paper. Microwave on high power for about 90 seconds, or until hot. Serve the pudding drizzled with the sauce.

CHOCOLATE SYRUP

It's mostly drizzled on ice cream, but chocolate syrup can be an extremely versatile condiment. Plus, it's fat-free. Here are a few ideas.

1. **Chocolate-Cinnamon Pears:** Drizzle chocolate syrup over cinnamon-poached pears.

2. **Chocolate Trifle:** Make a chocolate trifle with layers of ladyfingers, vanilla pudding, and chocolate syrup.

3. **Hot Mocha:** Mix 2 tablespoons chocolate syrup, ¼ cup brewed coffee, ¾ cup milk, and ¼ teaspoon vanilla extract in a microwaveable mug. Microwave for 1 to 2 minutes, stirring once or twice, until hot. Top with whipped cream and a dash of cinnamon. Makes 1 serving.

4. **Chocolate Fruit Dip:** In a food processor, puree 1 package (8 ounces) cream cheese with ¼ to ⅓ cup chocolate syrup (just enough to make a thin, puddinglike consistency). Use for dipping fruit and pound cake. Makes about 1¼ cups.

5. **Easy Chocolate Glaze:** Mix 3 tablespoons chocolate syrup and ⅔ cup confectioners' sugar until smooth. Use to glaze the top of a store-bought angel-food cake. Makes about ½ cup.

6. **Effortless Chocolate Sorbet:** Mix 1 cup chocolate syrup, 1 cup brown sugar, 2 tablespoons corn syrup, and 2 cups water until smooth. Freeze in a metal cake pan until crystals form. Break up and stir the crystals, then refreeze for 4 to 6 hours, or until solid. Scrape off servings with a spoon. Makes 4 to 6 servings.

CHOCOLATE-WALNUT-CHERRY TART

Serve this rich confection within a few hours of baking so the flaky crust remains crispy. Don't worry about storing leftovers; there won't be any.

Hands-On Time: 5 minutes

Total Time: 25 minutes (plus 2 hours cooling time)

Makes 12 servings

1 sheet frozen puff pastry, thawed

1 egg

1 jar (12 ounces) hot-fudge sauce

1 bag (2 ounces) chopped walnuts, finely chopped in a food processor

½ cup cherry preserves

1 tablespoon sugar

Whipped cream

Preheat the oven to 375°F.

Fit the puff pastry into a 9" pie pan. The edges will overlap. Set aside.

With a fork, beat the egg in a mixing bowl. Add the fudge sauce. Stir and then beat until smooth. Stir in the walnuts. Pour into the prepared crust. Dollop the preserves over the filling, swirling lightly. Fold the crust points over the filling (it will not be completely covered). Sprinkle the sugar over the crust.

Bake for about 25 minutes, or until the pastry is browned and puffed. Allow to cool on a rack for about 2 hours, or until just warm. Serve with whipped cream on the side.

DEEP-DISH GOLDEN DELICIOUS APPLE PIE

The mythical Mom's apple pie was a labor of love. Mixing and rolling flaky dough for the crust. Peeling and slicing apples by hand. Measuring cinnamon, nutmeg, and allspice to combine with the sugar and cornstarch. This streamlined all-American dessert will have even Mom asking for seconds.

Before 2 hours and 20 minutes

After 1 hour and 40 minutes

Time Saved 40 minutes

Makes 8 servings

Photo on page 312

1 cup brown sugar

¼ cup cornstarch

1 tablespoon apple pie spice

½ stick (¼ cup) butter, cut into chunks

2 pounds unpeeled, Golden Delicious apples, cored and cut into quarters (4 large apples)

1 cup unsweetened chunky applesauce

1 box (15 ounces) refrigerated piecrusts (2 crusts)

1 teaspoon granulated sugar

Preheat the oven to 425°F.

In a mixing bowl, combine the brown sugar, cornstarch, apple pie spice, and butter. With a fork, mash the butter into small bits.

In a food processor fitted with the shedding blade, shred the apples. Add to the bowl. Toss to combine. Add the applesauce. Stir to combine.

Fit one crust into a 9" deep-dish pie pan. Spoon in the apple mixture, mounding in the center. Top with the second crust. Fold the edges of the top crust under the bottom crust. Pinch to seal. Pierce the top crust several times with a sharp knife.

Bake for 20 minutes. Sprinkle with the granulated sugar. Cover with aluminum foil. Reduce the heat to 375°F. Bake for 1 hour, or until thickened filling bubbles from the slits in the crust. Cool in the pan on a rack for several hours.

- Shredding unpeeled apples in the food processor instead of peeling apples by hand and slicing

- Using refrigerated piecrusts instead of mixing dough from scratch and rolling by hand

- Adding a small amount of jarred applesauce to jump-start the cooking of the filling in the oven

- Using prepared apple pie spice instead of searching the pantry for, and separately measuring, cinnamon, nutmeg, and allspice

SOUTHERN SOUR CREAM-COCONUT LAYER CAKE

Majestic is the word that best describes this dreamy old-fashioned layer cake. Offer it for a special occasion or serve it simply to make the occasion special.

Hands-On Time: 15 minutes
Total Time: 45 minutes

Makes 8 to 10 servings

1 box (18 ounces) white cake mix

1⅓ cups sour cream, divided

¾ cup whole milk

3 egg whites

⅓ cup + 3¾ cups confectioners' sugar

1½ tablespoons coconut extract

¾ cup solid vegetable shortening

1 cup flaked sweetened coconut, divided

Preheat the oven to 350°F. Coat two 9" round cake pans with cooking spray. Dust with flour, shaking out any excess.

In the bowl of an electric mixer, combine the cake mix, 1 cup of the sour cream, the milk, egg whites, ⅓ cup of the sugar, and the coconut extract. Blend for about 30 seconds, or until the dry ingredients are moistened. Beat at high speed for 3 minutes, or until smooth and fluffy. Pour into the reserved pans. Bake for 30 to 35 minutes, or until the cake springs back when pressed with fingertips. Cool in the pans for 10 minutes on a rack. Run a knife between the cake sides and pans. Turn the layers onto a cooling rack to cool completely.

Meanwhile, in the bowl of an electric mixer, combine the remaining 3¾ cups sugar, the shortening, and the remaining ⅓ cup sour cream. Blend for about 1 minute, or until the sugar is moistened. Beat at high speed for 3 minutes, or until smooth and fluffy.

Place one cake layer on a serving plate. Frost the top. Sprinkle with ¼ cup of the coconut. Top with the second layer. Frost the sides and top. With the palm of one hand, press about 1 tablespoon of coconut at a time onto the side of the cake. Continue while rotating the cake until the sides are coated. Sprinkle the remaining coconut over the top.

TIRAMISU CHEESECAKE

Five Ingredients or Less!

The cream, coffee, and chocolate flavors of traditional tiramisu
really pop in this oh-so-easy
cake. If you can plan ahead,
allow the cheesecake to thaw
slowly in the refrigerator to produce a creamier texture.

Hands-On Time: 5 minutes

Total Time: 5 minutes

Makes 6 servings

1 New York-style frozen cheesecake (1 pound 14 ounces),
   thawed

1 container (8 ounces) coffee-flavored mascarpone cheese

¼ cup (2 ounces) miniature semisweet chocolate morsels,
   divided

1 tablespoon cocoa powder

1 tablespoon confectioners' sugar

Remove the paper collar from the cheesecake. Place the cake on
a serving dish. Stir the mascarpone until smooth. Add 2 tablespoons of the morsels. Spread over the cheesecake. Sprinkle
the remaining 2 tablespoons of morsels over the top.

Combine the cocoa and sugar in a small fine sieve or dredger.
Cut the cake into wedges and place on plates. Dust the cake and
surrounding plate with the cocoa-sugar mixture.

Shelf-Ready Shortcuts

BAKING MIXES

Biscuit mix, muffin mix, cake mix, cornbread mix, cookie mix, and brownie mix can all give you a
head start on making more-elaborate, impressive desserts. Transform a simple box of brownie
mix into a luscious chocolate torte. Doctor up cake mixes with your favorite flavors like coconut,
whiskey, or bananas and use them to make snacking bars as well as layer cakes. Use biscuit mix
or cornbread mix to make a sweet coffee cake. The possibilities are endless. See the recipes
throughout this chapter for more examples.

MAPLE CREAM-PEACH PARFAITS
WITH TOFFEE TOPPING

Five Ingredients or Less!

For a frosty touch, you can place these prepared parfaits in the freezer for 1 hour before serving.

Hands-On Time: 8 minutes

Total Time: 8 minutes

Makes 6 servings

1   carton (15 ounces) ricotta cheese

⅓   cup maple syrup

1   jar (24 ounces) peaches in light syrup or 1 can (29 ounces each) peaches in syrup, drained and patted dry

½   cup bagged crushed toffee bits

In a food processor fitted with a metal blade, combine the cheese and maple syrup. Process for 3 minutes, scraping the sides of the bowl occasionally, or until very smooth.

Dollop about 1 tablespoon of maple cream into 6 parfait dishes. Top each with 2 or 3 peaches. Repeat with the maple cream and peaches. Top with the remaining maple cream. Sprinkle the toffee bits on top.

PUMPKIN PANNA COTTA

Pumpkin pie mix can be used for a whole lot more than Thanksgiving. This sophisticated Italian restaurant dessert is deceptively simple. Your guests will never guess you prepared it in less than 5 minutes with fewer than 5 ingredients.

Hands-On Time: 4 minutes

Total Time: 4 minutes (plus 2 hours chilling time)

Makes 10 servings

1 cup whole milk

1 box (3 ounces) orange gelatin mix

1 carton (1 pint) half-and-half, divided

1 cup canned pumpkin pie mix

Whipped cream

Set 10 custard cups or small bowls ($\frac{1}{2}$ cup each) on a tray.

Place the milk in a large microwaveable measuring cup with a pour spout. Microwave on high power for 2 minutes, or until steaming hot. Whisk in the gelatin until dissolved. Whisk in the half-and-half and the pie mix. Pour into the reserved cups. Cover with waxed paper and refrigerate for at least 2 hours or as long as overnight, or until set. Garnish with whipped cream.

RASPBERRY SUNDAES IN FUDGE-GLAZED WAFFLE BOWLS

Five Ingredients or Less!

Crispy waffle cones, in the shape of flat-bottomed bowls, become elegant sit-down fare in this uncomplicated treat.

Hands-On Time: 10 minutes

Total Time: 10 minutes

Makes 10 servings

1 jar (12 ounces) hot-fudge sauce

1 box (about $\frac{1}{2}$ ounce) waffle bowls (10 bowls)

$\frac{1}{2}$ cup all-fruit chunky raspberry spread

2 tablespoons frozen orange-juice concentrate

1 pint French vanilla ice cream, soft enough to scoop

Place the hot-fudge sauce in a microwaveable measuring cup. Microwave on high power for 2 minutes, or until pourable. One at a time, drizzle the hot fudge sauce into the waffle bowls. Tilt the bowls to coat the inside surfaces evenly.

In a small bowl, combine the spread and juice concentrate. Stir to mix. Scoop the ice cream into each waffle bowl. Top with the raspberry sauce.

MAKE AHEAD FOR THE FREEZER: The sundaes can be prepared ahead of time. Place the bowls on a freezerproof tray, cover loosely with plastic wrap, and freeze for up to 24 hours. Allow to stand at room temperature for 10 minutes before serving.

TROPICAL-FRUIT CREAM PIE

This refreshing and creamy concoction tastes really good after a grill meal like Charred Flank Steak with Picadillo Relish (page 166).

Hands-On Time: 6 minutes

Total Time: 6 minutes (plus 1 hour chilling time)

Makes 6 to 8 servings

1 box (6 ounces) instant vanilla pudding

2 cups whole milk

1 tablespoon spiced rum (see note)

1 prepared graham cracker piecrust (6 ounces)

1 banana, quartered lengthwise, cut into small chunks

2 kiwifruit, quartered lengthwise, cut into small chunks

½ cup drained canned pineapple chunks in light syrup

¼ cup sweetened flaked coconut

In a mixing bowl, whisk the pudding, milk, and rum. Pour half into the piecrust. Scatter the banana, kiwi, and pineapple evenly over the pudding. Cover with the remaining pudding mixture. Place the clear plastic crust cover upside down over the pie. Refrigerate for at least 1 hour, or until set.

Meanwhile, place the coconut in a medium heavy skillet. Cook over medium-high heat, stirring constantly with a fork, for 2 minutes, or until golden brown. Allow to cool. Sprinkle over the pie.

NOTE: If spiced rum is not available, replace it with 1 teaspoon of rum extract and a dash of apple pie spice mix.

BANANA-GLAZED PECAN ICE-CREAM SUNDAES

Five Ingredients or Less!

When your family is in the mood for something special, there's no need to run to the supermarket. Everything you need is probably in your kitchen.

Hands-On Time: 5 minutes
Total Time: 5 minutes

Makes 6 servings

½ cup brown sugar

2 tablespoons butter

2 bananas, cut diagonally into thick slices

1½ pints vanilla ice cream

½ cup bagged glazed pecans

In a skillet, combine the sugar and butter. Cook, stirring, over medium-high heat, for 2 minutes, or until bubbling. Add the bananas. Stir gently to coat with the sugar mixture. Set aside.

Scoop the ice cream into 6 dessert bowls. Top with the banana sauce and pecans.

RAINBOW-SORBET ANGEL CAKE

Five Ingredients or Less!

When strawberries, raspberries, or blueberries are in season, scatter some on each serving of this refreshing dessert. For a special occasion, garnish each plate with a mint leaf or a slice of fresh lime.

Hands-On Time: 10 minutes

Total Time: 10 minutes (plus several hours freezing time)

Makes 12 servings

1 prepared angel-food cake (10 ounces)

1 pint strawberry or raspberry sorbet, soft enough to scoop

½ pint mango or peach sorbet, soft enough to scoop

½ cup confectioners' sugar

3 tablespoons frozen limeade concentrate

With a serrated knife, cut the cake into 3 equal layers. Place the bottom layer, cut side up, on a freezer-proof serving plate. Spread on the strawberry or raspberry sorbet in an even layer. Top with the second cake layer. Spread the mango or peach sorbet in an even layer. Top with the last cake layer. With a spatula, smooth any sorbet on the sides of the cake, like frosting. Cover with plastic wrap. Freeze for several hours or as long as several days.

To serve, let stand at room temperature for 20 minutes. In a bowl, whisk the sugar and limeade concentrate. Drizzle over the cake, allowing it to run down the sides. Cut with a serrated knife.

CHAPTER 15

QUICK-COOKING MENUS

This chapter includes 2 weeks of great dinners, complete with menu plans, total cooking times, and weekly shopping lists. The times listed let you know how long each meal will take so you can plan ahead. (Don't worry; most meals take less than 30 minutes.) The shopping lists are categorized by section of the typical grocery store, so you can get in and out of the store in record time. In short, here is everything you need to make shopping and cooking for the week a breeze.

WEEK ONE DINNER PLAN

DAY OF WEEK	DINNER PLAN	TOTAL PREP AND COOKING TIME
Sunday	Breaded Dijon Chicken Breasts (page 238)	35 minutes (10 minutes hands-on)
	Southern Greens with Bacon (page 296)	10 minutes
	Cooked instant rice	10 minutes
Monday	Thai Catfish Curry with Green Beans and Rice (page 184)	20 minutes
Tuesday	Provençal Chicken-and-Vegetable Main Dish Salad (page 240)	12 minutes
Wednesday	Bistro Steaks with Mushrooms and Onions (page 192)	1 hour and 35 minutes (10 minutes hands-on)
Thursday	Curried Peppercorn Pork with Cauliflower and Potatoes (page 190)	20 minutes
Friday	Grilled Fennel Salmon with Sun-Dried Tomato–Orange Butter (page 155)	12 minutes
Saturday	Heartland Pork, Potato, and Apple Bake (page 218)	1 hour (5 minutes hands-on)
Total Prep and Cooking Time for Week:		3 hours and 34 minutes (includes only 1 hour and 49 minutes hands-on time for the week)

Shopping List for the Week

Canned and Jarred Foods

- ☐ 1 cup chunky unsweetened applesauce
- ☐ ½ cup jarred roasted red bell peppers
- ☐ 1 can (14 ounces) coconut milk
- ☐ 1 tablespoon Thai red curry paste (jarred or from an envelope)

Bottled Sauces and Dressings

- ☐ ½ cup Dijon mustard
- ☐ 2 tablespoons stone-ground mustard
- ☐ ¾ cup French vinaigrette salad dressing
- ☐ 1 cup steak-house marinade and sauce

Pasta, Grains, and Cereals

- ☐ 1 cup instant brown rice
- ☐ Cooked instant rice

Oils, Vinegars, and Broth

Cooking spray
- ☐ ¼ cup olive oil
- ☐ 1 cup vegetable oil
- ☐ 1 tablespoon cider vinegar or white wine vinegar
- ☐ ½ cup chicken broth or water
- ☐ ½ cup vegetable broth or water

Spices, Seasonings, and Baking Items

- ☐ 3 cups dried bread crumbs
- ☐ 1 tablespoon curry powder
- ☐ 2 teaspoons herbes de Provence
- ☐ 2 teaspoons paprika
- ☐ 1 teaspoon fennel seeds
- ☐ 2 teaspoons salt
- ☐ 2 teaspoons ground black pepper

Meat and Poultry

- ☐ 4-4½ pounds boneless, skinless chicken breast halves
- ☐ 2½ pounds premarinated peppercorn pork tenderloin
- ☐ 2-2½ pounds boneless beef bottom round steaks or other braising steaks
- ☐ ¼ cup (1 ounce) bagged crumbled real bacon

Produce and Refrigerated Produce Section

- ☐ 2 apples, preferably Golden Delicious
- ☐ 2 cups prechopped onions
- ☐ 1-2 bags (1 pound each) pretrimmed green beans (3 cups)
- ☐ 1 package (8 ounces) presliced fresh mushrooms (4 cups)

- [ ] 2 bags (8 ounces each) cauliflower florets
- [ ] 1 bag (1 pound) collard greens or kale (16 packed cups)
- [ ] 1 bag (5 ounces) spring salad mix
- [ ] 1 bunch scallions
- [ ] 3 tablespoons preminced oil-packed garlic
- [ ] ½ cup prechopped oil-packed sun-dried tomatoes
- [ ] 3 pre-hard-cooked eggs
- [ ] ¼ cup fresh parsley or cilantro (optional)
- [ ] ½ cup fresh basil leaves (optional)

Bags and Wraps

- [ ] Waxed paper
- [ ] Plastic wrap
- [ ] Large zipper-lock bags

Seafood

- [ ] 2 pounds catfish fillets
- [ ] 2-2½ pounds boneless, skinless salmon fillets

Dairy, Cheese, and Eggs

- [ ] 2 tablespoons butter

Frozen Foods

- [ ] 2 cups (8 ounces) frozen potato wedges
- [ ] 1 pound (4 cups) frozen French-onion oven-roast potatoes
- [ ] 1 tablespoon frozen orange-juice concentrate

DAY OF WEEK	DINNER PLAN	TOTAL PREP AND COOKING TIME
Sunday	Leg of Lamb Roasted with Herbs and Red Wine (page 256)	1 hour 55 minutes (15 minutes hands-on time)
	Risotto with Cheese and Peas (page 301)	10 minutes
	Tossed salad	5 minutes
Monday	Gyros with Creamy Cucumber-Dill Sauce in Pita (page 257)	8 minutes
	Chunky Broccoli-Spinach Soup (page 89)	12 minutes
Tuesday	Tex-a-Cajun Jambalaya (page 172)	25 minutes (7 minutes hands-on time)
Wednesday	Rigatoni Carbonara with Peas (page 176)	18 minutes (6 minutes hands-on time)
Thursday	Mediterranean Tilapia and Spinach in Spicy Tomato Sauce (page 181)	20 minutes (5 minutes hands-on time)
Friday	Pork Chops Italiano with Peppers and Onions (page 164)	25 minutes (7 minutes hands-on time)
Saturday	Chicken Pot Pie with Biscuits (page 216)	1 hour (15 minutes hands-on time)
Total Prep and Cooking Time for Week:		4 hours and 58 minutes (only 1½ hours hands-on time for the week)

Shopping List for the Week

Canned and Jarred Foods

- ☐ 2 cans (14 ounces each) diced pepper-onion seasoned tomatoes
- ☐ 1 can (14 ounces) diced Italian-seasoned tomatoes
- ☐ 2 cans (10 ounces each) sage and black pepper chicken gravy

Bottled Sauces and Dressings

- ☐ Salad dressing (your choice, for salad with Sunday Leg of Lamb meal)
- ☐ ½ cup bottled Italian salad dressing
- ☐ 1 teaspoon hot-pepper sauce

Pasta, Grains, and Cereals

- ☐ 1½ cups Arborio rice
- ☐ 12 ounces uncooked rigatoni

Bread and Refrigerated Dough

- ☐ 4 pitas (6"-wide)
- ☐ 1 tube (16 ounces) large-size refrigerated biscuits (8 biscuits)

Oils, Vinegars, and Broth

- ☐ ¼ cup olive oil
- ☐ 6 tablespoons extra-virgin olive oil
- ☐ 1 cup beef broth
- ☐ 9 cups vegetable broth
- ☐ 1 cup chicken broth

Spices, Seasonings, and Baking Items

- ☐ 1 teaspoon Italian seasoning
- ☐ 1 tablespoon chili powder
- ☐ 1 teaspoon red-pepper flakes
- ☐ 1 teaspoon poultry seasoning
- ☐ 2½ tablespoons salt
- ☐ 1¼ teaspoons ground black pepper
- ☐ ¼ teaspoon dried dillweed
- ☐ 6 tablespoons flour

Produce and Refrigerated Produce Section

- ☐ Salad greens and fixings from salad bar (your choice)
- ☐ 1½ bags (10 ounces each) baby spinach leaves
- ☐ 1 bag (8 ounces) broccoli florets
- ☐ ½ bag (1 pound) baby carrots
- ☐ 1 container (7 ounces) prechopped tricolor bell pepper (1 cup)
- ☐ 2 containers (7 ounces each) presliced onion and bell pepper (4 cups)
- ☐ ⅓ English cucumber (15 ounces)
- ☐ 1 cup prechopped celery

- [ ] 2½ cups prechopped onion
- [ ] 1 bunch scallions
- [ ] 4½ tablespoons preminced oil-packed garlic
- [ ] 1 teaspoon lemon juice

Meat and Poultry

- [ ] 1 rotisserie chicken or 1 pound boneless roasted chicken
- [ ] 3½-4 pounds boneless leg of lamb
- [ ] 4 to 6 boneless premarinated Italian-seasoned pork chops (2 to 3 pounds)
- [ ] ½ pound smoked fully cooked kielbasa sausage
- [ ] ½ cup (2 ounces) bagged precooked crumbled real bacon

Seafood

- [ ] ¾ pound medium peeled, deveined shrimp
- [ ] 2-2½ pounds tilapia fillets

Dairy, Cheese, and Eggs

- [ ] 6 tablespoons butter

- [ ] 1¾ cups preshredded Parmesan-Romano cheese
- [ ] 2 tablespoons preshredded Romano cheese
- [ ] ½ cup (4 ounces) plain yogurt or sour cream
- [ ] ⅓ cup sour cream
- [ ] 4 eggs

Frozen Foods

- [ ] 3¾ cups (about 16 ounces) frozen petite peas
- [ ] 2 cups (8 ounces) frozen pearl onions

Wine, Spirits, and Beer

- [ ] ½ cup dry red wine

Bags and Wraps

- [ ] Plastic wrap
- [ ] Aluminum foil
- [ ] Large zipper-lock bags

INDEX

Note: Underscored page references indicate boxed text.
Boldfaced page references indicate photographs.

Conversion Chart

These equivalents have been slightly rounded to make measuring easier.

Volume Measurements

U.S.	Imperial	Metric
¼ tsp	–	1 ml
½ tsp	–	2 ml
1 tsp	–	5 ml
1 Tbsp	–	15 ml
2 Tbsp (1 oz)	1 fl oz	30 ml
¼ cup (2 oz)	2 fl oz	60 ml
⅓ cup (3 oz)	3 fl oz	80 ml
½ cup (4 oz)	4 fl oz	120 ml
⅔ cup (5 oz)	5 fl oz	160 ml
¾ cup (6 oz)	6 fl oz	180 ml
1 cup (8 oz)	8 fl oz	240 ml

Weight Measurements

U.S.	Metric
1 oz	30 g
2 oz	60 g
4 oz (¼ lb)	115 g
5 oz (⅓ lb)	145 g
6 oz	170 g
7 oz	200 g
8 oz (½ lb)	230 g
10 oz	285 g
12 oz (¾ lb)	340 g
14 oz	400 g
16 oz (1 lb)	455 g
2.2 lb	1 kg

Length Measurements

U.S.	Metric
¼"	0.6 cm
½"	1.25 cm
1"	2.5 cm
2"	5 cm
4"	11 cm
6"	15 cm
8"	20 cm
10"	25 cm
12" (1')	30 cm

Pan Sizes

U.S.	Metric
8" cake pan	20 × 4 cm sandwich or cake tin
9" cake pan	23 × 3.5 cm sandwich or cake tin
11" × 7" baking pan	28 × 18 cm baking tin
13" × 9" baking pan	32.5 × 23 cm baking tin
15" × 10" baking pan	38 × 25.5 cm baking tin (Swiss roll tin)
1½ qt baking dish	1.5 liter baking dish
2 qt baking dish	2 liter baking dish
2 qt rectangular baking dish	30 × 19 cm baking dish
9" pie plate	22 × 4 or 23 × 4 cm pie plate
7" or 8" springform pan	18 or 20 cm springform or loose-bottom cake tin
9" × 5" loaf pan	23 × 13 cm or 2 lb narrow loaf tin or pâté tin

Temperatures

Fahrenheit	Centigrade	Gas
140°	60°	–
160°	70°	–
180°	80°	–
225°	105°	¼
250°	120°	½
275°	135°	1
300°	150°	2
325°	160°	3
350°	180°	4
375°	190°	5
400°	200°	6
425°	220°	7
450°	230°	8
475°	245°	9
500°	260°	–